Properties of Modernity

Properties
of Modernity

Romantic Spain, Modern Europe,

and the Legacies of Empire

Michael Iarocci

Vanderbilt University Press

NASHVILLE

10 09 08 07 06   1 2 3 4 5

Printed on acid-free paper
Manufactured in the United States of America

Publication of this book has been supported by a generous subsidy
from the Program for Cultural Cooperation between
Spain's Ministry of Culture and United States Universities.

Library of Congress Cataloging-in-Publication Data

Iarocci, Michael P.
Properties of modernity : romantic Spain, modern Europe, and
the legacies of empire / Michael Iarocci.—1st ed.
    p. cm.
    Includes index.
    ISBN 0-8265-1521-5 (cloth : alk. paper)
    ISBN 0-8265-1522-3 (pbk. : alk. paper)
    1. Spanish literature—18th century—History and criticism.
2. Spanish literature—19th century—History and criticism.
3. Romanticism—Spain. 4. National characteristics, Spanish,
in literature. 5. Cadalso, José, 1741–1782—Criticism and
interpretation. 6. Rivas, Angel de Saavedra, duque de, 1791–
1865. Don Alvaro. 7. Larra, Mariano José de, 1809–1837—
Criticism and interpretation. I. Title.
PQ6071.I37 2005
860.9'145'09033—dc22
                                              2005022927

Contents

Acknowledgments

Friends, students, family, and colleagues have been the companions to this project over the last several years, and I am deeply grateful to them all for the frequent encouragement they have given me, often without knowing it. Conversations with several of my colleagues in the Department of Spanish and Portuguese at Berkeley—in particular, Estelle Tarica, José Luis Passos, José Rabasa, and Dru Dougherty—provided me with an early, much appreciated sounding board for ideas when they were still taking shape. Graduate seminars have been a stimulating forum of dialogue and exchange, and the energy and enthusiasm of undergraduates at Berkeley has been a source of inspiration. A Humanities Research Fellowship from the University of California afforded me invaluable time to finish the manuscript, and I feel privileged to work at an institution that foments intellectual inquiry in so many ways. At the same time, I would like to express my gratitude to my colleagues in eighteenth- and nineteenth-century Spanish studies across the country; the field is unique for the way it draws so many first-rate scholars who, as it happens, are also generous interlocutors. To Jesús in Montreal and to Charlotte in Portland, here it is. I would also like to thank Betsy Phillips, who supported this work from the time she first read it, and Vanderbilt University Press for its continuing commitment to the mission of academic publishing. I feel fortunate that my work has found such a wonderful venue. Finally, I would like to thank Debarati Sanyal, whose energy, brilliance, and companionship made the closing months of this project—and the days that have followed—an unexpected joy.

Introduction

Struggling against the News

A twenty-four-hour news channel on a television screen, somewhere in America; increasingly, anywhere in the world. Return from commercial. Dramatic theme-music fades out. A talking head beams with info-youth—a combination of makeup, imaging software, and cosmetic surgery. Below the head, the movement of multiple data streams. Above it, to the left, a graphic. The head reads a teleprompter with the studied exaggeration and emphatic cadences of newspeak. The story begins, "IN EUROPE TODAY. . . ." The graphic is a map that represents the silhouettes of Britain, France and Germany. . . . Britain, France, and Germany . . . Europe . . . a curious synecdoche.

Not long ago, it may have seemed odd to begin a book dedicated to the literary production of romantic Spain by evoking the Anglo-international twenty-four-hour news. In the increasingly corporate Information Age that some would simply sum up as the present, however, and as calls for literary and cultural studies to globalize eerily begin to echo neoliberal demands for the unhindered movement of capital across the planet, the twenty-four-hour international news is a paradoxically apt vehicle of introduction for the material I will be taking up in the pages that follow.[1] As a media phenomenon that, among other things, produces a sense of the contemporary, the perennial news-flow of our times speaks to what might be termed the *presentism* of the digital age. It points to the beguilingly depthless, technologized temporality of a news cycle whose ultimate horizon is always a relentless, hypnotic *now*, a now for which the past is by definition yesterday's news, or perhaps at best tomorrow's miniseries. The twenty-four-hour news is in this regard a peculiarly telling, contemporary negation of historical time and of the questions with which most attempts to think historically have had to grapple—How can the past speak? Whose past is it? What claims might it have on the present? Whose present? Indeed, presentism is another name for the threat to which Walter Benjamin famously referred when he wrote that "to articulate the past historically . . . means to seize hold of a memory as is it flashes up at a moment of danger" (*Illuminations* 255).

The moment of danger for Benjamin was the present—any present—for he knew that the stakes of historical thinking are always high and that the task of the historian is therefore an urgent one. He saw the ease with which the now of the present can be made to legitimize abhorrent forms of power, and he knew all too well that accounts of the past have often been scarcely veiled apologies for the ideology of "just the way things are." It is for this reason, among others, that the Benjaminian conception of history is fundamentally agonistic and that his call to cultural historians is an injunction to struggle. "In every era," he writes, "the attempt must be made to wrest tradition away from a conformism that is about to overpower it" (255). As the image of a relentlessly packaged present, and as shorthand for a particular kind of conformism, the twenty-four-hour international news—or to be fairer, my account of it thus far—is in many ways the antithesis of one of the aims of this book, which is to take up the challenges of historical thought by asking what cultural memories might yet be seized as they flash up in a series of texts that were written in Spain between the 1770s and the 1830s. They are works that, like much modern Spanish literature, remain largely unknown outside of the Spanish-speaking world, texts that have rarely drawn attention from a purportedly international comparative literature.

The news, however, is of course much more than merely a figure of what I have called presentism. It is also a phenomenon that unambiguously manifests the power of representation in the era of the image. It is not difficult to recognize in the global telecommunications industry—news channels, for example, whose distribution spans from Cuzco to Calcutta, from Montreal to Madrid—the kind of power that ever-increasing networks of data delivery are capable of realizing. My evocation of the twenty-four-hour news is thus also meant to take up broadly the question of representational dominance; that is, the power of those images, narratives, or modes of thought that by sheer repetition have taken on the appearance of common knowledge, *idées recues*, which, like the graphic on the newscast I have sketched, hover for a moment on the cusp of aware-ness, unquestioned. The ubiquity of these thought-structures can easily overpower the complexities of thinking about the past. In the context of rethinking Spanish romantic writing through the texts that I take up in the chapters that follow, the dominant narrative that I have inevitably confronted—the historical news with which I have repeatedly grappled—is the story of European modernity and of Spain's seemingly sui generis relationship to that grand narrative, its symbolic position throughout most of the modern era, somewhere off to the side of modern Europe.

The end of Spanish hegemony in the late 1600s entailed not only a diminishment of Spanish power within the European political arena, but also the forfeiture of Spain's ability to represent and successfully project its history and culture internationally. A country that had been one of the privileged sites for the enunciation of European history in the early modern era had by the eighteenth-century increasingly become an object of representation—and symbolic subordination—for a newly dominant northern Europe. If the Renaissance Zeitgeist came to be viewed as radiat-ing from Mediterranean Europe, the spirit of Enlightenment and its after-math in contrast was represented as an almost entirely northern affair. The effect of this fundamental geopolitical shift, of Spain's becoming the first posthegemonic European nation-state, could not have been more pro-found. From the late seventeenth to the late twentieth century, Spain was displaced to the periphery of the modern within the European imaginary, and by the early nineteenth century, as the majority of Spain's romantics began to write, Spanish culture was for the most part imagined to exist on the outskirts of the "modern history" of Europe.

Another aim of this book is to struggle with this legacy of representa-tion—a legacy that only the last decades have begun to rewrite—in order to comprehend better the relationships between Spanish romantic culture and the category of the modern. Indeed, one of the basic contentions of this project is that Spanish romantic writing and the subsequent history of its critical reception were shaped in fundamental ways by Spain's symbolic location on the periphery of the symbolic map of European modernity. It is a map—Britain, France, Germany—that invisibly subtends the idea of Europe, even today, as a circle of gold stars on a blue field becomes the new continental emblem and the likely twenty-first-century news graphic. The reason this symbolic geography of the modern is fundamental to rethinking the texts I will be taking up is not difficult to surmise. If "European romanticism" has largely been conceived as a cultural phenomenon that arose in dialectical tension with the modernity of Enlightenment, the symbolic positioning of Spain on the outskirts of the modern tacitly called into question the very possibility of conceptualizing "Spanish romanticism." If, as the dominant narrative implied, Spain was never quite modern enough, how could Spanish culture possibly have produced its own romanticism? The answer for northern Europe was, of course, that it did not. Indeed, for the north, Spain did not *produce* romanticism; it simply *was* romantic. A newly hegemonic northern gaze transmuted Spanish "backwardness" into romantic mystique, and in place of "Spanish romanticism," nineteenth-century Britain, France, and Germany repeatedly conjured up the image of "romantic Spain," the most proximate "outside" to northern modernity. Like the graphic on the news, Spain was just beyond the borders of modern Europe.[2] To rethink romantic writing in Spain is to struggle against this news, not only in the interest of documenting—as numerous scholars of Spanish culture have—the history of a Spanish modernity that was occluded by this symbolic geography, but also in order to register the historical life of this ideological structure itself within Spanish romanticism and its theorization.

If the graphic with which we begin reveals a contemporary thought-pattern that reflects the way modern Europe has been imagined since the eighteenth century, however, it also gestures to a very different phenomenon that will be equally important in the pages that follow. Needless to say, the information industry to which the news belongs is a transnational commercial enterprise for which images and sounds are, first and foremost, merchandise. The twenty-four-hour news consequently offers an emblematic face of the postindustrial present, with its relentless consumption of images and simulacra, and in this sense the news rather clearly remains embedded in the story of modern capitalism, the very story that what I have called "presentism" so often seeks to erase. The twenty-four-hour news belongs to a history, I would like to suggest, with which romanticism was itself intimately bound in an earlier moment, and it is a history against which romanticism in Spain struggled in ambiguous and often contradictory ways. My discussion of the newscast-as-commodity is in this regard also meant to recall romanticism's historical other: the life-world of business, markets, commerce, and exchange, a world whose shadow was in the end perhaps romanticism's closest companion.

The dense web of relationships between Spanish romantic discourse and the transformation of Spain's political economy during the first half of the nineteenth century has only begun to be explored.[3] This is so in part because, as we shall see in the first chapter, one of the effects of the northern European narrative of the modern was to channel analysis away from this fundamental sphere of inquiry into other, more immediately visible areas, such as the aesthetic and political polemics that were etched into the surface of early nineteenth-century Spanish letters. The attention that such skirmishes received—neoclassicists versus romantics, progressive versus moderate liberals—was useful, to be sure, but it often came at the expense of examining the relationship between Spanish romantic discourse and the more fundamental sociocultural transformation to which it belonged. Another of the aims of this book is to make clearer the position of Spanish romantic discourse—particularly the representation of romantic subjectivity—within the secularizing political, economic, and cultural machinery of late eighteenth- and early nineteenth-century Spain. While Spain was not at the center of those upheavals that would become metonymic emblems of European modernity—the French, the Scientific, and the Industrial Revolutions, respectively—its peripheral status makes it a unique, albeit often overlooked, site of inquiry from which to think about the familiar European narratives of modernity and romanticism.

Finally, I have evoked the twenty-four-hour news in order to recall by way of contrast that *information,* the life-blood of the news and the new currency of the times, could scarcely be more removed from the deeply affective rhetorical registers that characterize Spanish romantic writing. The texts I will be taking up repeatedly stage a radical disjunction between fact and feeling, datum and impression. They are texts that register the increasing divergence between a world of empirical certainties on one hand, and more subjective claims to knowledge on the other. In this split are the traces of a division of labor within psychic life that is itself a symptom of what Max Weber would come to call the rationalization of the world, and at the level of romantic expression such a rift bears witness to the widening gap between the language of science and the language of art; it speaks to the double character of language in modernity (Horkheimer and Adorno, 17–18).

Such observations in turn raise fundamental questions for readers and critics at the beginning of the twenty-first century, for in its recoiling from the values of data and information, romantic discourse carries with it a cautionary tale that may still speak to the Information Age and its "knowledge-workers." There is within romantic discourse a tacit warning concerning the limits of empirical thought, a warning that the more reductive or scientific strains of contemporary cultural theory might do well to heed. To process romantic discourse primarily as "information" is not only to disregard the discursive specificity of the cultural production that has come to be known as "literature"; it is also to participate in the ongoing reification of culture by limiting accounts of the literary to a delivering of the news, as it were.[4] Far from the realm of fact, language is, among other things, a site of struggle—what Voloshinov referred to as "the inner dialectic quality of the sign" (24)—, and in the analyses that follow I have attempted to register the complex and highly dynamic ways in which Spanish romantic discourse engages both its sociohistoric and its symbolic locations.

Against presentism, this book thus aims to raise a multilayered conception of the historical, particularly as it pertains to a pivotal moment of Spanish cultural history (1770s to 1830s); against the legacy of "modern Europe," it will attempt to take up the challenges of thinking about "Spanish modernity"; against the backdrop of Spain's emergent, nineteenth-century liberal political economy, it aims to understand the contradictory status of romantic subjectivity; and against the temptation of reading culture primarily as a product, it will posit a series of more complexly mediated relationships. In many ways, the exegetical ideal of this project is something similar to what Clifford Geertz has called "thick description," a kind of reading that takes into account the dense, polysemic nature of the material under scrutiny, even as it tries to accord such material intelligibility within a broader analytic framework.

At the same time, I have purposefully attempted to engage a hermeneutics that is neither systematically suspicious nor programmatically redemptive. No serious reader today can be unaware of the ways in which literary discourse has repeatedly participated in any number of execrable power formations, but neither can such a reader seriously entertain the notion that complicity is the only mode of relationship that obtains between discourse and power. The common, vaguely Foucauldian stance from which literature is read solely as part of the discursive construction of social life is in danger of forgetting that Foucault himself was keenly aware of the polyvalent functions of discourse:

We must make allowance for the complex and unstable process whereby discourse can be both an instrument and an effect of power, but also a hindrance, a stumbling-block, a point of resistance and a starting point for an opposing strategy. Discourse transmits and produces power; it reinforces it, but also undermines and exposes it, renders it fragile and makes it possible to thwart it. (*The History*, 101)[5]

Similarly, the kind of wholesale indictment of the past that at times rears its head within certain sectors of a socially committed cultural criticism might yet benefit from recalling the enigmatic qualities of historical time as evoked, for example, in Benjamin's "Theses on the Philosophy of History." In this work one can find, to be sure, the following well-known image of "the angel of history": "His face is turned toward the past. Where we perceive a chain of events, he sees one single catastrophe which keeps piling wreckage upon wreckage and hurls it in front of his feet" (*Illuminations* 257). But there is also a Benjamin for whom "the past carries with it a temporal index by which it is referred to redemption" (254). "By dint of a secret heliotropism"—he writes in the fourth thesis—"the past strives to turn toward the sun which is rising in the sky of history" (254–55). For Benjamin, the urgency of historical thought demands the rare "gift of fanning the spark of hope in the past" (255). In the chapters that follow, I have consequently attempted to avoid narrowly deterministic conceptions of both discourse and of history. In practical terms, this has meant that in examining the idea of the modern, I have tried to acknowledge the critical potential—the spark of hope in the past—that dwells within the more emancipatory impulses of romantic aesthetics in Spain while also pointing to its ideological limitations. Readers who wish to exempt the literary from social history and those who wish to reduce it to that history will, I hope, be equally disappointed.

The book is comprised of four chapters followed by a brief afterword. The first chapter, "From the Narratives of Modernity to Spanish Romanticism," expands on the issues I have raised here by means of an extended inquiry into Spain's position within the standard historical theorization of Western modernity. In recent years it has become a critical commonplace to acknowledge that, from the eighteenth century onward, Spain and its cultural production became peripheral to the idea of "modern Europe." The history of Spain's shifting status within the West's historical imagination, however, has rarely been examined as a centuries-long process with deep roots in Spain's own early modern, imperial era.[6] Drawing on classic sociohistorical theories of modernity (Weber, Durkheim), on the philosophy of history (Hegel), on world-systems analysis (Wallerstein), and on recent debates within postcolonial historiography (Mignolo, Dussel, Quijano), this chapter attempts to place the question of Spanish modernity within a deeper historical matrix than it has traditionally been granted. It then proceeds to examine the effects of this historical structure on Spain's romantic literature, on the history of its critical reception, and on its ongoing contemporary theorization. After analyzing such effects, the chapter sketches possible new terms of dialogue between "romantic Spain" and "modern Europe."

Subsequent chapters attempt to demonstrate how such a dialogue might begin to be carried out in practice at the level of textual analysis. Each chapter takes up the question of modernity through the work of a different Spanish author: José Cadalso (1741–1782), Angel Saavedra [Duke of Rivas] (1791–1865), and Mariano José de Larra (1809–1837). Although they are well-known—indeed canonical—figures within Spanish literary studies, these writers have been utterly absent from the canon of "modern European literature." My hope is that discussion of their work in the pages that follow will prompt additional interest in them, not only because they still have much to teach us about the question of modernity in Spain, but also because, as each analysis suggests, their works offer fascinating sites from which to question longstanding assumptions about the nature of Western modernity itself.[7]

Readers who are familiar with the oeuvre of each of these writers will find a sustained attempt to take each author into new critical and theoretical terrain. Chapter 2 is a meditation on the links between modern subjectivity and melancholy in one of Spain's more notorious gothic texts, *Noches lúgubres* [Lugubrious Nights] (1774). Drawing on psychoanalytic and political theory, it highlights the emergence of a distinctively modern form of affect in Cadalso's work and charts its significance for the romantic era in Spain. Chapter 3 engages the relationships between liberal modernity, colonialism, and empire in *Don Alvaro o la fuerza del sino* (1835), a play that would become internationally famous by way of Giuseppe Verdi's opera, *La Forza del Destino*. It explores the socially symbolic dimensions of the play's form and then proceeds to examine the work through the overlapping frameworks of Spain's waning colonialism and modern Europe's growing cultural imperialism. Chapter 4 examines the relationship between death and the modern in a series of 1836 essays that Mariano José de Larra penned shortly before committing suicide in the winter of 1837. The chapter takes up key notions from Marxian cultural theory in order analyze the links between the figure of death in Larra's writing and the emergence of modern liberalism. A brief afterword explores the ways in which reading Spanish romanticism against the narratives of Western modernity may yet speak to our present, particularly as the familiar tale of civilization against barbarity once again seems to structure the contemporary international politics of our day.

The mode of argumentation throughout the book is purposefully incremental. Arguments are designed to accrue, and my hope is that the intensity of critical predication builds as readers proceed through each chapter. In the chapters dedicated to individual works, the direction of analysis intentionally moves from literary textuality to other discourses (history, psychoanalysis, philosophy, political theory, etc.) in order to produce a kind of "working through" each text. My interest in proceeding this way has been to engage the works under scrutiny as, among other things, modes of thought worthy of protracted engagement in their own right. The etymology of the word "theory" teaches us that it is fundamentally a mode of seeing; at times, however, it is easy to forget that the texts that we have traditionally called "literature" share this basic feature with the models of inquiry that we bring to them. In the chapters that follow, my objective has been to grant both kinds of insight their due as we explore the intersections between romanticism, modernity, and empire in late eighteenth- and early nineteenth-century Spain.

CHAPTER I

From the Narratives of the Modernity
to Spanish Romanticism

In the closing lines of his 1990 Nobel Lecture, "La búsqueda del presente" [The Search for the Present], Octavio Paz openly grapples, like others before him, with the elusive character of the modern. "Perseguimos a la modernidad en sus incesantes metamorfosis"—he writes—"y nunca logramos asirla. Se escapa siempre: cada encuento es una fuga" [We pursue modernity in her incessant metamorphoses, yet we never manage to get a hold of her. She always escapes: each encounter ends in flight] (20).[1] Moments later, as Paz brings his observations to an end, the quest for the modern, which he has figured in the language of Eros throughout the lecture, finally comes to find its object in the paradox of evanescence itself, a sense of the fleeting that, once acknowledged, becomes the threshold of an epiphany:

> La abrazamos y al punto se disipa: sólo era un poco de aire. Es el instante, ese pájaro que está en todas partes y en ninguna. Queremos asirlo vivo pero abre las alas y se desvanece, vuelto un puñado de sílabas. Nos quedamos con las manos vacías. Entonces las puertas de la percepción se entreabren y aparece el otro tiempo, el verdadero, el que buscábamos sin saberlo: el presente, la presencia. (22)

> [We embrace her and she disappears immediately: it was just a little air. It is the instant, that bird that is everywhere and nowhere. We want to apprehend it alive but it opens its wings and vanishes, transformed into a handful of syllables. We are left empty-handed. Then the doors of perception open slightly and the *other time* appears, the real one we were searching for without knowing it: the present, the presence.]

In its rapturous figuration of the modern as the ever-vanishing trace of the present, this formulation and the modernist poetic tradition to which it belongs eloquently bear witness to the challenges of coming to terms with a word-thought that is most at home in the impermanence we call time.[2] The convergence of modernity and the present in Paz's lecture, however, also speaks to an intuitive understanding of the modern as a particular way of conceptualizing contemporary times, a manner of distinguishing the way things are now from the way they were then. The concept of modernity is born under the sign of discontinuity. It is, among other things, an attempt to transect historical time into a before and an after such that the two moments no longer recognize their family resemblance. It entails an othering of past and present; but the irony behind modernity-as-discontinuity is that the discontinuous itself then becomes a category capable of binding disparate historical times. Modernity comes to share something fundamental with the very past it would eschew. It shares its passing, for the today from which the modern looks over its shoulder to tell the past, "we are different, you and I," is a moment to which tomorrow will also be able repeat the same words. Like Paz's bird, the modern appears to be everywhere and nowhere.

As an abstract, formal relation to the past, the modern flirts with temporal ubiquity. Paz comments, for example, that "la modernidad rompe con el pasado inmediato sólo para rescatar al pasado milenario y convertir a una figurilla de fertilidad del neolítico en nuestra contemporánea" [modernity breaks with the immediate past only to recover an age-old past and transform a tiny fertility figure from the Neolithic into our contemporary] (22), and the poet seems to smile wryly at the claims of a postmodernity that is often unaware of the way it apes the hallmark proclamation of the modern, *now things are really different*. "¿Pero qué es la postmodernidad"—Paz asks—"sino una modernidad aún más moderna?" [But what is postmodernism if not an even more modern modernity?] (14). And yet, as if to remind us of the longstanding quarrel between Poetry and History, this aesthetic sense of a modernity in perpetual flight is almost immediately countered by the weight with which the modern has been imbued as one of the fundamental categories of Western historiography. For history, modernity is not just any perceived break with the past, not just any moment of discontinuity. Clio does not easily tolerate a ubiquitous modernity-as-vanishing-act that would leave her empty-handed. History tells us in no uncertain terms that the modern is no mere relational category; it has substance, it is there, the traditional Western narrative reminds us, early modernity is there at the end of the European Middle Ages.

It is precisely this narrative and Spain's symbolic position within it that I would like to reconsider in this chapter in order to begin to understand the many contradictions and paradoxes that subtend the idea of Spanish modernity and by extension the idea of Spanish romanticism. Without forgetting the aesthetic challenge that Paz's protean, mobile modernity poses to history's need to fix the past in place, I will consequently focus on the dominant Western sociohistorical narrative of modernity and on Spain's peculiar position within it. The reason behind such a choice is as simple as it is profound, for Spain's seemingly ambiguous relationship to the history of Western modernity has been one of the central features of Spanish culture from the late seventeenth century to recent times. Moreover, as we shall see, the question of historical modernity has largely defined the parameters of literary-critical engagement with Spanish romanticism almost since the movement's inception. The idea of the modern has in a sense been the field in which most discussions of Spanish romanticism have—wittingly or not—tended to unfold up to the present. This chapter will thus take up the intersections between what Jürgen Habermas has called "the philosophical discourse of modernity" on the one hand, and the history of the theorization of Spanish romanticism on the other.

My objective is neither to provide a new theory of modernity nor to offer a new history of Spanish romanticism, but rather to bring these two spheres of inquiry into productive dialogue with one another. In doing so, I hope to question several prevailing assumptions about Spanish romantic writing and its relationship to both its historical moment and to "the history of the West." Part of such a process entails embedding romantic Spain within a far deeper history than the subject has habitually elicited; indeed, it calls for a historical horizon that harks back several centuries before European romanticism itself. What follows will in this regard be a critical retelling of the story of the modern with a view to charting more fully Spain's shifting positions within this macronarrative. My aim is not only to situate the question of Spanish romanticism within a broader historical framework than it has habitually been accorded, but also to reflect on the ways in which a centuries-long pattern of thinking about Spain shaped a significant portion of its romantic production as well as critical inquiry into the culture of romantic Spain to this day. By the end of my tale, the reasons for which all but the most intrepid of comparative romanticists are likely to be reading these lines will, I hope, become rather clear. For those who are such comparative romanticists, as well as for those who might want to address them, I will also attempt to demonstrate that Spanish romanticism can and should be read as a heuristic on the ideological limits within which entities as formidable as "Western modernity," "European romanticism," and "modern European literature" have been constituted.

Eclipse: Spain and the History of Modern Europe

Our starting point will be the classic sociohistorical conception of the modern. If the dawn of modernity has traditionally been positioned by historians at end of the Middle Ages, this interpretation has in large measure been predicated on a series of phenomena—Discovery, Renaissance, and Reformation—whose cumulative effect is thought to have produced a significant rupture within the history of European social life. Drawn by these three midwives of the modern, Hegel, in his *Lectures on the Philosophy of History*, famously placed modernity's birth at the beginning of the sixteenth century. The profound impact of the discovery of a new continent, the resurgence of humanistic thought, and the new Protestant understanding of religious subjectivity announced for Hegel something new and unprecedented.[3] Almost a century later, Max Weber's foundational twentieth-century inquiry into European modernity, *The Protestant Ethic and the "Spirit of Capitalism,"* would reaffirm this temporal location of the modern by making the Reformation the touchstone of his well-known thesis. In reviewing these and other classic conceptions of modernity, Habermas has summarized their basic features by invoking the key Weberian concept of *rationalization*, a process thought to be at work throughout the various historical tumults that the Europe of the 1500s was undergoing.

> Weber understood [modern rationalization] as the institutionalization of purposive-rational economic and administrative action. To the degree that everyday life was affected by this cultural and societal rationalization [. . .] traditional forms of life were dissolved. [. . .] Emile Durkheim and George Herbert Mead saw rationalized lifeworlds as characterized by the reflective treatment of traditions that have lost their quasinatural status; by the universalization of norms of action and the generalization of values [. . .]; and finally by patterns of socialization that are oriented to the formations of abstract ego-identities. [. . .] This is in broad strokes how the classical social theorists drew the picture of modernity. (*Philosophical*, 2)[4]

In such an account of the modern, the overarching effect of the geographical, literary-philosophical, and psycho-religious upheavals of the sixteenth century comes to be understood as part of a broader denaturalizing cultural machinery that undermines a putatively stable medieval culture, thus marking a signal moment within the history of European social life. This template for organizing European history has proved remarkably stable since its consolidation in the early nineteenth century, and despite the myriad challenges that have been directed at the chronology—usually from within the disciplines of postmodern philosophy and cultural theory—in departments of history, where the practical matter of writing historical works continues to overshadow protracted theoretical reflection on the possibility of such writing, the traditional division of Western history into antiquity, the Middle Ages, and the modern era remains firmly in place today. The historical conception of the modern is not easily dislodged; like other icons of Western culture, its inertia has been extraordinary.

Even as Hegel was locating modernity in sixteenth-century Europe, however, he had become aware of a fissure that seemed to be opening up within his own present. The Enlightenment and the French Revolution had given the modern—already a three-century-long epoch—a decidedly novel inflection. The Hegel of *Phenomenology of Spirit* thus acknowledges in 1807 that something new has been stirring within *Geist*:

> It is surely not difficult to see that our time is a birth and transition to a new period. The Spirit has broken with what was hitherto the world of its existence and imagination is about to submerge all this in the past; it is at work giving itself a new form. [. . .] This gradual crumbling [. . .] is interrupted by the break of day, that like lightning, all at once reveals the edifice of the new world. (cited by Habermas, *Philosophical*, 6)

The rift to which Hegel refers here has of course also been codified in the traditional historiographic distinction between early modern and modern Europe. On the face of it, however, the appearance of a new modernity—the modern Europe of the Enlightenment and its aftermath—would seem to thwart modernity's historical claim to be *the* irreparable break with the past. The familiar historiographic solution to this conundrum is equally curious, for two very different historical upheavals come to be scripted as moments *within* a vaster modern era that remains intact.[5] Such a solution to the problem of modernity's doubling suggests that the "edifice of the

new world" of the 1800s that Hegel saw flash up before him was ultimately not grasped as a radical historical rupture with the past. Rather, it
seems to have been represented as a shift—profound, to be sure—within
an ongoing historical process whereby, in a characteristically Hegelian maneuver, quantitative accretion leads to the recognition of a new qualitative
form. Hegel himself would observe moments after the passage quoted
above that "this new world is no more a complete actuality than is a new-
born child" (50). In construing the passage from early modern to modern
Europe in these terms, the history of modernity, so often apprehended in
terms of its own inaugural break with the past, thus begins to reveal its
penchant for continuity. The familial metaphor Hegel uses is significant,
for although new, the paternity of Hegel's "child" is never in question; it
is simply the new face of Spirit. Indeed, by Europe's eighteenth century,
modernity dons the mask of Progress in order to stage a play in which its
own unfolding becomes the primary engine of History.[6] Through an extraordinarily deft sleight-of-hand, rupture begets a narrative of continual
development, and the modernity of Enlightenment thus comes to be apprehended as an intensification of an ongoing rationalization and disenchantment of the world reputed to have begun in Europe circa 1500.[7]

Viewed from a present that remains wary of grand narratives, any
number of caveats regarding this historical tale might of course be articulated. Like most narratives of origin, the ruptural moment of modernity's
birth is difficult to pin down, and upon close scrutiny its temporal location often dissolves into an historical *longue durée*. For their part, reason and rationalization, particularly in their totalized, instrumentalized,
and strategic incarnations, have long been suspect entities in projects that
range—to mention one genealogy—from Nietzsche and Heidegger, to
Franco-American postmodernism more generally. Similarly, the tale of historical progress, in many ways the paradigmatic metanarrative whose end
Lyotard notes in *The Postmodern Condition*, seems to have withered away
over the course of the second half of the twentieth century, as if discredited
by, among other things, the prima facie case that the century itself made
against such a notion.[8] The idea of progress as a historical force claims few
devotees within the academy today, except perhaps as the necessary villain
within an ongoing romance of postmodern theoretical conflict. Indeed, it
is suspicion of narrative epistemology itself, more specifically of narrative's
teleological propensities, that seems to have become one of the defining
gestures of the newer forms of contemporary literary-historical thought.[9]

The majority of the battles that postmodern theory waged with the modern, however, remained squarely within the house that modernity built.[10] Until recent years, what tended to pass unquestioned in the myriad attempts to redesign—if not dismantle—the house of the modern was the open secret of all real estate: the question of location. In large measure it has fallen on postcolonial studies—and even more recently on "global literary studies"—to insistently put the theoretical question of *place* on the table as part of a broader ongoing critique of Eurocentrism. The European claim to universality that Max Weber famously posed as a question in the prefatory remarks to his *Collected Essays in the Sociology of Religion* has consequently been at the heart of recent postcolonial engagements with European thought. "What chain of circumstances"—Weber asks—"led to the appearance in the West, and only in the West, of cultural phenomena which—or so at least we like to think—came to have universal significance and validity?" (*Protestant* 356). The presumption of a uniquely Western universal significance has of course been directly challenged from any number of non-European localities, and one of the central issues within contemporary postcolonial studies is the epistemological dance it maintains with Western categories of thought that have become "both indispensable and inadequate" (Chakrabarty, 6).[11] At the same time, however, the privileging of place within postcolonial epistemologies has slowly worked its way back to the European continent itself as scholars have increasingly asked just where this universalizing "West" was located.

The answer already present in Hegel's lessons on universal history is revealing, and, as we shall see, its implications for an understanding of the position of modern Spanish culture (late seventeenth to twentieth centuries) within a broader European context could not be more fundamental. Walter Mignolo has recently summarized Hegel's geography of the modern and its relationship to the Iberoamerican Atlantic world:

> Europe as conceptualized by Hegel in his lessons on universal history had a center and several peripheries. [. . .] And he divides the pie as follows. The first part is southern Europe. The mountain chains that run through France separate Italy from France and Germany. He adds, "Greece also belongs to this part of Europe. Greece and Italy long presented the theater of the World's History; and while the middle and north of Europe were uncultivated, the World-Spirit found its home here." ("Rethinking," 165)

"You many notice," Mignolo observes, "that Spain and Portugal are absent in Hegel's scheme." It is an omission whose significance is progressively magnified:

> The silence becomes even louder when Hegel mentions that the second portion is the "heart of Europe." "In this center of Europe"—Hegel clearly stated—"France, Germany and England are the principal countries." That is, these were the three countries in the process of becoming the new colonial powers, replacing Spain and Portugal. The third part of Europe (the northeastern states) presents a new scenario that connects Europe with Asia. ("Rethinking," 165)

For Mignolo, Hegel's omission of Spain, Portugal, and, by extension, the colonial Atlantic world is symptomatic of the "imperial difference" that from the eighteenth century forward came to characterize the conceptualization of European modernity. "The imperial difference"—he observes—"is the silence in Hegel's southern Europe. [. . .] At the time that Hegel was writing, it was already clear that Spain and Portugal, on the one hand, and Russia, on the other were on the margin of Europe or the West" ("Rethinking," 165). Leopoldo Zea puts it even more plainly when he observes that for the modern Europe of the eighteenth and nineteenth centuries, "Spain and her colonies had merely become part of the non-Western world, spoils of war to be conquered as Asia, Africa, and Oceania had been before" (125).

This symbolic amputation of Spain from "modernity," "Europe," and the "West" was arguably among the most profound historical determinants in defining modern Spanish culture. Indeed, it is difficult to imagine another European country in which the crisis of (non)modernity has played as central a role in the cultural history of the nation as it did in the case of modern Spain.[12] This is so, not only because Spain became the first posthegemonic European nation-state—with a memory of its early modern centrality—but more importantly because its loss of hegemony was in fact intimately linked to the transition from early modern to modern Europe. In fundamental ways, modern Europe was born out of the material and discursive defeat of early modern Spain. The "edifice of the new world" that Hegel intuited in 1807 was, as Mignolo suggests, another name for the ascent of the *Kulturwelt* of Britain, France, and Germany as the new European powers; these powers in turn became the new agents of universal history, the heart of modern Europe. Tellingly, only seven years after Hegel's words were first published, Spain would officially "come to be considered by the diplomats and statesmen who gathered in Paris in 1814, as *un cour secondaire*, a second-class nation" (Carr, 1). Moreover, if it is a truism that history is generally written from the perspective of the victor, Spain's geopolitical defeat and the ensuing northern European hegemony called modern Europe would render something even more formidable, History—with a capital H—an entity to which the Iberoamerican world, along with the rest of the non-European world, would, by definition, not belong.[13] From the eighteenth century forward, the message was consistent: If the rational spirit of History was to inhabit the Luso-Hispanic world, it would have to radiate outward from its home in northern Europe. As fortune would have it, the new powers were more than willing to demonstrate their generosity in this civilizing mission.[14]

The birth of modern universal History could not have taken place, however, without the prior erasure of a significant portion of early modern European history. In order for the genealogy of Western civilization to coalesce into the familiar temporal and geographical progression that moves seamlessly from ancient Greece and Rome, to Renaissance Italy, to modern Europe, the north first needed to engage in a profound kind of historical housecleaning; and it did so by extirpating its greatest early modern rival—and the source of much of its own wealth—from the history of modernity. Examining these events from the global perspective of world-systems theory, Enrique Dussel has recently charted the key features of this process.[15] Echoing the rift in Hegel's sense of historical time that we considered earlier, Dussel observes that "there are at least two modernities," two ostensible thresholds of grand historical change, which traditional historiographies have simply named Renaissance and Enlightenment:

> the first is Hispanic, humanist, Renaissance modernity, still linked to the old interregional system of Mediterranean, Muslim and Christian. In this [modernity] [. . .] Spain "manages" centrality as domination through the hegemony of an integral culture, a language, a religion (and thus, the evangelization process that Amerindia will suffer); as military occupation, bureaucratic-political organization, economic expropriation, demographic presence (with hundreds of thousands of Spaniards and Portuguese who will forever inhabit Amerindia), ecological transformation (through the modification of

the fauna and flora), and so on. This is the substance of the world empire project, which [. . .] failed with Charles V. (13)

In this first moment, as manager of the world-system, Spain is in fact at the center of the modern to the extent that conquest and colonization are modernity's engines; but as power increasingly drifts northward, replicating the flow of wealth that passed from the Americas through Spain to the Low Countries, another modernity emerges, a modernity that will make its own claims to exclusivity:

> Second, there is the modernity of Anglo-Germanic Europe, which begins with the Amsterdam of Flanders and which frequently passes as the *only* modernity (this is the interpretation of Sombart, Weber, Habermas, and even the postmoderns, who will produce a "reductionist fallacy" that occludes the meaning of modernity and, thus, the sense of its contemporary crisis). This second modernity, [in order] to be able to manage the immense world-system suddenly opening itself to tiny Holland [. . .] must accomplish or increase its efficacy through *simplification*. (13)

The simplification to which Dussel refers is nothing other than the world of Cartesian/Spinozan rationalism and, at a later moment, the new empirical sciences of Enlightenment. Its characteristics thus coincide roughly with the attributes of the abstract, instrumental reason necessitated by the need to coordinate the world-system.[16]

While Dussel mounts a compelling materialist challenge to the genealogy of Western reason—rationalization here is revealed to be merely a function of a world-system managerial problem—his account also makes manifest the ways in which the concept of modern Europe, the Europe of Enlightenment, served to efface the enormous debt that an emergent north owed to the early modern, Luso-Hispanic, transatlantic world. For Dussel, on a planetary scale, the exploitation of the Americas accorded to Europe "*the definitive comparative advantage* with respect to the Muslim, Indian, and Chinese worlds" that had competed with and often surpassed it during the Middle Ages (12). His answer to Weber's question—Why Europe?—is quite simply the conquest and colonization of the Americas.[17] Yet, as we saw in Hegel, it was precisely the Luso-Hispanic Atlantic that would be written out of History in order to establish the image of an autonomous (northern) "European Spirit" unfolding through time.[18] Akin to the pristine houses that dot the suburban landscape of the postindustrial West today, the imported materials and labor that made the edifice of Hegel's 1807 modernity possible would be submerged below the threshold of visibility. And by the time of Weber's 1905 analysis, the historical cleansing of the modern becomes even clearer. Of the old triad—Discovery, Renaissance, and Reformation—the first two terms fade into subordinate positions, while the third is brilliantly elevated to become the central interpretive category. Although a diffuse rationalizing spirit might be acknowledged in other times and places, the true catalyst of the modern for Weber—the moment that really matters—is to be found in the ethno-religious subjectivities of Protestantism. Moreover, the narrative of linear progress that, as we saw, bridges Europe's two modernities into a single, cohesive modern era, made possible a fascinating and remarkable kind of historical back-formation. Gazing upon the child of Hegel's "new age," there was little doubt about its lineage. Any civilized person could see it plainly. It was in the child's face. Surely the modern had been northern all along.[19]

The Land That Time Forgot

Spain, however, was not purged from the history of modernity solely by way of the omissions that characterize the "imperial difference" of Hegel's modern Europe. Even as the Spanish Empire declined, it remained a political and economic reality that could not easily be overlooked by the rising powers to the north. In order for modern Europe to constitute its autonomy as the agent of universal History, it was not enough to merely sidestep the Iberoamerican Atlantic and its legacy. The modernity of early modern Spain had to be expressly refuted—rewritten as something else— and northern Europe displayed an almost inexhaustible energy in pursuing this task.[20] Indeed, it mounted a campaign so successful that even today, among relatively educated nonspecialists, "Spanish Inquisition" is as familiar an expression as "Spanish Enlightenment," for example, is a strange one. "Spanish barbarity" seems to have a natural ring to it in English that "French barbarity" and "British barbarity" do not. These are the ideological remnants of over three centuries of northern European historical representation, and the cumulative effect of this historical juggernaut was to render until very recently the terms "Spain" and "modernity" antithetical to the Western ear.

This history of northern European representation can be grasped in three distinctive phases that align themselves roughly with the Reformation, Enlightenment, and romanticism, and a review of these moments will prove useful in understanding the deeper context in which Spain's romanticism has been imagined. Almost from its inception, the Reformation's struggle against early modern Spain was carried out on symbolic as well as material terrain. The wars of the early modern era were not only conflagrations fought with armies, but also representational battles waged with the printed word, the new warrior on a battlefield that, since Gutenberg, had become a fundamental site of ideological struggle. In this context, Spain's ultimate defeat in its confrontation with Protestant Europe meant, among other things, a profound diminishment of its power to define itself and its history internationally. From the position of an enunciating agent of European history, Spain became the object of northern European historical enunciation. From the seventeenth century forward, it would have little or no control over its image abroad; instead, it would increasingly respond defensively to a modern Europe whose power to define Spain and Spanish history only grew stronger with time. What emerged from Spain's struggles against a burgeoning north was thus a series of stereotypes—the Inquisition, the Black Legend, and, in the eighteenth century, a more general portrait of uncivilized backwardness. The common denominator to each of these images was the tacit expulsion of Spain from European history; or, to put it more precisely, from the celebratory history of Western rationalism.[21]

To the extent that they would become paradigmatic, each of these stereotypes helps to illuminate the symbolic place Spain was accorded within the discursive construction of modern Europe. The mythmaking around the Inquisition, for example, afforded Protestant Europe a powerful ideological tool that was central to its own self-definition. Political conflict was collapsed into the convenient ethical binaries that have invariably accompanied war in the West: The Spanish Inquisition became the image of a Catholic evil against which to define Protestant goodness.[22] As Henry Kamen has recently concluded, the depiction of the Tribunal as an omnipotent instrument of tyranny, intolerance, and barbarity was, for the most part, the product of a highly effective Reformation propaganda campaign:

The printing-press, one of the most powerful weapons taken up by the Reformation, was used against the tribunal. For the first time, in the 1560s images of the dreaded [. . .] auto de fe were reproduced as proof of the terrible fate awaiting the enemies of Rome. Protestant pens depicted the struggles of heretics as one for freedom from a tyrannical faith. Wherever Catholicism triumphed, they claimed, not only religious but civil liberty was extinguished. The Reformation, according to this interpretation, brought about the liberation of the human spirit from the fetters of darkness and superstition. Propaganda along these lines proved to be strikingly effective in the context of the political conflicts of the period. (305)

"Bearing in mind the very small numbers of Protestants ever executed by Spanish tribunals"—Kamen notes—"the campaign against the Inquisition can be seen as a reflection of political and religious fears rather than as a logical reaction to a real threat" (305). The political expedience of making Spain and the Inquisition synonymous with one another was of course considerable, and the fact that the vast majority of the Inquisition's victims had been people of Jewish and Muslim origin was easily overlooked. What mattered most in the north was to marshal opposition to the more immediate political threat that Spain posed to the Reformation. At the same time, converting Spain into the antonomasia of religious intolerance was an extremely useful way of drawing attention away from northern Europe's own dark history of religious persecution.[23]

Coupled with this image of the Inquisition was the characterization of Spain's colonial history that has come to be known as the Black Legend.[24] Drawing from Fray Bartolomé de las Casas's well-known indictment of Spain's conquest and colonization of the Americas, northern Europe put the *Brevíssima relación de la destrucción de las Indias* [A Very Brief Relation of the Destruction of the Indies] (1552) to the service of establishing the image of Spain as a *singularly* barbaric and oppressive nation. Although antecedents to this discourse can be found in earlier Italian resistance to Spanish dominion, its flourishing accompanied the revolt of the Netherlands in the sixteenth century, and it grew with the religious wars of the seventeenth. In the *Apologia* (1580) that William of Orange wrote in response to his Proscription by Phillip II, for example, Spaniards are represented as the height of cruelty, a "bloody people, more cruel than Palaris, Busiris, Nero, Domitian, and all similar tyrants" (47). Several years later, the anonymous author of *A Treatise Paraenetical* (1597) would hold "that tyranny is as proper and natural to the Castilian as laughter to a man; and that all which he hath in any part of the world hath been usurped, either by his predecessors or by himself, unjustly and by plain tyranny" (48).[25] The idea that Spaniards were naturally ignorant and barbaric, along with its unspoken correlate—that northern Europe was not—would remain a central feature of anti-Spanish discourse. It appears repeatedly throughout the propaganda that accompanied the Thirty Years' War, and it is not difficult to find in the years to follow, as English rivalry with Spain intensified. Oliver Cromwell's speech at the opening of Parliament in 1656 offers a revealing synthesis of the "natural" place that Spain and Spaniards would be accorded within Europe's "second modernity" (Dussel 13):

> Why, truly, your great enemy is the Spaniard. He is. He is a natural enemy, he is naturally so. He is naturally so, throughout, as I said before, throughout all your enemies, through that enmity that is in him against all that is of God that is in you, or that which may be in you, contrary to that that his blindness and darkness, led on by superstition and the implications of his faith in submitting to the See of Rome, acts him unto. (57)

Underlying such characterizations was the more fundamental fact of protracted military and political conflict. Under the Hapsburg dynasty, Spain had risen to preside over the largest, most powerful empire in Europe since Rome, and as this imperial order slowly unraveled, Spain paid the price of prior dominion. "No great empire," Maltby observes, "can avoid incurring the wrath of its neighbors; and the wide range of Spanish activities, not only against England, but in the Netherlands, France and Italy, left Spain particularly vulnerable to hostile criticism" (139). Moreover, the common struggle against Spain generated a kind of consensus among the otherwise competing countries of the north:

> When the honest Englishman turned to his neighbors for enlightenment [concerning Spain], he found his worst suspicions confirmed and the prejudice of his countrymen justified. For all their differences, England's cultural ties with France and the Netherlands have always been close, and their separate strains of anti-Hispanism tended inevitably to reinforce each other. It was in this way that the legend of Spanish barbarism was allowed to grow and become part of the intellectual baggage of the Western man. (Maltby, 139)

To put it more simply, the vilification of Spain was sufficiently widespread so as to take on the appearance and function of a common truth. The ideological work that this truth performed for northern Europe was, in symbolic terms, considerable. The images of Spanish inquisitorial and colonial barbarity did much more than simply condemn a political foe. They also elided modern Europe's roots in the Iberoamerican Atlantic by marking the Spanish Empire as modernity's exterior. Spain became a non-European Europe, a non-Western West. It is for this reason, among others, that as Dussel noted, Europe's "second modernity" has so often passed as the only one and that its pre-Enlightenment pedigree was carefully circumscribed to the Reformation. The modernity of the Luso-Hispanic transatlantic was quite literally made unthinkable, thus clearing the way for the narrative of a self-contained, unfolding, modern European history. Within the West's emergent symbolic self-understanding, Spain had become the image of everything modern Europe was not, and this Manichean logic was integral to the rhetoric of modern colonialism: If Spain was barbaric, oppressive, fanatical, ignorant, bigoted, violent, and superstitious, modern European imperialism would imagine itself as civilized, liberating, tolerant, educated, fair-minded, peaceful, and rational. Moreover, as it assumed the center of the world-system, modern Europe ensured that these wonders, the new masks of its power, were spread across the planet.

Northern Europe's representation of Spain, however, was not a static affair. As early modern Europe entered the second modernity of Enlightenment, Spain's symbolic expulsion from the modern also entered a new phase. While the country had been successfully portrayed as distinctively tyrannical and barbaric in the sixteenth and seventeenth centuries, by the eighteenth century Spain was represented as an embarrassingly backward, uncivilized place that the spirit of progress had forgotten. Perhaps for this reason, it remained a de rigueur reference for the majority of the writers of the French Enlightenment, all of whom seem to have felt compelled to cast a disapproving eye southward.[26] The images of Spanish culture that had emerged from the heat of the religiously inflected wars of the early modern era were thus replaced with a decidedly secular form of cultural disparagement. In place of Protestant diatribes against a fanatically Catholic Spain, it was now enlightened Reason—the sibling of Protestantism after all, Weber would later proclaim—that patrolled the boundaries of modern Europe, making clear at all times that Spain's position remained south of the border. María Carmen Iglesias sums up the overall effect of this shift:

> [T]he writers of the [French] Enlightenment, whether or not they had the opportunity to travel in Spain [. . .] accepted the black legend and gave it a place within a coherent history of Europe, thereby creating the definitive stereotype of the Spanish essence for the modern world, and bestowing upon it the weight of their authority [. . .] [and] the appearance of a foregone rational conclusion. (144)

At the same time, under the cool gaze of French reason, the definition of Spain's national character underwent a metamorphosis that would have a considerable impact on the nineteenth-century understanding of Spanish romanticism. As northern Europe became more powerful, the earlier paradigm of Spanish tyranny, barbarity, and fanaticism was fused with a new "naturally" Spanish vice that, not surprisingly, was far less formidable. For the French Enlightenment, the problem with Spain was simply that, although famously proud, Spaniards were inherently lazy. Over the course of the 1700s, a pseudoempirical psychology of climate begins to naturalize northern European power, and within this new scheme Spain becomes part of a mythically unproductive, slothful, and indolent south. Montesquieu's *The Spirit of the Laws* (1748) offers a revealing example of the new symbolic geography of modern Europe and its distinctive north–south divide. The superiority of northern Europeans is for Montesquieu a natural state of affairs, for it is simply a function of the colder climate in which they live:

> Therefore, men are more vigorous in cold climates. The action of the heart and the reaction of the extremities of the fibers are in closer accord, the fluids are in a better equilibrium, the blood is pushed harder toward the heart and, reciprocally, the heart has more power. This greater strength should produce many effects: for example, more confidence in oneself, that is, more courage; better knowledge of one's superiority, that is, less desire for vengeance; a higher opinion of one's security, that is, more frankness and fewer suspicions, maneuvers, and tricks. Finally, it should make very different characters. [. . .] The peoples in hot countries are timid like old men; those in cold countries are courageous like young men. (232)

The political valences of the geographical divide that Montesquieu begins to sketch in the opposition between northern vigor and southern fear are subsequently made more explicit when the author turns to consider the question of liberty:

> We have already said that great heat enervates the strength and courage of men and that there is in cold climates a certain strength of body and spirit that makes them capable of long, arduous, great and daring action. [. . .] Therefore, one must not be surprised that the cowardice of the peoples of hot climates has almost always made them slaves and that the courage of the peoples of cold climates has kept them free. This is an effect which derives from its natural cause. (278)

While such passages have often been discussed in terms of the justification they provided for the slave trade and for modern Europe's transoceanic colonialism, this psychopolitical geography was applied to the European continent as well. Thus when Montesquieu evaluates early modern Europe's political and religious conflicts, he sees a struggle between a north that naturally loves liberty and a south that is climatologically conditioned to love subservience:

> When, two centuries ago, the Christian religion suffered the unfortunate division that divided it into Catholic and Protestant, the peoples of the north embraced the Protestant, and those of the south kept the Catholic.
> This is because the people of the north have and will always have a spirit of independence and liberty that the people of the south do not, and because a religion that has no visible leader is better suited to the independence fostered by the climate than is the religion that has one. (463)

Similarly, when Montesquieu's gaze turns specifically to Spain, the quintessentially southern flaw of laziness plays an important role in explaining Spanish decadence. While acknowledging that Spaniards are honest, Montesquieu argues that this virtue is tempered by an aversion to work that is ultimately injurious to national life:

> The faithfulness they had of old they still have today. All the nations that trade in Cadiz entrust their fortunes to the Spanish; they have never repented of it. But this admirable quality joined to their laziness forms a mixture

whose effects are pernicious to them; before their very eyes the peoples of Europe carry on all the commerce of their monarchy. (313)

Curiously, however, for Montesquieu Spain's sloth is not incompatible with its barbarity; one image seems to overlay rather than annul the other, despite the contradiction.[27] Consequently, even as he attributes Spain's decline to its naturally defective southern character, Montesquieu also reminds his readers that at its height Spain was never really part of the civilized world. Ventriloquizing his observations through the voice of a Jew of the past, whom he imagines addressing the Inquisition, Montesquieu formulates the following admonition to Spain:

> We must warn you of one thing; it is that, if someone in the future ever dares to say that the peoples of Europe had a police [i.e. was civilized] in the century in which we live, you will be cited to prove that they were barbarians, and the idea one will have about you will be such that it will stigmatize your century and bring hatred on all your contemporaries. (492)

Written in the mid-eighteenth century, this fictively retrospective placement of prophecy was, of course, a way of telling history; but whereas Montesquieu suggests that the idea of European civilization had been compromised by Spanish barbarity, the exquisitely refined and civilized authorial "Je" of *The Spirit of the Laws* tacitly reassured readers that this was not the case. Montesquieu, and northern European representations of Spain more generally, had in fact managed to turn the tables on the formulation. It was not that European civilization was barbaric. The problem—the north suggested—was that Spain had never been sufficiently European.

This idea was such a commonplace by the 1700s that it was structurally embedded into one of the cornerstones of eighteenth-century upper-class education, the Grand Tour of Europe. While Italy was a focus of interest because ancient Rome—presumably despite its southern sloth—had managed to contribute to Western civilization, Spain did not merit a stop on the tour. Behind Spanish indolence there was only the earlier image of barbarity, and the Grand Tour was expressly designed to educate the traveler in the ways of the *civilized* world. In his classic study of the British Grand Tour in the eighteenth century, Mead recalls the standard travel itinerary of the 1700s, an itinerary that presages Hegel's map of world history:

> The grand tour was, at least in intention, not merely a pleasurable round of travel, but an indispensable form of education for young men in the higher ranks of society. When made with a competent tutor, the grand tour meant a carefully planned tour through France and Italy and a return journey through Germany and the Low Countries. (3)[28]

A general consensus had formed regarding the countries that were not worth visiting:

> Spain and Greece and countries east of Prague or north of Hamburg were rarely visited, because the Tourist felt little drawn to territories [. . .] where, as he was led to believe, there were no sights or artistic treasures worth the exhausting effort of reaching them. [. . .] When in 1776 Voltaire spoke about Spain to Martin Sherlock he expressed a common enough opinion. "It is a country of which we know no more than of the most parts of savage Africa, and it is not worth the trouble of being known." (Hibbert, 25)

Toward the end of the eighteenth century, however, the dominant European view of Spain would undergo another significant change. As historical consciousness intensified over the course of the second half of the 1700s (Gilmore, 95–96), and as the French Revolution and the Napoleonic Wars fed what would become nineteenth-century romantic historicism (Lukàcs, *Historical*, 23–24), the north's image of Spain was once again imbued with new meaning.[29] In the transition from the eighteenth to the nineteenth centuries, the hegemonic gaze of modern Europe began to see something new in the uncivilized south; it began to see the past. Just as the civilized world of the eighteenth century had clear geographical boundaries, in the nineteenth century historical time itself began to be conceived in spatial terms.[30] If the strangeness of past epochs was increasingly conceived as what David Lowenthal has called "a foreign country," the converse was also true; foreign countries—and particularly a country as foreign and as proximate to modern Europe as Spain—had begun to be grasped as living examples of the past. The past that modern Europe saw in Spain, however, was not the past with which Petrarch had wrestled in what is traditionally taken to be the inaugural moment of humanist historicism, nor was it the past that subtended the famous *Querelle des Anciens et des Moderns* or, more generally, eighteenth-century classicism. The past that captured the civilized world's attention and that a new kind of traveler increasingly sought out in nineteenth-century Spain was the very past with which Europe had putatively broken at the dawn of modernity. It was the mystified past of the Middle Ages.

The celebrated travel writer, Richard Ford, whose three-volume *Handbook for Travellers in Spain* (1845) would become a nineteenth-century classic, articulates the common northern European view of Spain in the 1800s. For Ford, the country was a living example of an exotic, barely Western, medieval world, a world much akin to the Orient against which—to recall Said's formulation—the modern West habitually imagined itself. "The key to decipher this singular people," Ford writes, "is scarcely European, since this *Berberia Cristiana* is at least a neutral ground between the hat and the turban, and many contend that Africa begins even at the Pyrenees." He adds:

> Test her, therefore, and her natives by an Oriental standard, how analogous does much appear that is strange and repugnant, if compared with European usages! This land and people of routine and habit are also potted for antiquarians, for here Pagan, Roman, and Eastern customs long obsolete elsewhere, turn up at every step in church and house, in cabinet and campaign, as we shall carefully point out. (3)

To the extent that orientalism had become one of the handmaidens of Western colonialism in the nineteenth century, Ford's description is, in symbolic terms, a confirmation of Spain's political, economic, and cultural subordination to modern Europe. In the passage above, such power relations are reflected in the unidirectional tourist gaze, and they are implied by the logic of collection: An entire "land and people" has been "potted"—that is, preserved—for the consumption of the antiquarian tourist-collector.[31]

Ford's observations, however, also seem to speak to the limits of a purely orientalist understanding of Spain's symbolic place within the northern European imagination. His injunction for readers to test Spain "by an Oriental standard" suggests that this was not in fact the way that his readers had habitually engaged Spanish culture. The figure of Spain as "between the hat and the turban" acknowledges a quasi-European status that rarely appears in the West's construction of the Orient, and Ford entices the British tourist by suggesting that what awaits the traveler in Spain is an experience of the exotic within the familiar. If there is little doubt that nineteenth-century Spain was orientalized by northern Europe, what also seems clear is that orientalism converged with the earlier stereotypes of Spanish national identity and with a vestigial northern European awareness that Spain had once been part of modern Europe's own past.

As a contemporary theoretical formulation, orientalism does not fully account for the specificity of Spain's distinctive position—that is, its centrality within the first world-system as the empire of early modernity—and it occludes the symbolic function that the image of a nonmodern Spain played within the constitution of the idea of modern Europe. At the same time, the concept tends to disregard the fundamental structural homology that the nineteenth century's exoticizing representations of Spain share with sixteenth- and seventeenth-century images of Spanish barbarity and with eighteenth-century representations of uncivilized Spanish indolence. Northern European orientalism in Iberia was simply the new face of a centuries-old paradigm by which Spain and modernity had been divorced within the historical imagination of the West. Underpinning most of modern Europe's nineteenth-century images of Spain, orientalized or not, was a more fundamental assumption that Spain was a country that time had forgotten. As late as 1861, the British historian Henry Thomas Buckle summarized the commonplace: "There she lies, at the furthest extremity of the Continent, a huge and torpid mass, the sole representative now remaining of the feelings and knowledge of the Middle Ages" (138). For Buckle, as for the vast majority of northern European and North American writers throughout the nineteenth-century, Spain remained on the other side of Hegel's threshold of modernity; it was imagined as a land untouched by three centuries of historical time.[32]

What's Past Is Prologue: Romantic Historicism in Spain

With this long history of Modern Europe's representation of Spain in view, and with the image of "medieval Spain" on the horizon, we arrive finally at the historical juncture that traditional accounts of Spanish romanticism have taken as their point of departure: the early 1800s and the introduction into Spain of German romantic historicist ideas.[33] In turning to this moment, we also shift from the broad field of a generalized north-ern European cultural discourse about Spain to the narrower confines of romantic literary theory and historiography. In the preceding pages, the passages we considered were selected from sources habitually regarded as nonfictive (i.e., political texts, historical and philosophical works, travel writing, etc.) in order to draw attention to the pervasive nature of northern Europe's discursive expulsion of Spain from the modern. In what follows, we will be turning to the ways in which nineteenth-century understand-ings of Spanish romanticism and twentieth-century critical receptions of the movement have been shaped by this long legacy of representation.

The inaugural moment cited in most histories of Spain's nineteenth-century romanticism is the famed *querella calderoniana* between Nicholas Böhl von Faber and José Joaquín de Mora.[34] A reactionary German immi-grant who was familiar with the writings of the Schlegel brothers, Böhl is credited with introducing several of the key tenets of romantic historicism to Spanish readers.[35] For the most part, Böhl sought to reassert the cultural and aesthetic values that his German mentors had "discovered" in Spain's seventeenth-century theater, particularly in the theater of Calderón de la Barca. The core values that Böhl celebrated in his defense of a "romantic" Spanish baroque theater were consequently a somewhat mystified Chris-tian spirituality and a dramaturgy thought to be unrestrained by clas-sicist norms. The apology of these values has habitually been considered to represent a significant romantic break with the poetics of the classical tradition, and critical accounts of the *querella* and of its significance for Spanish romanticism have consequently drawn attention to the contrast between Böhl's affirmation of a historically distinctive Christian, chival-ric, national Spanish character and the more universalizing, cosmopolitan premises of Mora's classicism. In addition, scholars of the debate have productively situated the polemic in its most immediate political contexts (Pitollet; Juretschke, *Origen*; Carnero, *Orígenes*), and they have empha-sized both the reactionary ideology to which nationalist historicism lent itself (Carnero) and the subsequent importance of historicism within the more conservative strains of Spanish romantic theory (Flitter).

The broader meaning of romantic historicism itself and its relation-ship to the cartography of modernity we have sketched, however, has until recently remained on the sidelines of discussions of Spanish romanticism.[36] More often than not, romantic historicism has simply been approached as a preconstituted given whose introduction and subsequent dissemination in Spanish letters is then documented and analyzed. What such conceptions of Schlegelian historicism elide, however, is the broader, transnational context in which the phenomenon unfolded, as well as the power relations that informed that context. Romantic historicism was not simply one more northern European intellectual export to Spain; it effected a profound redistribution of values on the symbolic map of modern Europe and its peripheries. Spain was, in this sense, not simply the recipient of this discourse; in many regards it was integral to its very formulation. For with Herder and the Schlegels, northern European literary historiography begins to register its own ambivalence about the historical narrative of modernity, and this disquiet manifests itself by turning precisely to those realms—symbolic and geographical—that a future-oriented, cosmopolitan Progress had seemingly spurned. Romantic historicism consequently carries out a well-known symbolic reversal of the values embedded within the narrative of the modern, in what amounts to one of the West's early, ambiguous responses to its own modernity.[37] The key maneuvers of the romantic historicist paradigm that, as Wellek recalls, became dominant during the first half of the nineteenth-century are not difficult to identify: In place of an ever-ascendant common civilization, it posits the irreducible difference of each nation's *Volkgeist*; in place of the promise of the future, it seeks to commune with its fantasies of the past; and in place of the celebratory pursuit of material progress, it aims to dwell in the world of spirit.[38] Rather than embracing modernity's break with the Middle Ages, romantic historicism longs for a symbolic return to that age, which it thoroughly mystifies.

As we have seen, however, one of modern Europe's collective fantasies in the nineteenth century was that the Middle Ages could still be found, just beyond its borders, to the south. Within the romantic historicist reversal of Enlightenment values, Spain's longstanding symbolic position outside of the modern is thus once again affirmed. What is novel in historical terms, however, is that the attributes for which Spanish culture had long been excoriated are for the first time in centuries *celebrated* by northern pens. When northern Europe—now ambivalent rather than triumphal about its modernity—turns its gaze to Spain once more, it discovers in the centuries-old image it has created the very values it wishes to embrace: a national spirit untainted by a now-suspect civilization, a land that is the very image of a now-desired past, the living incarnation of a now-mystified rather than reviled Middle Ages. In effect, the Schlegel brothers—Böhl's primary source—project into literary history precisely what writers like Ford would project onto their travels across the Iberian peninsula: the enchantments of a place outside of the modern. Like the tourist gaze, German historicism's perception of each nation's *Kuntsgeist*, or art-spirit, was thoroughly conditioned by its own northern perspective, and what northern Europe's romantic historicism saw in Spanish literary history was a national spirit that had heroically resisted a modern world that was now beginning to come into question.

A brief review of several passages from Schlegel's Vienna lectures will help elucidate this phenomenon. Drawing on the Herderian notion that the lifeblood of a nation is to be found in its language, August Wilhelm Schlegel characterizes the Castilian tongue as a medieval hybrid that is strikingly similar to Ford's later conception of the entire country.[39] For Schlegel, the Spanish language, its soul, is a seductive mixture of gothic and Moorish elements:

> It had not yet altogether lost the rough strength and cordiality of the Goths, when oriental intermixtures gave it a wonderful degree of sublimity, and elevated a poetry, intoxicated as it were with aromatic vapours, far above the scruples of the sober west. (340)

In a similar vein, he identifies the heart of Spanish cultural identity as an unwavering, idealized chivalric spirit that inheres in all authentic Spanish literature:

> The spirit of chivalry has nowhere outlived its political existence so long as in Spain. [. . .] This spirit propagated itself down to the flourishing period of their literature, and imprinted its stamp upon it in a manner which cannot be mistaken. (342–43)

Tellingly, the flourishing period to which Schlegel refers in this passage is the literature of early modern Spain—the sixteenth and seventeenth centuries—which for August Wilhelm remains essentially medieval in character. Inasmuch as the Christian Middle Ages are in and of themselves "romantic" within the Schlegelian system, it follows that Spain, which according to modern Europe's dominant historical narrative never managed to move beyond the Middle Ages, is by its very nature a romantic country. "If the feeling of religion, true heroism, honour, and love, are the foundation of the romantic poetry," Schlegel writes, a literature "born and grown up in Spain under such auspices [. . .] could not fail to assume the highest elevation" (344). For Schlegel, Spanish letters are thus poised to become a preeminent romantic literature in the nineteenth century if Spaniards can but learn to embrace once more the romanticism that has always been in their nature:

> Living nearly in an insular situation, they have slept the eighteenth century, and how could they in the main have applied their time better? Should the Spanish poetry again awake in old Europe, or in the other hemisphere, it would certainly have a step to make, from instinct to consciousness. What the Spaniards have hitherto loved from native inclination, they must learn to reverence on clear principles, and, unconcerned at the criticism which has in the interval sprung up, proceed to fresh creations in the spirit of their greatest poets. (351–52)

In short, Schlegel enjoins Spanish literature to wake up to its authentic, natural, medieval, Christian self, a position that Böhl would also take up over the course of his polemic with Mora.

In the context of the history of northern European representations of Spain, one ought not underestimate the rhetorical power of this injunction. Indeed, for all of its shortcomings, and despite the reactionary politics with which it was initially wed, German historicism entered Spain under the appealing guise of northern European approval and recognition, a celebration of Spanish culture that seemed to depart from almost three centuries of criticism and disparagement.[40] It was a kind of recognition with which broad swaths of Spanish society identified, and, as Derek Flitter has shown, the trajectory of historicist thought can be charted from Böhl through Spanish writers such as Agustín Durán, Alberto Lista, Ramón López Soler, Juan Donoso Cortés, and Enrique Gil, to the mid-century traditionalism of Böhl's daughter, Cecilia. What should also be noted, however, is the extraordinary affinity between Schlegelian romanticism and the other images of "romantic Spain" that northern Europe—from Vigny, to Merimée, to Gautier in France for example—repeatedly generated over the course of the nineteenth century. Common to such views was the assumption that Spanish national identity was fundamentally not modern, and to the extent that Spaniards themselves embraced such images, it is not unreasonable to conclude that modern Europe successfully interpellated a significant part of Spain's collective self-understanding.[41]

Against a broader historical canvas, these years represent a hallmark moment in the history of the representation of Spanish national identity, for Spanish romantic historicism firmly established a paradigm that, mutatis mutandis, would subsequently underpin not only nineteenth-century Spanish nationalism more generally, but also, in the early twentieth century, the *ideas madres* of the so-called Generation of 1898 and subsequently—with some modification—the basic conceptual framework that characterized Francoist historiography.[42] In this regard, if romantic historicism was an important feature of the early nineteenth-century conceptualization of romanticism in Spain, it quickly turned into much more, for the view of an essential, transhistorical, Catholic, "romantic" Spanish national character ultimately became the touchstone for later engagements—both critical and apologetic—with the cultural and historical "difference" of Spain in the modern era.

The power of this mode of thought—wrought over roughly three centuries of northern European representation of Spain—did not limit itself, however, to the confines of Spanish cultural politics. As we shall see shortly, its impact on subsequent *critical* receptions of Spanish romanticism was equally significant, for northern Europe's narrative of the modern did more than produce "romantic Spain." It also drew the boundaries of those fields of inquiry that would come to be known as "European romanticism" and, more generally, "modern European literature." In doing so, it profoundly shaped the perspective from which "Spanish romanticism" would come to be viewed, and it continues inform inquiry into the subject today. As any Hispanist with comparative interests soon discovers, the literary production of Spain's eighteenth, nineteenth, and—with some exceptions—twentieth centuries has largely been either entirely absent from, or at best, utterly peripheral to, the constitution of the entity known as "modern European literature."

This is so because the symbolic geography we have considered in the preceding pages shaped not only the way the West (Britain, France, and Germany) came to imagine itself as sole agent of History, but also the way it came to constitute its *cultural and literary history* as the most representative literature, the literature most worthy of study. As Edward Said comments in *Culture and Imperialism*:

The notion of Western literature that lies at the very core of comparative literary study centrally highlights, dramatizes, and celebrates a certain idea of history, and at the same time obscures the fundamental geographical and political reality empowering that idea. The idea of European or Western literary history contained in it and the other scholarly works of comparative literature is essentially idealistic and, in an unsystematic way, Hegelian. (47)

The fiction of a transcendent autonomous historical agency, which, as we considered earlier, characterizes the Hegelian vision of History generally, thus reappears in the constitution of the field of a self-contained modern European literature:

More and more reality is included in a literature that expands and elaborates from the medieval chronicles to the great edifices of nineteenth-century narrative fiction. [. . .] Class, political upheavals, shifts in economic patterns and organization, war: all these subjects [. . .] are enfolded within recurringly renewed structures, visions, stabilities, all of them attesting to the abiding dialectical order represented by Europe itself. (Said, *Culture*, 47)

What Said does not note here, however, is the degree to which Spain, and the European south and east more generally, had been made external to this "Europe" and its dialectical unfolding. Mignolo has recently discussed this exclusion more extensively within the framework of the "imperial difference" that transected the European continent in the eighteenth and nineteenth centuries. He thus underscores how northern European imperialism in fact shaped the very foundations of modern comparative literature:

Hegel's universal history spilled over into the history of literature. If the heart of Europe was the reference point for mapping universal history, so were the (national) literatures of England, France and Germany for the universal history of literature. Russia and Spain (the imperial difference) remained at the interior margins of the International Association of Comparative Literature. ("Rethinking," 165–66).

Over the course of the late twentieth century, comparative literary studies have, to be sure, slowly begun to move away from this model, and "world literature" now seems to be the most likely candidate to become the field's more proper horizon of inquiry.[43] Nevertheless, one cannot help but notice the persistence of the thought-structure called "modern European literature" within contemporary literary and cultural studies. As postcolonial theorists are well aware, "a certain version of 'Europe,' reified and celebrated in the phenomenal world of everyday relationships of power as the scene of the birth of the modern, continues to dominate the discourse of history. Analysis does not make it go away" (Chakrabarty, 28).

In the case of studies in Spanish culture, Spain's symbolic location on the periphery of modern European history generated a host of issues with which more than one generation of Hispanists has grappled. Indeed, as a discipline Hispanism has had to work through a series of fundamental doubts about its field of study. They are symptoms of Spain's symbolic amputation from the modern. Was there *really* a Renaissance in Spain or did it remain essentially medieval (Green, 3–26)? Was there *really* a Spanish Enlightenment and was it revolutionary, or was it insufficient, thwarted by an essentially medieval religious obscurantism (Herr, *Eighteenth* and *An Historical*; or Subirats, *Ilustración* and *Después*)? Was there *really* an important romantic movement in Spain, or was it simply a reaffirmation of an eternal romantic national character, over which exiles returning from modern Europe sprinkled a more revolutionary rhetoric that ultimately failed (Peers, *History*)?[44] An alternate formulation of the problem grudgingly acknowledges key Western cultural movements in Spain but only to qualify them quickly as "weak" or "derivative."

The point, of course, is not to revisit such issues here, but rather to note the common ground from which they spring. Such questions could not have been formulated to begin with had not Spain's tacit position beyond the borders of the West become a critical commonplace. One need only consider how strange it would seem to put such questions to French or British culture in order to note how thoroughly conditioned such considerations are by the geopolitics of culture. Entire agenda's of research in Peninsular studies have in fact been haunted by Spain's symbolic position on the periphery of European modernity, and the trope of Spain-as-a-living-Middle Ages (i.e., Spanish culture as constitutively nonmodern) is not difficult to identify throughout.

That the effects of eighteenth- and nineteenth-century northern European cultural imperialism continue to reverberate within the field of "European literature" today is evident in the asymmetry that still governs the constitution of the European canon. Even within an increasingly post-canonical critical landscape, and as the very idea of Literature is habitually put into question, it remains somewhat scandalous, for example, to call oneself a scholar of European romanticism while admitting that one has never read Wordsworth or Hölderin; yet utter ignorance of Spanish romantics such as José Espronceda (1808–1842) or Mariano José de Larra (1809–1837) generally passes without comment. There remains a mode of thinking that would consider Flaubert and Balzac indispensable to comprehending "the nineteenth-century European novel," whereas Spanish novelists such as Benito Pérez Galdós (1843–1920), Emilia Pardo Bazán (1852–1921), and Leopoldo Alas, "Clarín" (1852–1901), are at best viewed as interesting options.[45] This pattern of thought is undoubtedly familiar to any scholar working on those European cultures traditionally deemed exterior to modern Europe: Poland, Hungary, Romania, Bulgaria, Greece and the Balkans, Italy, and the like. Similar observations might also be made about the objects of reflection from which the classic works of literary theory would emerge, for they too were for the most part texts that belonged to modern Europe.[46] In this regard, as the postcolonial critique of Eurocentrism takes up the intellectual challenges of "provincializing Europe" (Chakrabarty), it will be important to recall just how much of the European continent had in fact already been "provincialized" within the Western imagination as a consequence of the northern hegemony that defined the "Age of Europe."

Schlegel's Progeny

If we return now to our original site of inquiry, Spanish romanticism's putative "primal scene"—that is, Böhl von Faber's dissemination of historicist ideas in Spain—it becomes evident that Spanish romantics who followed the Schlegelian injunction to be their naturally "romantic" (i.e., chivalric, Catholic, traditionalist) selves were implicated in a transnational power structure in which modern Europe hailed its periphery to wake up to and live out its backward enchantments. Spanish romantics who answered the call were, among other things, performing the "nonmodern" identity that northern Europe had habitually projected onto Spanish culture. Moreover, inasmuch as this Schlegelian "awakening" was carried out in writing, a significant portion of nineteenth-century Spanish romantic literary production in fact wound up confirming what modern Europe thought of Spain all along. Consequently, if Waldo Frank could argue as early as 1926 that "it is the German metaphysicians who invented the romanticism of Calderón" and that "it is Byron and the French aesthetes who created romantic Spain," it is nevertheless the case that the invention proved successful within Spain (245; cited by del Río, 234). Many Spanish romantics themselves came to believe and produce the northern fantasy about them within their own national literature. In this sense, Schlegelian historicism functioned as a powerful kind of self-fulfilling prophecy, and its success is a testament to the tremendous force that modern European culture exerted on the neighboring countries it traditionally viewed as its exterior.[47]

As we have seen, however, given the extent of modern Europe's cultural power well into the twentieth century, Spanish romantic historicists were not the only figures to internalize the Schlegelian paradigm. Twentieth-century critics and literary historians absorbed similar predispositions. In fact, a review of several key moments within the history of critical receptions of romanticism in Spain during the twentieth century reveals a curious kind of echo effect. If in the 1800s Spain was commonly viewed as a romantic "living Middle Ages" that did not belong to modern Europe, in the twentieth century many cultural critics and literary historians attempting to come to terms with the movement would similarly see only "romantic Spain" (or its affirmation by Spanish writers) as the core of the movement. As a result, much literary criticism and history would serve to confirm that, while intriguing, Spanish romanticism was at best an epiphenomenon in comparison to the modern titans of "European romanticism." Even recent, theoretically sophisticated work on romantic historicism has not remained untouched by this paradigm, and it will be useful to explore this critical history briefly.[48]

For many, E. Allison Peers's 1940 *A History of the Romantic Movement in Spain*, which was successfully marketed as the first full, book-length study of the movement, marks the inaugural moment in twentieth-century appraisals of Spanish romanticism. Its breadth of scope and detail assured the study a central role in subsequent appraisals of the movement. Examination of Peers's preliminary assumptions, however, manifests rather clearly that the work was fundamentally neoschlegelian in conception. In his opening chapter, "The Antecedents of the Romantic Movement," Peers reminds readers of the place that Spain had been accorded by German and French "critics of excellent judgement" during the nineteenth century:

> Ever since the word "romanticism" was invented, it has been used, by critics of excellent judgement, to describe a fundamental characteristic of literature and art in Spain. The leaders of the Romantic movement in France and Germany turned for inspiration to Spain. To the brothers Schlegel, Spanish drama, down to the time of Calderón, was "almost entirely Romantic," while Spanish poetry "remained purely Romantic throughout." Sismondi described Spanish literature as "much less Classical than that of other countries"—in fact, as "wholly Romantic and chivalric," creating "prodigies, adventures and intrigues in abundance," but only "for so long as it feels itself to be unrestrained by the bounds of the possible and the probable." (2)

Significantly, in this passage Peers marshals the figures of the Schlegels and Sismondi not in order to take historical distance from them, but rather to reaffirm the truth of romantic historicist views of Spain:

> Our considered judgement will hardly be less definitive than the judgement of these critics. In every phase and epoch of that literature [i.e., Spanish literature] the Romantic tendencies of the Spanish character find expression—most markedly so in the Middle Ages, when literature had hardly taken definite form [. . .] and in the period of Spain's fullest self-consciousness and most triumphant art, the so-called "Age of Gold." (2–3)

To put it in terms of the narrative we have been following, Peers's account of romanticism in Spain reproduces within twentieth-century literary historiography the "imperial difference" that romantic historicism had propagated more than a century earlier. In the passages cited above, Spanish literature is imagined and approved of as an expression of an enchanted medieval world that never crossed modernity's threshold. Just as the country had been imagined by northern Europe for centuries, Spanish literary production in Peers often becomes a field untouched by history: Medieval, renaissance, and baroque literature collapse into the transhistorical monad, "romantic Spain," an entity seemingly unmodified by historical time. Enlightenment and its consequences—the "new edifice" of modernity that Hegel intuited in 1807—are strikingly absent.

By the mid-twentieth century, numerous opposing views were in circulation, to be sure, but in a seminal 1948 essay, "Present Trends in the

Conception and Criticism of Spanish Romanticism," Angel del Río makes clear that research on the subject remained strongly influenced by Peers's romantic historicist presuppositions. "Scholars are still repeating"—he writes after recognizing Peers's *opus magnum*—"concepts and ideas formed in the nineteenth century and have not yet succeeded in reaching convincing conclusions as to the overall meaning of romanticism in Spanish literature or about the true place of the romantic movement in our total evaluation of that literature" (229). The "concepts and ideas" he has in mind are primarily Herderian and Schlegelian historicist tenets, and after reviewing the work of critics whose thinking openly diverged from Peers's neoschlegelian characterization of the movement—Castro, Frank, Tarr, and Adams, among others—del Río observes that

> [w]hile there have been attempts to rectify this one-sided image of Spanish literature as the embodiment of romanticism, nevertheless it still persists. [. . .] The conclusion is that we must exercise some restraint in handling these ideas, and not oversimplify a very complex and paradoxical period, so complex in fact that in it are involved the ever-present problems of modern Spanish culture. (234)

Despite the call for restraint, however, in the very same essay del Río affirms that a critical consensus remains regarding the idea of an essentially "medieval" quality within modern Spanish literature:

> At the root of this idea of the romantic tendencies of Spanish literature lies *a phenomenon that we know well today*: the persistence and perpetuation in modern literature (i.e. that which develops after the Renaissance) of medieval themes and attitudes. This explains the fact that . . . [foreign writers] found that in Spain the tradition, or at least many of its themes, were still alive. (232, my emphasis)

While waning, the idea that Spain's authentic, nonmodern, medieval character could still be found throughout its literature was a commonplace.

In this context, the publication of Hans Juretschke's 1954 essay, *Origen doctrinal y génesis del romanticismo español,* marked a decisive shift in coming to terms with German historicism, and the study firmly established the framework in which Schlegelian theory and historiography would be discussed for much of the latter half of the twentieth century.

In large measure, this was accomplished by putting the Schlegelian historicist genie back into its nineteenth-century bottle. In Juretschke's treatment of the subject, German romantic historicism no longer remained an unexamined filter through which Spanish literary history was viewed. Rather, it was treated as a doctrine, a discourse whose propagation in nineteenth-century Spain could be documented and measured. In effect, Juretschke's work, followed by later studies such as Guillermo Carnero's 1978 *Los orígenes del romanticismo reaccionario español: el matrimonio Böhl de Faber,* helped to reframe the historicist phenomenon by relocating it. It was no longer a question of whether Spanish literature actually *was* romantic throughout much of its history; it was more simply that certain German thinkers had believed this to be the case and that the dissemination of their ideas had successfully convinced a substantial number of nineteenth-century Spanish writers to view their cultural and literary past in a similar way. Within such a framework, critical debate was free to turn to questions concerning the relative importance of historicist thinking within Spanish romanticism.[49]

As the title of his study indicates, for Juretschke, German historicism was the principal progenitor of romanticism in Spain, but as we shall see shortly, in the years following his work a broad array of scholarship would increasingly point to other important forces at work in the movement's gestation: the dialectical turn of Spain's own Enlightenment, Napoleonic invasion, liberal revolution and reform, psychosocial crisis, and so on. Indeed, after breaking the historicist spell, for a time research into Spanish romanticism almost seemed poised to abandon the topic of German historicism altogether. Two recent book-length reexaminations of the problem of romanticism in Spain, however, have revisited the question in order to once again place romantic historicism at the center of current critical debates. Both projects aim to refute competing claims concerning the gravitational center of the movement by asserting the primacy of romantic historicist thought. In this sense, if Peers could be described as a neoschlegelian, these recent scholars—despite very different critical vocabularies—belong to what might aptly be termed a "neojuretschkean" line of thinking.

Derek Flitter's 1992 *Spanish Romantic Literary Theory and Criticism,* for example, effectively restates and expands Juretschke's thesis:

> My major contention is that it was the principles of Romantic historicism, stemming from the work of Herder and more fully expounded with reference to literary history by the Schlegel brothers, which dominated Spanish literary theory and criticism during the whole of the period under discussion. (3)

Writing expressly to rebut claims made about the relationship between liberalism and romanticism in Spain, Flitter regards exploration of the links between politics and aesthetics deleterious to a proper comprehension of literary historiography. Interdisciplinary inquiry itself seems for Flitter injurious to a purportedly autonomous aesthetic realm. "In this assumption that literary Romanticism and political liberalism were interdependent historical phenomena"—he writes—"the significance of Romanticism as a new literary and artistic sensibility becomes subordinate to events tangential to or wholly outside aesthetic formulae and creative endeavor" (2). In place of such endeavors, Flitter offers a fundamentally idealist literary historiography in which Schlegelian ideas arrive, are disseminated, are challenged by "liberal romanticism," and are ultimately reaffirmed, becoming dominant by the mid-century.[50] In this account of romantic theory, "aesthetic formulae and creative endeavor" are conceived as entities that are largely independent of social, political, and economic history. Thus, although Flitter describes romantic historicism in Spain as a movement that was "profoundly Christian in inspiration and orientation, characterised by an intense idealism and a belief in the potency of national traditions," his treatment of the subject remains within the framework of an ostensibly depoliticized "history of literary ideas" (150). August Wilhelm Schlegel spoke—Flitter's narrative suggests—and romantic Spain listened.

By contrast, the most recent book-length assessment of the romantic historicist legacy in Spain, Philip Silver's 1997 *Ruin and Restitution: Reinterpreting Romanticism in Spain,* is keenly aware—and deeply critical—of the political valences of the historicist paradigm, so much so in fact that the author questions whether the term "romanticism" should be used to describe it at all. Marked by profound revisionist ambitions, Silver's study purports to offer a fundamentally new historiographic framework from which to consider Spanish romanticism and its relationship to Spain's twentieth-century modernist poets. The key features of Silver's view—as summed up in the introduction—are the following:

First, that a conservative-liberal romanticism helped a nationalistic political centrism consolidate a factitiously unitary Spanish culture; second, that Spain produced no high romantic movement *per se*; third, that the discontinuity romanticism–contemporary poetry is compensated for by a piecemeal restitution of high romanticism [by Cernuda and others]; fourth, that this redefinition [. . .] will provide new understanding of many [. . .] [early twentieth-century] poets [. . .] and last, that a literary movement like romanticism, that evades all attempts to contain it, still has much to teach us. (*Ruin*, xv)

For Silver, the nationalist uses to which historicism was put by the conservative (i.e., *moderado*) elements of Spain's emergent liberal order seem to trump whatever interest historicism may have had in aesthetic terms.[51] To put it more simply, while Silver largely accepts the Juretschkean portrayal of a dominant Schlegelian historicism in Spain, he finds little within such a discourse worthy of the label "high romanticism." "There was a grudging experience of historical Romanticism"—he writes—"but no *high* romantic movement. Because Spain was culturally belated and peripheral, its reception of foreign romanticism coincided with an ongoing compulsion to reinterpret its historical past" (42).

Needless to say, for Silver *high* romanticism resides elsewhere; it dwells only in the Hegelian house of modern Europe. Summarizing René Wellek's arguments in favor of the concept of a unified "European" high romanticism, Silver observes:

[In response to Lovejoy's claim that there were a variety of romanticisms] Wellek answered that *especially the German, English and French romantic movements* did indeed form a coherent group as to style, theory, and philosophy, and that they all held essentially the same conception of the romantic imagination and of man's relationship to nature, as well as a similar use of imagery, symbol and myth. (*Ruin*, 55, my emphasis)

The author then charts the way in which this unified "European romanticism" generated some of the twentieth century's more powerful theoretical and philosophical engagements with romantic writing: Walter Benjamin, Meyer H. Abrams, Harold Bloom, Geoffrey Hartman, Virgil Nemoianu, the team of Phillip Lacoue-Labarthe and Jean-Luc Nancy, and—most notably for Silver—Paul De Man.

At the core of Silver's "*high* romanticism" are two compelling romantic paradigms. The first is Abrams's proposition—from *Natural Supernaturalism*—that "European romanticism" is fundamentally an internalized "secularization of inherited theological ideas and ways of thinking" (95–96); the second is De Man's deconstructive rewriting of the Abramsian paradigm as a narrative in which the romantic writing-subject ultimately comes to renounce the ontological stability she or he sees in nature in favor of a "self-consciousness in the form of temporal being" (*Critical,* 74; both passages cited by Silver, *Ruin,* 65). In light of the absence in Spain of both this tradition of high theoretical commentary and the high romanticism that prompted it (Rousseau/France, Hölderlin/Germany, and Wordsworth/Britain), Silver believes that what takes place over the course of Spain's nineteenth century—aside from romantic historicist nationalism—is "a dissemination of the detritus of European high romanticism" (71). In this view, it is not until Luis Cernuda, the so-called Generation of 1927, and Spain's early twentieth-century "Silver Age" more generally, that a full restitution of high romanticism to Spain takes place.

In many regards, Silver's study is an apt culmination of the historicist thesis and the contradictions it evinces, for if the Schlegelian vision of romantic Spain—and subsequently Peers's "romantic revival"—posits an essentially nonmodern Spanish culture, and if Juretschke—and later, Flitter—characterize the core of the movement in Spain as a second-degree affirmation of such a view on the part of Spanish writers, it is difficult to imagine that Spanish culture itself might have *produced* anything called romanticism. In the first instance Spain would simply be "romantic" by virtue of its nonmodernity; in the second, the heart of the movement would entail the reception, performance, and subsequent adaptation of a conservative script of national identity originally written by more powerful northern European cultures. It is no surprise, then, that Silver suspects that "there may be no Spanish romanticism at all" (68). In doing so he rightly emphasizes that nationalist historicism constitutes a rather impoverished content for the category "Spanish romanticism." But in supposing that the only possible content *worthy* of the name is Abramsian/De Manian "high romanticism," Silver also manifests the northern, Eurocentric bias that has structured studies in "European romanticism" since their inception.[52]

In this regard, Silver's framework is ultimately far less a revisionist project than it initially seems, for it reaffirms those longstanding tradi-

tional assumptions that we considered earlier, assumptions of a purportedly belated, derivative, or otherwise watered-down Spanish literary culture. Indeed, Silver's study, which is among the most theoretically dense
to be carried out on the subject of romanticism in Spain, is a wonderful
case study of the way in which the ideologies of "modern Europe" and
"European romanticism" have continued to be internalized by contemporary analysts of Spanish culture. Silver himself acknowledges that "much
more is at stake in the question of romanticism than literature," for as he
goes on to write, "unless a nation can be said to possess a high romanticism it does not seem European enough" (67). Although the author recognizes this notion as a "prejudice," his interest is rather clearly to reassert
rather than to dismantle the bias. Consequently, for Silver, authentic romanticism continues to dwell exclusively where Hegel located the spirit of
universal history, in the British, French, and German cradle of modernity.
In Silver's model, the culture of high romanticism, like modernity itself,
can only radiate outward from its high northern European source. It expands, his narrative suggests, in fragmented form, as the detritus of the
glorious edifice of "modern European culture," until unfortunate, backward cultures like Spain belatedly manage to flower by finally grasping its
complexity.

From Schlegel to Peers, through Juretschke, Flitter, and Sliver, Spain's
symbolic status as one of the most proximate exteriors to modern Europe
is repeatedly implied. This is so because despite divergent objectives, contrasting methodologies, and the considerable temporal distance that separates them (the early 1800s to 1997), each of these projects is thoroughly
structured by the *metageography* that northern European hegemony fashioned for itself in constructing the "modern Europe" of the Enlightenment and its aftermath.[53] If, as we have seen, one of the properties of the
modern, well into the twentieth century, was its circumscription to an exclusive, carefully patrolled northern European real estate, it is no surprise
that European romanticism continues to be imagined today within what
amounts to a trinational, gated community. Indeed, some of the most
effective policing of the territory has come from beyond the gates, as writers, literary historians, and cultural critics who have inhabited less-prized
real estate have internalized the dominant narrative that came streaming
across modernity's borders. The historicist thesis in Spain and its long
afterlife in twentieth-century Hispanic studies was one among many such

phenomena, and it has largely confirmed Spanish romanticism's status as a marginal event within nineteenth-century modern European literary studies.

In recent years, however, it has almost become a truism to observe that the grounds for particularly powerful insights are often to be found at the margins and borderlands of areas of inquiry that seem otherwise unproblematic, and reframing Spanish cultural history in terms the *privileged* perspective it might afford on the question of European modernity promises to be a fruitful direction of study. The question of Spanish romanticism has already begun to reveal, for example, that "European romanticism" itself is embedded in a deeper history concerning the power to narrate the modern and its locations. As we have seen, Spain's status as the first early modern European empire made it one of the more significant "others" within the discursive construction of "modern Europe" that accompanied the displacement of imperial power to northern Europe from the late seventeenth through the mid-twentieth centuries. In the process, Spain became the very emblem of a proximate "nonmodern" within the imagination of the West, and during the romantic era this status was transmuted into the image of an eternally romantic Spain.

The common denominator throughout this legacy of representation, from the eighteenth century forward, was the effacement of any sense of Spanish historical agency. The force of History was by definition elsewhere, and such assumptions produced a pattern of thinking that continues to linger within contemporary analyses of Spain's eighteenth- and nineteenth-century past today. It is the habit of mind by which modernity may have eventually arrived but could not have been produced in Spain; it is the thought-structure by which Spain could "be" romantic or "act" romantic in accordance with northern European expectations, but its writers couldn't possibly have generated a romanticism worthy of inclusion within "European romanticism." Even as the European Union attempts to come together—under the shadow of new forms of North American empire, to be sure—the question at hand seems to be whether this legacy of representation will continue to shape future inquiry into the cultural and literary history of Spanish romanticism and the literature of "peripheral Europe" more generally, or whether the gates of "European romanticism," "modern European literature," and their respective histories will come down in order to reveal a more complex geography, perhaps an entirely new neighborhood.[54]

Counterhistories and the Limits of Liberalism

There are of course several ways of rethinking the narrative of "modern Europe," and each carries with it particular consequences for reconceptualizing "Spanish romanticism." One might, for example, want to dismiss the story of Western modernity altogether by denouncing it as sheer ideology. The account of the modern that we have reviewed is, after all, a kind of storytelling that is remarkably akin to one of the traditional conceptions of ideology as the method by which a dominant power—here, northern Europe—symbolically attempts to

> legitimate itself by promoting beliefs and values congenial to it; naturalizing and universalizing such beliefs so as to render them self-evident and apparently inevitable; denigrating ideas which might challenge it; excluding rival forms of thought, perhaps by some unspoken but systematic logic; and obscuring social reality in ways convenient to itself. (Eagleton, *Ideology*, 5–6)

In such an account, "Western modernity" would be an extraordinarily thorough and successful mystification of the simple, brutal fact of modern European power, and there is considerable evidence for such a reading. If, however, one were reluctant to reduce the story of the modern to merely "one of the West's big lies," one could approach the narrative with more nuance, as an illustration, for example, of "mythic" discourse in the sense of the term that Roland Barthes famously explored in *Mythologies*. In such a view, the tale of northern European modernity would be exposed as a classic example of the way myth installs itself within language, in this case the language of history. Indeed, it would not be difficult to grasp the Hegelian narrative of the modern as a "second order semiological system" in which, far from a simple register of what happened, historical facts become signs of something altogether more grand (Barthes, 114).[55] Within this framework, one would not need to deny the differential patterns of scientific, economic, and political development and revolution that have traditionally been taken to separate modern Europe from its peripheries; but one could nevertheless express profound skepticism over the way in which such a history was transmuted into the story of an exclusively Western rational spirit unfolding through time and expanding outward from its northern European center to the rest of the world.[56]

Alternatively, one might challenge the tale of the modern more directly by following the lead of postmodern thinkers such as Bruno Latour, who suggests that, at its core, modernity has always been more a matter of irrational belief than a matter of science. Readers of his *We Have Never Been Modern* may recall that for Latour, several of the centerpieces of Western rationality, such as the distinction between nature and culture, or the distinction between the human and the nonhuman, rely on an unquestioned faith in the purity and separability of such spheres, whereas the world and the actions that take place in it increasingly seem to suggest a very different, hybrid, and fundamentally mediated affair. In a similar vein, skepticism about the modern might be expressed with the smile of the ironic pragmatist, in the manner of Richard Rorty when, following Nietzsche and Wittgenstein, he enjoins readers to put Western rationality in its place as a curious, utterly contingent, haphazard phenomenon that has no particular claim to truth:

> Old metaphors are constantly dying off into literalness, and then serving as a platform and foil for new metaphors. This analogy lets us think of "our language"—that is, of the science and culture of twentieth-century Europe—as something that took shape as a result of a great number of sheer contingencies. Our language and our culture are as much a contingency, as much a result of thousands of small mutations finding niches (and millions of others finding no niches), as are the orchids and the anthropoids. (16)

Modern Europe would in this view be the product of innumerable accidents rather than the teleological unfolding of the West's reason through time, and terms like "modern" and "modernity" would consequently only continue to be used with a wink and a nod, in order to mark these terms as rather dated language-tools for "our" more-knowing present.

What can be easily overlooked by adopting such options, however, is the impact of the narrative of the modern as a centuries-long representational legacy not easily forgotten, dismissed, or analyzed away by those who were not the subjects of the celebratory tale. From the perspective of the "nonmodern" or the "deficiently modern," identification with Rorty's "our," for example, is not necessarily a given. Indeed, the varying positions that one can occupy within the symbolic geography we have been examining account for many of the frictions between what might broadly be termed postmodern engagements with the idea of modernity, on the one hand, and postcolonial engagements, on the other. Whereas one tradition has increasingly emphasized the fictive, illusory, and aleatory nature of the modern, for the other the concept of modernity is so thoroughly en-meshed in the history of modern European imperialism that to supersede it seems a highly suspicious preemption of a more substantive historical reckoning.[57]

The rift between these two modes of conceptualizing modernity may be understood more clearly by imagining the following centuries-long conversation between modern Europe and its others. "You are not modern"—northern Europe proclaims in the seventeenth and eighteenth centuries—"you are barbaric, you are backward, you are lazy. We know, we are civilized." In the nineteenth century, modern Europe pauses for a mo-ment to add, "It's strange that we didn't see it earlier, but your backward ways have a certain charm, a romantic appeal that you really ought to cul-tivate. Be who you are! We just love it!" Gradually, however, over the sec-ond half of the twentieth century, modern Europe's global others begin to respond: "The modernity you celebrated, the modernity from which you so often judged us, it is not of your own making. It never was. Although you think of us as others, without us you never would have been modern to begin with." Modern Europe, sitting at an early twenty-first-century postmodern café blinks several times and responds in a slightly puzzled, patronizing tone: "Have you not realized that all our talk about modernity was a phantom, a language-game? We smile wryly at those of you who still want to make claims about the modern. If it weren't embarrassingly teleological, we would be tempted to call you backward. Whatever the case, do get over thinking that there really was ever anything called modernity. Accident and contingency, that's what history is about. We know, we are postmodern ironists."

The point of this satire is of course to highlight the fact that critical engagement with the modern has been and continues to be thoroughly conditioned by the symbolic site of enunciation from which such en-gagement takes place. If, as we have seen, postcolonial and world-systems critiques of an exclusively northern European genealogy of the modern aim to show that modernity and coloniality are two sides of the same coin, or that modernity never truly had an outside, or that modernity had no singular location of origin, this is not necessarily because such projects are enthralled by the modern while more rigorous, postmodern luminaries have been able to see through it. It is because the need to re-conceptualize the modern—to wrest it away from the dubious history of its deployment—is perceived to be more urgent than the need to dismiss it altogether. To put it another way, if the narrative of the modern was a Wittgensteinian language-game, the rules of the game were written so that the winner for roughly three centuries was modern Europe. In such a context it is scarcely surprising that certain postmodern calls of *game over* have been met with suspicion and resistance by a chorus of voices for whom the cry of *foul*, along with investigation into how the game was rigged and substantive discussion of how to proceed in light of such unfairness, are far more pressing historical exigencies.[58]

For those countries and cultures in Europe that were not part of the grand historical tale of modern Europe, there may still be much to learn from such gestures. Considerable modification of the postcolonial paradigm is undoubtedly in order, however, when it comes to conceptualizing the effects of modern European imperialism on the European periphery. The dominance of modern Europe over less powerful European nations cannot be fully equated with the more outright forms of empire and colonialism that Britain and France, for example, practiced elsewhere on the globe. There are, after all, important differences between a European subordinate, such as Spain, and a colony.[59] Even so, as I have attempted to suggest in the preceding sections of this chapter, several of the insights of the postcolonial framework can be brought to bear on the challenges of thinking about Spain, about the historically peripheral status it has occupied within the narrative of "modern Europe," and about its implications for analyses of Spanish romanticism and modern Spanish culture more generally. There is, at the least, considerable room for a historical reckoning with the image of Spain as the quintessential emblem of nonmodern Europe in the eighteenth and nineteenth centuries.

Such a reckoning involves the simple, fundamental enterprise of reclaiming the category of the modern as a phenomenon not merely experienced by Spanish culture, but produced by it as well. As Fredric Jameson concludes at the end of a recent study on the figure of modernity, "when applied exclusively to the past, 'modernity' is a useful trope for generating alternate historical narratives, despite the charge of ideology it necessarily continues to bear" (*Singular*, 214). This is so because at the level of rhetoric, "modern" and "modernity" carry within them a series of important tacit ideas. Among them are the notion of historical agency (as opposed to the passive reception of "History"), an intense awareness of historical change (as opposed to the affirmation of unwavering tradition), and a dynamic sense of historical flux (as opposed the image of historical stasis). As a trope, the modern can work to recover precisely those characteristics that the metageography of "modern Europe" had attempted to deny its exterior.

This process of rather profound historiographic revision has been underway in Spain, intermittently, for roughly the last half-century, and, during the last thirty years in particular, historical scholarship has explicitly called into question Spain's symbolic exile from the modern in a true bourgeoning of alternate historical narratives or counterhistories. In the wake of, among other hallmarks, Franco's death and the end of dictatorship, the transition to democratic governance, and Spain's integration within the European Union, the question of a wayward Spanish modernity has, like the Freudian repressed, returned with particular insistence. Echoing a passage from José Saramago's *The Stone Raft*, Alvarez Junco notes, for example, that it is as if in the short span of a few decades, the Iberian Peninsula, long adrift in the Atlantic, had suddenly awoken to find itself reattached to the European continent (Introduction, 1). Spain's recent history has in turn nourished a broader reconceptualization of Spain's modern era in significant ways. Raymond Carr has observed, for example, that the historiographic revision currently underway "can be seen as a rejection of any treatment of Spain as an exceptional case. It should be studied as one would study the history of any other major European country" (1).

Within the field of literary and cultural studies, a generation of scholars— Aguilar Piñal, Andioc (*Teatro*), Carnero, Caso González, Glendinning, Hafter, Herr, López, Polt, Rudat, Sarrailh, and Sebold, among others— painstakingly laid the framework for the shift away from a the tragic historiography of "two Spains"—in which tradition inevitably thwarted or hindered the possibility of change. In its place, *dieciochista* researchers documented the process of political, economic, cultural, and literary transformation that the forces of Enlightenment reform and secularizaton achieved in Spain during the 1700s. While acknowledging the distinctive features of Spain's eighteenth century, such work successfully began to dismantle the idea of a "weak" or "derivative" Spanish Enlightenment, and it tacitly challenged the presumption of a failed or absent Spanish modernity.[60] Studies in the history of Spain's early nineteenth century have similarly underscored the legacy of Enlightenment's offspring—the politics and culture of liberalism—as key phenomena for properly conceptualizing "modern Spain" (Artola, Fontana, García Sanz, Simon Segura, Tortella).

Historians now overtly challenge the traditional characterization of Spain's modern era as a kind of historical failure. Adrian Shubert concludes his *A Social History of Modern Spain*, for example, by observing that "in the nineteenth and twentieth centuries Spain was fully part of the European mainstream" (262). More recently, David Ringrose argues that Spain is best understood as "a long-term participant in the continent-wide process of accelerating economic expansion" (31), and that "Spain's dramatic economic transformation in the second half of the twentieth century is best understood as the extension and culmination of two centuries of remarkably persistent economic growth that began around 1700" (53). In the context of studies of romanticism in Spain, reclaiming the modern has taken the form of unambiguously affirming Spanish Enlightenment (Sebold), Spanish liberalism (Llorens; Shaw, "Towards"; Abellán; Navas Ruiz), or, increasingly, the broader category of "bourgeois revolution" (Kirkpatrick, *Románticas,* 37–61; Zavala; Escobar, "Larra y la Revolución") as the romantic movement's most apt historical matrices. Despite their many differences, these lines of inquiry have participated— knowingly or not—in a broader process of historical revision that has replaced earlier notions of "backward Spain" with more complex accounts of the history of modern Spanish culture. Together, such projects have forged a discourse in which modern Europe's imperial ghost—that is, the story of *what Spain was not*—is slowly being exorcized in order to begin to reveal the landscape of a Spanish modernity that was neither monumental nor ruinous.

In turn, such reconfigurations have given rise to a series of newer questions concerning romanticism in Spain. They are questions pertaining to the relationship between Spanish romanticism and its late–eighteenth- and early nineteenth-century modernity. Like the historicist theses considered earlier, the genealogy of the critical tradition that has linked romanticism and enlightened liberalism also finds its early formulations in the romantic era itself, principally in Victor Hugo's 1827 *Preface to Cromwell.* Widely read as a manifesto of "romantic liberalism," the text famously analogizes the classicist-romantic polemics in theater with the broader sociopolitical conflicts between the Ancien Régime and a revolutionary liberalism. The author affirms that "il y a aujourd'hui l'Ancien Régime littéraire comme l'Ancien Régime politique. Le dernier siècle pèse encore presque de tout point sur le nouveau" [There is today a literary as well as a political Ancien Régime. The last century weighs on the new one at almost every point] (314). Within this framework, romanticism is for Hugo an expression of freedom against the weight of tradition. He thus envisages romantic theater as the defense of "la liberté de l'art contre le despotisme des systèmes, des codes, et des règles" [the liberty of art against the despotism of systems, codes, and rules] (292). Hugo's defense of artistic freedom in the preface would subsequently become a rallying point for nineteenth-century romantic playwrights across Europe.

In the twentieth century, literary history and criticism has, again, echoed and amplified this line of reasoning. Within the field of studies of Spanish romanticism, the liberal-romantic equation has become one of the more commonly accepted views of the movement. Ricardo Navas Ruiz's *El romanticismo español*—arguably the most widely disseminated study of the movement in Spain—affirms the link between liberalism and romanticism in no uncertain terms, characterizing Spain's romantic writers as follows:

> Abrazaron con entusiasmo la causa de la libertad, porque ser romántico y liberal era estar a la altura de los tiempos, a tono con la circunstancia histórica.
>
>   Y ésta fue básicamente la misión de la generación romántica [. . .] democratizar a España; europeizar al país; abrirlo a la libertad; incorporarlo a las ideas literarias, sociales y políticas de las naciones más avanzadas; darle un fuerte empuje de modernización en un momento en que su imperio acababa de hundirse. Si existe una España moderna, ésa arranca, con todos sus logros y todos sus fracasos, del romanticismo. (48–49)

> [They enthusiastically embraced the cause of liberty, because to be romantic and liberal was to be with the times, in tune with historical circumstance.
>
>   And this was basically the mission of the romantic generation { . . . } to democratize Spain; to Europeanize the country; to open it to liberty; to incorporate it in the literary, social, and political ideas of the more advanced nations; to give it a strong push of modernization at a moment in which its empire had just collapsed. If a modern Spain exists, it springs, with all its successes and failures, from romanticism.]

In a similar vein, Susan Kirkpatrick has studied the conceptual nexus between romantic rhetoric and liberal ideology. The privileging of the subjective within romantic discourse, she argues, was in effect the artistic analogue to the privileging of the individual within bourgeois liberalism:

> Romanticism's part in the formation of bourgeois culture was precisely that: to figure subjectivity as individual self, in a form and content through which readers could interpret their immediate and concrete experience in terms of a scheme that distinguished the perceiving, desiring subject from the surrounding social and physical world. (*Las Románticas* 9)

In the more specific context of early nineteenth-century Spanish history and culture, Kirkpatrick notes that "romanticism was central to the cultural agenda of the liberal movement of the 1830s, for the artistic cult of individual subjectivity supplied imaginative and emotional meanings for the new structures that the liberals sought to constitute in Spanish society" (*Románticas,* 40). The self-interested subject affirmed by liberal economics, the autonomous individual whose inalienable rights were posited by liberal politics, and the representation of the richness and complexity of inner life in romantic discourse were part of a mutually reinforcing liberal cultural machinery.

Such views of the movement in Spain initially appear to sit somewhat uneasily next to the historicist paradigm, according to which Spain's romanticism is at its core an affirmation of a quintessentially nonmodern cultural identity. Indeed, some critics have treated the two paradigms as irreconcilable conceptions of romanticism in Spain.[61] It is worth noting, however, that romantic historicism and liberalism belong to entirely different categories of analysis, and debates in which one must opt for either a "historicist" or a "liberal" heart of the movement simply present a false choice. This is so not only because as David Gies has noted, one can always follow Lovejoy's injunction to conceive of romanticisms in the plural ("Plurality"), but also because liberalism and romantic historicism are by no means mutually exclusive terms. Liberalism's ideological antagonist in Spain was not romantic historicism; it was Fernandine absolutism, followed by Carlism. Conversely, romantic historicism's conceptual adversary was not liberalism, but rather the cosmopolitan, humanist historiography of the eighteenth century. Liberal romantics in Spain and across modern Europe often espoused historicist ideas, even as they fought against absolutism. Opposing the Ancien Régime and embracing a nationalist mythology was by no means a contradiction.

As Silver makes plain, romantic historicism was in fact a key facet of the nationalism that aided *moderado* liberals—the most conservative, authoritarian wing of the liberal movement—in consolidating their political hegemony during the 1840s and 1850s. It is for this reason, perhaps, that most critics defending the liberalism/romanticism equation have subsumed romantic historicism into their accounts.[62] To conceive of Spain's romanticism within the broader culture of an emergent liberalism affords additional clarity concerning the way that historicist discourse circulated in Spain. Initially the product of a centuries-long metageography of modern Europe, the idea of "romantic" Spain was—despite its early association with Böhl von Faber's absolutist politics—ultimately internalized by Spanish liberals and deployed as an important tool of *moderado* nation building. The historicist fantasy of medieval Spain operated internationally (Schlegel), among Spanish traditionalists, and among many Spanish liberals, particularly conservative liberals. Its ideological use clearly varied according to context, and in this regard historicist thinking was neither the indispensable core of romanticism in Spain nor an utterly reactionary, absolutist ideology. It was part of the profound nationalism that accompanied nineteenth-century European history and cultural politics more generally.[63]

There is, however, a more fundamental conceptual challenge posed by postulating a basic consonance between liberalism and romanticism. For while the identification of romanticism and liberalism reclaims the modern as a key trope for understanding Spanish history, it tends to efface romanticism's dialectical relationship to modernity itself. In conceiving of Spanish romantic discourse as an agent of liberal modernization, analysts of the movement have set up a puzzling conceptual impasse, a contradiction that stems from the fact that, taken as a whole, liberalism was very much a continuation of eighteenth-century Enlightenment ideals. Liberalism struggled against absolutism and the late-feudal structures of the Ancien Régime in order to *rationalize* politics, economics, and the social order. The representatives who in 1812 drafted Spain's first liberal constitution in Cádiz were the intellectual heirs of the Spanish Enlightenment (Abellán, 55–94), and while their passions might have accorded them a "romantic" demeanor, their programs—inspired by John Locke and Adam Smith, among others—belonged to traditions that could scarcely be described as romantic. As Kirkpatrick, Escobar, and other scholars have noted, Enlightenment, and liberalism after it, are both part of what Jameson has described as

> a properly bourgeois cultural revolution, in which the values and the discourses, the habits and the daily space, of the Ancien Régime were systematically dismantled so that in their place could be set the new conceptualities, habits and life forms, and value systems of a capitalist market society. (*Political*, 96)

In Spain, this systematic process effected profound changes over the course of the first half of the nineteenth century. Indeed, it is difficult to imagine a prior moment of Spanish history in which such fundamental change took place in so short a span of years:

> Between 1808 and 1843 the entire socio-economic order of the Spanish Ancien Regime was dismantled. The nobility and the clergy lost their legal privileges and the equality of all male citizens before the law was proclaimed. Entails, seigniorial rights and the tithe were abolished. The lands of the Church were disentailed and sold at public auction, the guilds were suppressed and economic freedom established. The Inquisition was dissolved and the Church's legal jurisdiction in civil affairs eliminated. The absolute power of the monarch was replaced by a parliamentary system based on popular sovereignty. (Burdiel, 17)

While romanticism undoubtedly flourished in Spain during this historical period, the term "romantic" would have to be stretched far beyond even its notoriously ample semantic field to convincingly describe activities such as drafting a new legal code, establishing the rudiments of a market economy, or auctioning disentailed land. If the modernity of the bourgeois cultural revolution was romanticism's home in Spain, conflating the movement with its historical moment overlooks the fact that romanticism was often a rather disgruntled tenant within the house of liberal modernity.

Twentieth-century political theorists such as Nancy Rosenblum have offered useful insight into the reasons for this inherently uneasy relationship between liberalism and romanticism. Rosenblum shows that romantic sensibilities often speak to the insufficiencies of liberalism; they highlight those areas of subjective experience that liberalism tends to mute, despite its celebration of the individual:

> Liberalism is legalistic. It values regularity, impersonality, and impartiality; preoccupied with securing expectations, it inhibits spontaneity and self-expression. Liberal theory gives a fearful, self-protective rationale for limited government. It gives an instrumental rationale for a sphere of personal liberty. [. . .] Liberalism portrays men and women as legal persons bearing rights or as possessive individualists, but these representations acknowledge only what is general among people, not what makes them unique, various, and original. In short, liberalism does not take individuality, spontaneity and expressivity into account. Its political society is cold, contractual and unlovely—without emotional or aesthetic appeal. (Rosenblum, 2)

It is for this reason, among others, that critics such as Sebold (*Rapto*, 157–69), Shaw ("Towards"), and Kirkpatrick ("Spanish") have pointed to spiritual malaise, quasi-existential angst, and *mal du siècle* disaffection as important romantic symptoms of the crisis prompted by enlightened liberalism. Such examples suggest that while romantic rhetoric often affirmed liberal values, it also highlighted limitations within liberalism itself. It was not simply part of the symbolic machinery of liberalism; it was also the ghost within that machine, a sort of pained, bad conscience that accompanied the upheavals of liberal modernity. To the extent that the politics and economics of liberalism—now neoliberalism—have become increasingly dominant on a global scale since the nineteenth century, such a critique continues to resonate in the present (Argullol; Escobar, "Ilustración"). Not by coincidence, however, it is precisely this facet of the movement, at once participating in the liberal project and critical of it, that both the conception of "romantic Spain" as a quintessentially nonmodern phenomenon and the revisionist characterization of romanticism as an agent of liberal modernity have tended to occlude.

Facing modern Europe's centuries-long "you are not modern," Spanish literary historiography seems to have been forced down one of two equally narrow paths, the path of acquiescence to the dominant narrative (i.e., romanticism as nonmodern tradition) or the path of counterhistorical resistance (i.e., romanticism as the affirmation of liberal modernity). Given such choices, it was difficult to entertain the notion that one of Spanish romanticism's lasting legacies might be the cautionary tale it tells about liberal modernity itself. Chief among the features of the modern in nineteenth-century Spain, for example, was the institution of private property along with the new world of social relations that liberalism inaugurated;[64]

and as Spanish liberalism slowly implemented an entirely new system of ownership, commerce, and exchange, romantic writers bore witness to many of its alienating effects. In this sense, as we shall see in subsequent chapters, the romantic critique of liberalism was not always reactionary or even conservative. It often came from some of the more progressive liberals of the moment, and although such writers could at times engage in nostalgia for a world that was disappearing, they did not desire to return to the past. Their plaints were more complex, and they often functioned as a kind of immanent critique, a voice of concern, anger, and even desperation, from within the emergent, modern, liberal world.

As the history we have reviewed in this chapter suggests, thinking about works from the romantic era in Spain entails engagement with both the very visible, social, political, and economic upheavals of the late eighteenth and early nineteenth centuries, and with the deeper, broader, centuries-long history of conceptualizing the modern. Reappraisal of Spanish romantic texts seems to demand multiple, flexible hermeneutic frames that allow for movement from questions of more immediate significance, to considerations belonging to vaster historical time scales, to contemporary metacritical observations. Similarly, while the narrative of modernity has monumentalized the act of drawing lines—between past and present, and between north and south, as we have seen—reexamination of Spanish romantic texts appears to call for a more textured and perhaps self-conscious approach to history, an acknowledgment that the historical domain is "necessarily complex in character, never belonging to a single mode (continuity/discontinuity) or temporality" (Mulhern, 22).[65]

Precisely because Spanish romanticism, its conceptualization, and its critical reception have been so strongly marked by the line with which modern Europe expelled Spanish culture from the modern, the struggle with this legacy cannot be limited to simply affirming what was denied—that is, "Spain *did* have an Enlightenment, there *was* a liberal cultural revolution." Such responses are often forced to mimic the gaze they would oppose, and they prompt a tit-for-tat kind of exchange—"yes, but Spain was not as important as . . ."—when the more pressing need, it seems, is to imagine entirely new terms of dialogue. If such a dialogue is to take place, the pattern of thought whereby "European literature" is always already superior must begin to be dismantled, not only from the postcolonial world, but from the European periphery as well.

In turn, such a process poses a conceptual challenge that is as straight-forward as it is daunting, for it necessitates the perhaps impossible task of conceptualizing difference *qua difference*, without succumbing to the hierarchical impulse that so often shadows the perception of historical and cultural alterity. It might begin simply by asking what can be learned from the romanticisms of the periphery that would not be gleaned as easily in the romantic titans of modern Europe. What does southern Europe's path to the modern have to say, for example, to the grand historical narratives that sustain "European romanticism"? What would it mean to conceptual-ize and accord value to romanticism in the *absence* of an Abramsian/De Manian poetics? What would be the consequences of approaching Spanish romantic texts without assuming that their relationship to the modern is any less complex than what one finds in modern Europe? What if one openly questioned whether "European romanticism" should remain the transnational standard against which the cultural production of peripheral Europe should be judged?

To explore such questions is to take the initial steps from out of the shadow of modern European cultural imperialism. In this relatively new context, one might begin to read Spanish romantic texts for traces of the modernity of the Luso-Hispanic Atlantic that was so successfully erased by the dominant narrative we have considered; or one might point to a utopian strain of Spanish romantic thinking that, while bounded within historically conditioned ideological constraints, still has much to say to modern Europe. Readings in this vein would tacitly question the northern European monopoly on the modern, on romanticism, and on its symbolic locations, while simultaneously attending to the distinctive features of Spanish cultural history.

The readings that follow are an attempt to begin such a process, and among other things, they are intended to suggest that liberating the idea of modernity from the Hegelian metageography of modern Europe re-mains an unfinished task. While few scholars today would openly em-brace the idea of a universal History radiating from northern Europe, the effects of this construct continue to shape critical presuppositions con-cerning both the nature of "Europe" and the cultural production of the European periphery.[66] In the case of Spanish romanticism, we have seen such effects reverberate throughout the twentieth-century reception of the movement. Even today, Spanish romantic production tends to be seen, at best, as a phenomenon that might illuminate an interesting moment of Spanish history, while the romantics of modern Europe retain a vestigial, universalizing aura (i.e., Wordsworth speaks to modernity while Espronceda speaks to nineteenth-century Spain). As this legacy of representation diminishes—if it diminishes—it will be important to grasp romanticism and the modern as the highly mobile historical concepts they are. These word-thoughts often still bear the signs of centuries of crippling captivity in a northern European cage, but they have increasingly begun to take flight. Indeed, Octavio Paz's sense of the modern as "the instant, that bird that is everywhere and nowhere" may one day come to be seen not merely as a poet's fanciful imaginings but as a deeply egalitarian, profoundly historical claim after all.

CHAPTER 2

Beginnings without End

José Cadalso and the Melancholy of Modernity

In moving from questions of history and metahistory to the first work we shall consider, let us imagine for a moment a gathering, the coming together of a literary *tertulia* sometime in the summer of 1775. A group of young literati assembles in the university town of Salamanca to hear a new work that José Cadalso, friend and mentor to many of them, has sent. There is some expectation, for the manuscript has been circulating, albeit guardedly. In the correspondence that accompanies the papers Cadalso has forwarded to his protégé Juan Meléndez Valdés, the author calls for discretion in the dissemination of his work: "Supongo en Vmd, o mejor decir, creo y me consta en Vmd, bastante discreción para no fiar este papel a mucha gente, ni leerlo al profano vulgo" [I suppose, or better said, I believe and know for a fact that you have enough discretion not to entrust this sheet to many people or to read it to unthinking commoners] (Cadalso, *Escritos*, 102). The text to be read is a dialogue, but if its form recalls classical and Renaissance philosophical antecedents, its tone and content quickly signal that dispassionate inquiry is not among its most immediate concerns. Indeed, as the reading begins, the opening words of the text's protagonist, Tediato, conjure a world that could hardly seem more distant from Enlightenment ideals of lucid, rational exchange:

> ¡Qué noche! La oscuridad, el silencio pavoroso interrumpido por los lamentos que se oyen en la vecina carcel, completan la tristeza de mi corazón. El cielo también se conjura contra mi quietud, si alguna me quedara. El nublado crece. La luz de esos relámpagos . . . ¡qué horrorosa! [. . .] No hay hombre que no se crea mortal en este instante . . . ¡Ay si fuese el último momento de mi vida! ¡Cuán grato sería para mí! ¡Cuán horrible ahora! ¡Cuán horrible! Más lo fue el día, el triste día que fue causa de la escena en que ahora me hallo. (Cadalso, *Cartas marruecas. Noches lúgubres*, 229)

[What night! The darkness, the frightful silence interrupted by the laments heard in the nearby jail, they complete the sadness of my heart. The heavens too conspire against my restfulness, should any of it remain. The storm clouds grow. The flash of those lightning bolts . . . how horrible! { . . . } There is no man who does not believe himself mortal in this instant . . . Oh, if it were the last instant of my life! How pleasant it would be for me! How horrible it is now! How horrible! It was even more horrible on that day, on that sad day that was the cause of the state in which I now find myself.]

The work in question is Cadalso's *Noches lúgubres* [Lugubrious Nights], which along with his *Cartas marruecas* [Moroccan Letters] stands not only as one of the most edited and critically discussed eighteenth-century Spanish texts, but also as the centerpiece of a longstanding historiographic debate within Hispanism concerning "the origins" of Spanish romanticism.[1] Its basic plot is disturbingly simple: Over three consecutive nights, a gentleman dialogues with a gravedigger he has hired to exhume the body of his dead beloved. His aim is to return to his home, lie with the corpse, and commit suicide, but the work ends before readers learn if he accomplishes his objective. My intention in sketching the hypothetical scene of reading with which we begin, however, has been to foreground the role that historical imagination—the imagining of a particular past in which the text might be located—has played in modern critical appraisals of the work. For to notice that this scene of reading is, in a sense, already a map of some of the work's potential meanings—the seemingly antithetical status of its "goyaesque" nocturnal with respect to Enlightenment rationality (Helman, "Caprichos"; Sebold, *Noches*, 163; Ilie, *Age*, 371); its semipublic, primarily aural mode of reception (Lama, "Noches"); and its influence on the so-called "poetic school of Salamanca" (Real de la Riva)—is to acknowledge that the qualities ascribed to the past in which this text is imagined have often defined the parameters of subsequent inquiry into its interpretation.

I recall this historicist truism primarily because a review of the debates concerning the status of romanticism in *Noches lúgubres* suggests that the conflicting critical characterizations of Cadalso's text—a spectrum that runs from nonromantic, to preromantic, to fully and unabashedly romantic—have been predicated on two fundamental and perhaps ultimately incompatible imaginings of the late eighteenth-century Spanish cultural matrix to which the work ostensibly belongs. They are competing stories concerning the texture and range of possible meanings of the historical *where* of *Noches lúgubres*. On one hand is the narrative of an innovative moment in Spanish cultural production, a moment that parallels Germany's Sturm und Drang, a moment that is at the vanguard of the general sentimental shift in late eighteenth-century Western European aesthetic sensibility. On the other hand is the tale of a culture beholden to religious traditions and imported neoclassical literary paradigms, a Spain in which the sentimentalism of *Noches lúgubres*, like the Enlightenment culture to which it pertains, can only be imagined as derivative. And behind the scenes, structuring the terms of the debate from the outset, are the set of issues we discussed in the previous chapter, the peripheral status of Spanish modernity vis-à-vis the dominant European narratives of the modern. To be sure, one might attempt to reconcile this opposition—"modern" versus "backward" Spain—by tacking to a middle ground that recognizes "tradition and change" or "influence and originality" in both Cadalso's text and its historical moment, but such a splitting of the difference would seem to renounce rather than to resolve the problem of historical discrimination posed by these competing interpretive frames.

For to follow the debates concerning the historiographic implications of *Noches lúgubres* is precisely to marvel at the capacity with which participants on either side have been able to marshal intelligent close readings, meticulous source studies, and painstaking historical research to the service of their respective arguments. Independent of one's particular critical allegiances, it would seem prudent to conclude that no set of "data" has been able to put this question to rest. Inasmuch as it involves aesthetic and historical judgment, the question seems beyond the scope of any apodictic, empirical verification, and if the persistent return to this issue within the criticism of the last three decades is any indication, it very well may be that the question of an eighteenth-century romanticism in *Noches lúgubres* is in fact destined to be asked repeatedly, in a cyclical, open-ended fashion that eerily resonates with the structure of the work itself, a structure, it is worth recalling, that famously ends where it begins, its putative task unaccomplished.

This is not to propose that the structure of *Noches lúgubres* somehow prefigured the open-ended nature of the historiographic quandaries it would ultimately engender, but it is to suggest that already in Cadalso there are insights that might productively be brought to bear on the recent history of the text's critical reception. In the work's scandalously "incomplete" ending, for example, it is not difficult to see a certain resistance to the final word. In the multiple, apocryphal closings that would later be appended, like patches on a wound the text seems rather intent on keeping open, may be the elements of a cautionary tale regarding literary, psychological, and historical closure. And in the injunction to keep moving that is the text's last gesture—"andemos, amigo, andemos" [let's go, friend, let's go] (255)—there may be a largely unheeded invitation to approach this work not as a historiographic problem to be solved, but rather as a site in which something will always remain to be unearthed. In short, many of the discursive features of *Noches lúgubres* seem to suggest what more recent theoretical projects—that is, the deconstruction of historical origins, antipositivist conceptions of genealogy, the increasingly rhetorical understanding of history—have made explicit: that behind the taxonomies of traditional literary history and behind its seemingly nominalist quarrels are a series of perhaps more searching questions.

It may indeed be time to dispense altogether with the question of whether or not *Noches lúgubres* is best thought of as romantic, not only because the stakes of the question seem somewhat smaller within a critical landscape no longer dominated by the rhetoric of historiographic classification, but also because the historical *where* of *Noches lúgubres* itself quickly moved beyond the contentious boundaries of eighteenth-century literary historiography. As the work of numerous critics has made increasingly clear, while scholars may be destined to continue quarreling over Cadalso's romanticism, as a matter of record *Noches lúgubres* circulated amply and quite successfully as a text that was perfectly in consonance with the new sensibility of the romantic reading public of the 1820s, 1830s, and 1840s. One need only recall the enormous commercial success of the work in the first half of the nineteenth century (Camarero, "Noches"), or the exemplary status of the text for romantic writers (Dowling, Rodríguez), or its disturbing influence on the young readers of the early 1800s (Helman, Introducción, 54, Schurlknight, "Another") in order to appreciate the very contemporary appeal of the work for the readers of the first half-century. And this romantic reception of *Noches lúgubres* suggests that more pressing perhaps than the question of Cadalso's romanticism is the question of how a text written in the early 1770s and published posthumously in the *Correo de Madrid* in 1789 could have gained such purchase on the nineteenth-century romantic imaginary.

To be sure, any number of characteristics might be summoned to explain the appeal of *Noches lúgubres* to a romantic reading public. The macabre tenor of a plot structured around the attempt to unearth the body of a beloved would certainly have resonated well with the gothic literary vogue of the 1830s as represented, for example, by Agustín Pérez Zaragoza's twelve-volume bestseller of 1831, *Galería fúnebre de espectros y sombras ensangrentadas* [Funereal Gallery of Specters and Bloodied Shades]. Similarly, the autobiographical legend surrounding the text—the notion that it was confessional, that Cadalso had indeed attempted to disinter his recently deceased lover, María Ingacia Ibáñez—clearly converged with the expressive poetics and the rhetoric of authenticity that were in the process of becoming hallmarks of romantic discourse. (As late as the mid-century the work continued to be published as literary autobiography in editions such as Marés's 1852 *Historia de los amores del coronel don José de Cadalso, escrita por él mismo* [The History of Don José Cadalso's Loves, Written by Himself]). At the same time, the ostensibly incomplete nature of the text, the fact that it seemed to end abruptly, without the accomplishment of Tediato's declared goal, marked the text as a fragment, an increasingly appealing aesthetic form in the wake of translations at the turn of the century of Macpherson's "discovery" of Ossian. It also invited many a nineteenth-century writer to pick up where Cadalso appeared to have left off, and to respond to such an invitation was, among other things, to grant the work citizenship as a nineteenth-century literary text.

The claims of *Noches lúgubres* on its romantic readership, however, seem to run deeper than these characteristics and the historical resonance they may have had. For even in the aggregate, such features do not fully account for the text's predominant rhetorical effect, which is the incitement of the passions that classical rhetoric would have named *pathopoeia*. Indeed, there is a more fundamental place to look for the production of such an effect. In *Noches lúgubres* that place is the place of the subject, as suggested in Tediato's opening words—in the nexus they posit between the external and the internal, between night and the heart—in short, between the realm of nature and the realm of affect. By subject I mean to invoke here three interrelated understandings of the term. First and foremost my concern will be the self, the mind, or consciousness—in this case Tediato's inner word, the representation of which famously dominates in *Noches lúgubres*. I will also engage the meaning of subject that refers to the state of being in submission or under dominion, as, for example, Tediato's subjection to the relentlessly adverse fortune in which he perceives himself. At the same time, I hope to retain the term subject as a way of naming the basic matter or theme of a literary work, which at its most general might in this case be described as the representation of desire and its suffering. These dimensions of the work, so intimately bound to one another, make the most powerful claim on the romantic imaginary. They do so in large measure because one of the few commonalities that seems to subtend a romanticism whose concept often threatens to crumble into disparate, irreconcilable discourses is the representation of subjectivity itself (Kirkpatrick, *Las Románticas* 9–23); and beyond the eighteenth-century sentimentalism in which *Noches lúgubres* might initially have been apprehended (Rudat, "Lo prerromantico" and "Artificio"; Quinziano), there is little question but that nineteenth-century readers saw in Cadalso's text an example of such representation, an impressive staging of subjectivity and its vicissitudes.

An examination of the tale of subjectivity that *Noches lúgubres* encodes—that is, the story it seems to tell about the subject it constitutes—may consequently offer a useful lens through which to reappraise Cadalso's text. Of particular interest will be questions concerning the shape of the self that is figured in *Noches lúgubres*; that is, the contours of interiority as represented in this text, its relationship to the idea of a "modern self," and its legacy for nineteenth-century representations of romantic subjectivity. Such questions may provide a new way of understanding Cadalso's text, its historical import, and its intersections with *ochocentista* sensibilities. More broadly, an examination of these issues might make clearer the reasons for which *Noches lúgubres* and the question of its romanticism seem persistently to haunt the contemporary critical-historical landscape.

The Subject of Loss

The very fact that, as highly subjective, lyrical prose, *Noches lúgubres* represents a phenomenological arena strikingly similar to what had increasingly become the central subject matter of eighteenth-century loco-descriptive poetry—that is, the representation of consciousness in contact with the world—speaks to its affinities with both romanticism's "poetic" rewritings of the classical genres and with the movement's well-known literary mappings of the psyche (Bloom, 3). Even so, it is worth recalling just how extraordinary a self Tediato would have represented to late eighteenth- and early nineteenth-century readers by virtue of his rather anomalous affective disposition. As Randolph Pope has humorously observed, the wish to unearth one's beloved in order to carry the cadaver home, lie with it in bed, and then slowly turn to ash in an act of self-immolation "no es normal" (21). The observation serves as a useful reminder that Tediato makes his appearance initially under the sign of the pathological; what is most beguiling about him at first is precisely his distinctively morbid, seemingly infirm relationship to nature, to civil society, and to his other, the gravedigger Lorenzo. Yet, as we shall see, one of the more subtle and powerful rhetorical maneuvers of *Noches lúgubres* is to suggest that ultimately Tediato's pathologies are less sui generis than they appear. The pathological in this work carries with it an implicit indictment of the normative order that names it, or, to put it more simply, Cadalso is careful to insinuate that there is a collective, social dimension to the highly individual, exquisitely personal pain that the text represents. In addition, Tediato's condition has significantly been conjured not in order to deliver a narrative of exemplary cure, as would have been prescribed by neo-Horatian poetics, but rather to underscore the intractable nature of the disease, a compulsion whose only promise—as Tediato's closing words to Lorenzo suggest—is to open itself endlessly into the future.

But what is this pathology, this extraordinary disposition that in its persistence curiously begins to take on a predictable, almost familiar quality? At its most immediate, one might certainly read *Noches lúgubres* as a representation of the trauma of personal loss, whether understood as a coded autobiographical reference to the death of María Ignacia Ibáñez—Cadalso himself would acknowledge a certain "parte verdadera" [truthful part] to the work (Cadalso, *Escritos*, 102)—or taken in discursive terms, as the "pretextual" death of a beloved that defines Tediato's enunciative context (Godin, 132). Already in the opening lines of the work this loss makes its first, somewhat veiled appearance when Tediato's description of the horrors of the night are described as a partial, insufficient image in comparison with "el triste día que fue causa de la escena en que ahora me hallo" [the sad day that was the cause of the state in which I now find myself] (229). Shortly thereafter Tediato repeats the notion that the tortured memory of his loss surpasses his manifestly macabre surroundings in its horror: "¡Memoria! ¡Triste memoria! Cruel memoria, más tempestades fromas en mi alma que esas nubes en el aire" [Memory! Sad memory! Cruel memory, more tempests do you form in my soul than do those clouds in the air] (230).

These initial examples of hyperbolic *comparatio*, along with the euphemistic figures by which "triste día" and "memoria" are made to stand in for the unmentionable loss, establish a rhetorical paradigm that will extend itself throughout *Noches lúgubres*, where the beloved is repeatedly invoked as somehow beyond full representation. Echoing the longstanding conventions of amorous poetry, and in consonance with the work's widely acknowledged sublime style, the beloved's predominant modes of appearance will be fragmentary and metonymic, as if to suggest that she can only be known proximately, by a contiguity that denies full access even as it promises to unite, or by synecdochic vestiges that name her as an absent whole in the act of evoking her.[2] In an ironic twist on the conceit by which the fragmented beauty of the beloved is figured as ultimately unrepresentable, the full presence of the beloved in *Noches lúgubres* is unavailable, not because it defies representation, but because it literally is no more. For Tediato, the beloved is a trace that bears witness to its passing, "un pecho" [a bosom] that no longer exists (230); her gravestone stands in metonymically for the contact it prohibits—"la losa que he regado tantas veces con mi llanto y besado tantas veces con mis labios" [the gravestone I have watered so many times with my weeping and kissed so many times with my lips] (234).

Even the remains that lie beneath the stone, ostensibly the very telos of Tediato's quest, offer less than one might suspect, for if the disturbing plans to unearth the beloved—revealed at the end of the "Noche Primera"—are concrete and feasible enough, Tediato has also tellingly confessed to Lorenzo that the actual object of his pursuits is, in truth, no longer a corpse: "ya no es cadáver" (238). It is an extraordinary admission that hints at the impossibility of Tediato's "empresa" [enterprise] from the outset. And it suggests that the thwarting of his plans each night by the vagaries of adverse fortune may in fact be the surface representation of a more fundamental impasse, an aporia in which what Tediato pursues is, by definition—ontologically—beyond his grasp. All there is to disinter— "montón de huesos asquerosos" [pile of disgusting bones] (241)—is itself a vestige, bodily remains that inertly testify to what is gone. To execute his plans would thus be merely to encounter yet another painful sign of absence. Only in the image of Tediato's self-destruction—in flames that consume and symbolically consummate—does the imagined realization of his desire make a fleeting, if fatal, appearance: "Morirá mi cuerpo junto a ti, cadáver adorado, y expirando incendiaré mi domicilio; y tú y yo nos volveremos ceniza en medio de las de la casa" [My body will die next to you, beloved cadaver, and as I expire I will set my home aflame; and you and I will turn to ash among the ashes of the house] (241). With its macabre echoes of nuptial union, the passage makes clear the final consequences of a logic by which painful loss has turned on the self, demanding its annihilation as the price of an imagined peace.

The historical name for this malady is, of course, *melancholia*, a term that not by coincidence falls within the semantic field of Cadalso's title adjective, *lúgubres*, which the *Diccionario de autoridades* renders as "triste, funesto y melanchólico; es voz latina *Lugubris*, y mui usada de los poetas" [sad, ill-fated, and melancholic; it is a Latin word, *Lugubris*, and very much used by poets] (438). Tellingly, the term *melancolía* itself makes more than one appearance in the text. In one of the opening lines of the "Noche Segunda," Tediato will explicitly refer to "mi melancolía," noting that the day he has had to endure before returning to the cemetery has in no way assuaged his suffering. Toward the end of the "Noche Tercera" the word appears once again: "El mismo horroroso conjunto de cosas de la noche antepasada vuelve a herir mi vista con aquella dulce melancolía" [The same horrifying assemblage of things as the night before last again wounds my gaze with that sweet melancholy] (254).

Melancholy would thus seem to be a privileged analytical concept in the work; and both the traditional conception of melancholy within the long-lived legacy of Hippocratic humoral theory (Klibansky) and its more modern psychoanalytic theorization offer intriguing vantage points from which to grasp the nature of Tediato's woes. In a sense, *Noches lúgubres* suggestively hovers between the two frameworks.[3] It is no coincidence, for example, that the well-known etymology of the term—from the Greek *melas* [black] and *khole* [bile]—names the symbolically charged color that appears to perennially shade Tediato's perceptual field. Nor is it especially surprising that his sepulchral fascination connotes the natural element—earth—that was traditionally associated with the melancholic. Cadalso is well aware of the classical valences of the iconography he deploys, and he makes a point of situating Tediato within this legacy. Darkness, coolness, dryness, and heaviness are among the traditional attributes that, as

Foucault noted, provide "symbolic unity" to melancholy's concept (Radden, 9). Cadalso's representation of melancholy, however, diverges considerably from the etiological dimensions of the Hippocratic tradition. Description appears to preempt diagnosis, and the traces of a classical melancholy in *Noches lúgubres* serve more to evoke a set of recognizable symptoms—persistent sadness coupled with quasi-manic exaltation, suicidal inclinations, a pessimistic outlook, and the like—than to affirm the traditional underlying physiological cause.

The etiology that does seem to have some bearing on *Noches Lúgubres* is the Freudian vision of melancholy. To be sure, in Cadalso the naturalistic framework of Freudian analysis does not even begin to make an appearance, but the ways in which *Noches lúgubres* announces the Freudian template of melancholy are nevertheless suggestive. For Freud, it is worth recalling, the distinctive features of melancholy come into view when it is juxtaposed with the work of mourning. According to the oft-quoted schema from the 1917 essay, "Mourning and Melancholia," whereas the work of mourning entails a form of reality testing that progressively liberates the ego from its libidinal attachment to the lost beloved in order to allow it to form new attachments, melancholy is a narcissistic response in which such liberation seems to have been arrested:

> The object-cathexis [. . .] was brought to an end. But the free libido was not displaced onto another object; it was withdrawn into the ego. There, however, it [. . .] served to establish an *identification* of the ego with the abandoned object. Thus the shadow of the object fell upon the ego, and the latter could henceforth be judged by a special agency, as though it were an object, the forsaken object. (Freud, *Freud*, 586)

There is thus a twofold mechanism at work: The ego identifies with the lost beloved, taking on its attributes, and a "special agency" within the self—in his later work Freud would name it the superego—begins to judge the ego as a forsaken object.

As Nigel Glendinning has observed, both this "shadow of the object" and the critical agency it inaugurates are not difficult to discern in Tediato (Introducción, 44–47). The protagonist frequently describes his inner world in terms that seem to equate him with his dead beloved. While waiting for Lorenzo, Tediato suggests, for example, that his heart is akin to the horrors of the cemetery: "no ve lo interior de mi corazón . . . ¡cuánto más se horrorizaría!" [He does not see the inside of my heart . . . How much more horrified he would be!] (229). Later he describes himself by noting his resemblance to a corpse—"sólo un resuello me distinguía de un cadaver" [only a breath distinguished me from a cadaver] (242)—and he imagines friends and associates speaking of him as if he were dying: "'Tediato se muere' dirían unos. Otros repetirían: 'Se muere Tediato' " ["Tediato is dying," some probably said. Others must have repeated: "Tediato is dying"] (243). The analogical thinking at work here—his imagining himself as dead because *she* is dead—becomes clear when Tediato makes his identification with the beloved explicit in the "Noche Segunda": "Eramos uno. Su alma, ¿qué era sino la mía? La mía, ¿qué era sino la suya? [We were one. Her soul, what was it but mine? And mine, what was it but hers?] (244). As we shall see shortly, the implications of this union of souls and the vestiges of religious dualism (body/soul) on which it depends will be far-reaching. For present purposes, however, suffice it to note that, in consonance with his literal pursuit of the beloved's remains, Tediato symbolically introjects the qualities of bodily death into his self-understanding. The Freudian "shadow of the object" that colors the ego— what Kristeva would later call "the shadow cast on the fragile self [. . .] by the loss of that essential other" (5)—is, at this level, the shadow of a corpse.

There are also traces of the kind of self-critical gesture Freud describes, in which the ego is seen as a forsaken object. Recalling how his friend Virtelio abandoned him after trying—without success—to lift his spirits, part of Tediato seems to turn on himself: "¿Quién no se cansa de un amigo como yo, triste, enfermo, apartado del mundo, objeto de la lástima de algunos, del menosprecio de otros, de la burla de muchos? ¡Qué mucho que me dejase!" [Who does not tire of a friend like me; sad, sick, detached from the world, the object of the pity of some, the scorn of others, and the mocking of many? It is no surprise that he left me!] (242–43). Even more pointed is the quasi-masochistic pleasure Tediato derives from his incarceration and the prospect of his unjust execution in the "Noche Segunda." Falsely accused of a murder to which he has accidentally been witness, he relishes the thought of his immanent death, and when the officer who has apprehended him informs him that "en breve tendrás muerte ignominiosa y cruel" [shortly you shall have an ignominious, cruel death], Tediato responds, "tanto más gustosa" [all the more pleasurable] (245). Adding to the officer's perplexity, Tediato specifies that "lo que me es gustosa es la muerte" [what is pleasing to me is death], and in anticipation of the pleasures of punishment he himself calls for more physical harm: "apuren los verdugos sus crueldades sobre mí" [let the executioners bring their cruelties on me] (245); "cargad más prisiones sobre mí, ministros feroces. Ligad más esos cordeles con que me arrastráis" [load me with more confinements, fierce officers. Tighten those cords with which you drag me] (245); "muera yo, muera yo en breve" [may I die, may I die shortly] (246). In short, Tediato's demeanor attests to that part of the self that turns on the ego in Freud's account of the melancholy subject.

To the extent that Tediato might consequently be read as a staging of melancholy, as the representation of the unfinished work of mourning and its various psychological permutations, one can begin to appreciate the claim it would have had on a nineteenth-century reading public steeped in the romantic rhetoric of affect. The work's rhetorical appeal, however, is not limited to the intrigue that melancholy might have held as the historically voguish affective disorder it had become in the early nineteenth century. It stems also from the particular rootedness of melancholy within the self in *Noches lúgubres*; that is, from the way the text suggests that melancholy is not simply something the subject *experiences* but also something deep within the structure of subjectivity itself. As the revisiting of Tediato's plight each night makes him increasingly known to the reader, as the initial shock and morbid intrigue of the "Noche Primera" yield to a different kind of readerly investment, and as a certain familiarity takes the pathological edge off of what initially appeared to be a highly anomalous demeanor, Tediato becomes an emblem, not of the solipsistic anguish one might at first have expected, but of a much broader, generalized—indeed, universalized—human suffering.

It is a sentiment that he himself will articulate toward the end of the "Noche Tercera": "Todos lloramos . . . , todos enfermamos . . . , todos morimos" [We all weep . . . , we all become sick . . . , we all die] (254).[4] In these words it is not difficult to hear a tacit invitation for readers to identify affectively with the pathos of Tediato's loss, and Tediato himself seems to model such an identification in his own rapprochement with Lorenzo by the end of the "Noche Tercera." Underpinning this implicit call to communion through shared human suffering, however, is a more fundamental proposition, the proposition that the experience of loss and the libidinal dynamic it inaugurates are in fact common, constitutive elements of subjectivity. To put it more plainly, *Noches lúgubres* suggests that loss is a founding structure of the self. In strictly discursive terms, the absent beloved is the causal sine qua non of the utterances by which Tediato constitutes himself as a subject. Without the lost beloved Tediato would not *be* Tediato; part of what he *is*, is a register of loss. Loss catalyzes the construction of his subjectivity.[5]

Freud himself would adopt a similar position with regard to the psyche as he began to understand melancholy not so much as the disorder he described in "Mourning and Melancholia," but rather as a common feature of psychic life generally. Thus, when the Freud of *The Ego and the Id* (1923) returns to his earlier thinking on melancholia, he finds it necessary to expand the scope of his treatment:

> At this point we must widen our range a little. We succeeded in explaining the painful disorder of melancholia by supposing that [in those suffering from it] an object which was lost has been set up again inside the ego—that is, that an object-cathexis has been replaced by an identification. At the same time, however, we did not appreciate the full significance of this process and did not know how common and how typical it is. *Since then we have come to understand that this form of substitution has a great share in determining the form taken by the ego and that it makes an essential contribution towards building up what is called its 'character.'* (Freud, *Freud*, 638, my emphasis)

Commenting on this passage, Judith Butler notes that "what Freud here calls the 'character of the ego' appears to be the sedimentation of objects loved and lost, the archeological remainder, as it were, of unresolved grief" (133). She explains further:

> In the earlier essay, Freud assumes that grief can be resolved through a de-cathexis, a breaking of attachment. [. . .] In *The Ego and the Id*, he makes room for the notion that melancholic identification may be a *prerequisite* for letting the object go. By claiming this, he changes what it means to "let an object go," for there is no final breaking of the attachment. [. . .] The lost object is, in that sense, made coextensive with the ego itself. (133–34)

Within this framework, *Noches lúgubres* is a rather remarkable staging of the absence of any "final breaking of the attachment." By figuring subjectivity as an inherently melancholic structure—by suggesting that to be a subject is in some sense a melancholy affair by definition—the work makes clear the reason that Tediato's wound will not heal, the reason his "disease" cannot be cured, and the reason there will always be more work to be done. To put an end to loss would be to put an end to the self, which is perhaps one reason, as Sebold has suggested, that ultimately suicide is much more appealing as an imagined prospect than as a reality (*De ilustrados*, 68–69); his psychic investment is channeled into suicidal ideation, not suicide itself. Suicide, like the beloved, seems to belong to the realm of the always already beyond grasp. In this regard, Tediato repeatedly performs the ways in which loss is paradoxically a building block of subjectivity, and in equating unfinished mourning with the self, *Noches lúgubres* implicitly hails its melancholy readers. You are like me, it beguilingly intimates, you too have felt a loss that you know to be part of you. "Todos lloramos . . . , todos enfermamos . . . , todos morimos" [We all weep . . . , we all become sick . . . , we all die] (254). It is a siren's call, an interpellation that appeals to melancholic affect as a common human bond, and to heed such a call—readers of Althusser will remember—is both an act of recognition (yes, that's me being hailed, that's who I am) and an act of renunciation (that's me being hailed, I am not something else). The appeal to universal human suffering in *Noches lúgubres* thus works powerfully to shape and circumscribe the parameters of readerly self-understanding.

That romantic readers were especially receptive to this call is evident not only in the work's aforementioned commercial success or in the fact that Tediato's demeanor was actually imitated by readers (Helman, Introducción, 54),[6] but also in the numerous measures that were deployed to quell its infectious, melancholy appeal. Tellingly, the common denominator shared by both conservative and liberal nineteenth-century "solutions" to Cadalso's work—that is, Tediato's repentance and punishment or, conversely, the realization of his macabre intent—was closure itself, the attempt to put to rest precisely what Tediato could not relinquish, the prepoetic loss that founds his subjectivity.[7] Given the historical weight of classical aesthetic norms predicated on artistic unity, it is not difficult to understand this generalized imperative to close. Such rewritings, however, were not merely the formal exercise they might seem. Imbedded in them was an attempt to manage the more threatening consequences of nonconclusion, for Cadalso's scandalous "end without an ending" imbued his work with a patently slippery sort of autonomy; in its open-ended call to readers were the seeds of inexhaustible repetition.

A Different Sort of "amor in morte"

Akin to the Petrarchan lyric subjectivity before it, the call in *Noches lúgubres*—its interpellation of melancholy subjects—threatened endless proliferation precisely because its object of mimesis was not in fact an object but a loss. As Cascardi has observed, "since 'Petrarchism' or the mode of subjectivity it initiates is founded on the mimesis, not of an object or of an action but of a desire and a lack, the Petrarchan text allows for the infinite renewal of that desire in the subsequent tradition." He continues:

> If the fundamental loss that founds Petrarchan subjectivity has played a uniquely productive role over the course of Western literary history, this may well be because the Petrarchan pursuit of the beloved is by definition the search for an object of desire that remains elusive. [. . .] The painful melancholia of this lyric subject thus proves remarkably productive in a literary-historical sense. (*Ideologies*, 249–50)

To situate *Noches lúgubres* within this "infinite renewal" is to recognize in the work the representation of a libidinal structure common to the modern era, but it is also to confront the question of how the Petrarchan legacy—frequently abstracted into a structural paradigm—might be conceived of historically. All too often, the invocation of "Petrarchism" suggests repetition rather than the kind of productive renewal Cascardi posits—that is, a renewal thoroughly conditioned by the differing loco-historical valences that "Petrarchism" acquired after its inception. In this regard, while it is useful to situate *Noches lúgubres* within the broad history of Petrarchan desire—as Graf recently has, for example—it is equally important to assess the kind of renewal the work carries out with respect to that legacy. Indeed, Cadalso's work represents a particularly compelling, historically pivotal reworking of a vestigial Petrarchan code, and it is precisely such a refashioning that was part of the text's particularly strong—perhaps foundational—claim on nineteenth-century Spanish readers.[8]

Before studying the salient features of that refashioning, it will be useful to assess the points of contact between *Noches lúgubres* and the tradition of Petrarchan lyric subjectivity, both in terms of the preceding analysis and in the more specific context of eighteenth-century poetics. Our discussion of Tediato in terms of an object-relations psychoanalysis, along with the classical resonance of a metonymically "fragmented" beloved, initially suggest that *Noches lúgubres* readily lends itself to being read within a historically late, neoclassical Petrarchism. The representation of melancholic desire in *Noches lúgubres* can certainly be inscribed within the culture of a very broadly conceived modernity, for example, if one recalls Freud's distinction between the ancients and moderns in his much-commented footnote to the *Three Essays on Sexuality*: "The most striking distinction between the erotic life of antiquity and our own [. . .] lies in the fact that the ancients laid stress upon the instinct itself, whereas we emphasize its object" (Freud, *Three,* 15). Similarly, if one considers the literary-historical use to which the Freudian distinction has been put in scholarship dedicated to early modern lyric subjectivity, such as William Kerrigan and Gorden Braden's influential *The Idea of the Renaissance,* it is not unreasonable to conclude that, in expressing the sorrows of an unattainable, ostensibly superior beloved, Cadalso's work displays a generally Petrarchan configuration of melancholy desire. To invoke such a broadly defined modernity and to make Petrarchism a five-hundred-year-long, epochal qualifier, however, is once again to run the risk of emptying these categories of any historical specificity, for modernity in this account would come dangerously close to designating everything that follows the Petrarchan shift toward the valorization of objects of desire.

Significantly, the Petrarchan legacy had by the eighteenth century gone through a series of important modifications. While Petrarchan lyric discourse continued to be emulated (Arce, 79–80), its status and function as the lingua franca of amorous lyric discourse had been transformed in fundamental ways. The models held up for poetic emulation—that is, the literary objects of a distinctly neoclassical mimesis—came from a wide array of sources, both ancient and modern. Moreover, it was primarily *national* poets who enjoyed preeminence as the new classics to be imitated (Sebold, Prólogo, 46–55). One might thus identify a Petrarchism marked by several degrees of removal, and even so, it is important to recall that the neoclassical codification of exemplary writers was itself part of a broader eighteenth-century cultural project aimed at curbing the perceived excesses of the baroque rhetoric that continued to hold sway during the first decades of the 1700s. As Ignacio de Luzán's foundational *Poética* (1737) had made clear, when it came to lyric expression, it was the Spanish poets of the sixteenth century—in particular Garcilaso de la Vega— who were recommended as a salutary corrective to what was taken to be sickly baroque excess.

Después del marqués de Santillana, fueron los primeros [en adaptar el endecasílabo italiano al castellano] Juan Boscán [. . .] y don Diego de Mendoza y casi al mismo tiempo Gutierre de Cetina y Garcilaso de la Vega, que se remontó más que todos y mereció ser llamado el príncipe de la lírica española. [. . .] *Tras estos, que se deben considerar y venerar como padres de las muas españolas,* florecieron en España, por todo el siglo décimo sexto, muchos y muy excelentes poetas; hasta tanto que, por no sé qué fatal desgracia, empezó la poesía española a perder su naturaleza bella, y su sano vigor y su grandeza degeneraron poco a poco en una hinchazón enfermiza y en un artificio afectado. (135, my emphasis)

[After the Marquis of Santillana, the first {to adapt the Italian hendecasyllable to Castilian} were Juan Boscán { . . . } and don Diego de Mendoza and almost at the same time Gutierre de Cetina and Garcilaso de la Vega, who soared further than all of them and deserved to be called the prince of the Spanish lyric. { . . . } *After these, who should be considered and venerated as fathers of the Spanish muses,* throughout the sixteenth century there flourished in Spain many and very excellent poets; until, for I know not what fatal misfortune, Spanish poetry began to lose her natural beauty, and her healthy vigor and her grandeur degenerated little by little into a sickly pomposity and an affected artifice.]

Given this foundational status of Garcilaso—and subsequently of Fray Luis de León—for the neoclassical lyric renewal of the second half of the eighteenth century (Menéndez y Pelayo 308; Real de la Riva, 332; Arce, 115–22), the presence of Garcilaso in *Noches lúgubres* is not especially surprising. Indeed, as corresponds to the subject matter, it is the Garcilaso of the Petrarchan *in morte* tradition—more specifically, Nemoroso's plaint in the Egloga I—that most frequently surfaces in the midst of Tediato's lamentations. Martínez Mata has recently annotated several examples of such intertexts (Notas, 383–84):

Noches lúgubres	Egloga I
"el día, el triste día que fue causa de la escena en que ahora me hallo" (229).	"¿Quién me dixiera, Elisa, vida mía / . . . / que avia de ver, con largo apartamiento / venir el triste y solitario día / que diesse amargo fin a mis amores?" (291).

[the day, the sad day that was the cause of the state in which I now find myself.]

"¡En qué estado estarán las tristes reliquias de tu cadaver! ¡A qué sentido no ofenderá la misma que fue hechizo de todos ellos!" (239–40).

[In what a state the sad relics of your cadaver must be! What sense will not be offended by she who bewitched them all!]

Para mí nunca sale el sol. Las horas todas se pasan en igual oscuridad para mí. (241).

[For me the sun never rises. All the hours pass in the same darkness for me.]

[Who would have told me, Elisa, my life, that after long separation I would see the sad, solitary day come that would put a bitter end to my loves?]

"¿Dó están agora aquellos claros ojos / . . . / ¿Dó está la blanca mano delicada / . . . / ¿Dó la columna que'l dorado techo / con proporción graciosa sostenía? / Aquesto todo agora se encierra, / por deventura mía, / en la escura, desierta y dura tierra" (290–91).

[Where are those clear eyes now? Where is the column that with graceful proportion held up the golden roof? All of this is now enclosed, to my misfortune, in the dark, deserted, hard earth.]

"tal es la tenebrosa / noche de tu partir en que é quedado / de sombra y de temor atormentado, / hasta que muerte'l tiempo determine / que a ver el desseado / sol de tu clara vista m'encamine" (292–93).

[such is the gloomy night of your parting in which I have remained, tormented by darkness and fear until death determines that I might set off to see the desired sun of your clear gaze.]

One might provisionally conclude that, to the extent that Petrarchism can be invoked in *Noches lúgubres*, it is distinctively "Garcilasan." These echoes, however, ought not be read solely as reverential deference to classical authority, for their rhetorical function in the work is not simply to

establish literary lineage. A more complex understanding of such citation emerges when one takes into account the particular poetic values
that Garcilaso represented for neoclassical writers. The qualities typically
ascribed to Garcilaso's poetry, the very attributes on which his eighteenth-
century exemplarity was predicated, were his famed expressive *restraint*,
his elegantly *measured* representation of affect, the *harmony* of his shep-
herds' "dulce lamentar" [sweet lamenting]. To evoke this subtext within
the macabre, gothic excesses of *Noches lúgubres* is rather clearly to mark the
distance between these two discursive universes and their representation
of loss. Indeed, the echoes of Garcilaso and of much of the Greco-Roman
and Spanish classical tradition in Cadalso's work—Ovid, Virgil, Fray Luis
de Granada, and so on—work to heighten the specificity of Tediato's
discourse by way of contrast. The classical intertexts of *Noches lúgubres*
differentiate, even as they authorize. And in the distance that mediates
between classical authority and eighteenth-century melancholy—between
Nemoroso and Tediato—is a profound historical shift in the representation of interiority, a shift that separates Petrarchan subjectivity from its
ostensible analogues within the increasingly rationalist, utilitarian, reform-
ist, late modernity of the European Enlightenment and its aftermath.

What are the distinctive features of this shift? By what operation has a
vaguely Petrarchan model of subjectivity been invested with significantly
novel valences? In short, how might the representation of subjectivity encoded in *Noches lúgubres* be understood as a *new* narrative? As a point
of entry into these questions, it will be useful to reflect on that realm of
experience which the language of psychoanalysis—as indeed, much of the
classical Western lyric tradition—all too easily seems either to excise from
its field of view or to presuppose as the transhistorical given of psychic life,
that is, the domain of social existence. Indeed, one of the central thematic
concerns in *Noches lúgubres* is precisely the relationship between Tediato's
painful inner life and the social structure he inhabits. The work's quasi-
Rousseauian depiction of the intersection of the psychological and the social in *agonistic* terms is arguably among the work's more striking and relatively novel features, for Tediato is represented not simply as the libidinal
"subject of loss" analyzed earlier, but also as a "subject-in-struggle," a self
in conflict with his social milieu. The ostensibly private sphere of Tediato's
amorous suffering and the public sphere of social action are represented
in dialectical relation to one another, as implicating and constituting one

another. Interiority in this context is thus not simply a space of reprieve from a troublesome exterior order, as it had tended to be, grosso modo, in the Horatian pastoral settings of (neo)classical Petrarchism. In *Noches lúgubres* interior life has initially been represented as *expressly antithetical* to the order it inhabits. More than a refuge from the ways of the world, the self here has become a site of indictment of that world. In consonance with this positioning of the self, the representation of Tediato's inner suffering in the "Noche Primera" is systematically coupled with an ostensibly misanthropic repudiation of social life as such, a repudiation all but absent from the tradition of Petrarchan lyric subjectivity.[9]

The framework in which this repudiation is carried out is fairly straightforward. Lorenzo, unaware of the object his employer pursues, hints at a number of possible goals, to which Tediato repeatedly responds in the negative. Lorenzo first mentions, for example, that perhaps Tediato seeks the grave of a recently buried aristocrat:

> Pensé que querías abrir aquel monumento alto y ostentoso, donde enterré pocos días ha al duque Faustotimbrado, que había sido muy hombre de palacio y, según sus criados me dijeron, había tenido en vida el manejo de cosas grandes. Figuróseme que la curiosidad u interés te llevaba a ver si encontrabas algunos papeles ocultos, que tal vez se enterrasen con su cuerpo. (232–33)

> [I thought you wanted to open that tall sumptuous monument, where a few days ago I buried Duke Emblazoned Splendor, who had been quite a palace man and, according to what his servants told me, had in life been in charge of great things. I figured that curiosity or interest was taking you to see if you would find some hidden papers, which perhaps were buried with his body.]

Tediato responds with a blanket invective against the living and the dead:

> Tan despreciables son para mí muertos como vivos; en el sepulcro, como en el mundo; podridos, como triunfantes; llenos de gusanos, como rodeados de aduladores. (233)

> [Just as despicable to me are the dead as the living; those in graves as those in the world, the rotted as the triumphant; those full of worms as those surrounded by flatterers.]

Lorenzo then comments on a second possibility, tacitly raising the question of Tediato's motivations once more:

> pues al túmulo inmediato a ese, y donde yace el famoso indiano, tampoco tienes que ir, porque, aunque en su muerte no se le halló la menor parte de caudal, me consta que no enterró nada consigo, porque registré su cadaver: no se halló siquiera un doblón en su mortaja. (233)

> [well you don't have to go to the grave next to that one, where the famous *indiano* lies, because, although upon his death not the least part of his fortune was found, I happen to know for a fact that he did not bury anything with himself, because I searched his cadaver: not even one doubloon was to be found in his shroud.][10]

Addressing Lorenzo's intimations more directly, Tediato retorts: "tampoco vendría yo de mi casa a su tumba por todo el oro que trajo de la infeliz América a la tirana Europa" [I wouldn't come from my house to his grave for all the gold he brought from wretched America to tyrannical Europe] (233). The third tomb Lorenzo mentions in this sequence belongs to a man who died precipitously: "murió de repente el sujeto que en ella [la sepultura] se enterró. Estas muertes repentinas me asombran" [the person buried in it {the grave} died suddenly. These sudden deaths amaze me] (234). In this case, Tediato dismisses Lorenzo's observation by means of quasi-ascetic observations regarding the fragility of life: "Debiera asombrarte el poco número de ellas. Un cuerpo tan débil como el nuestro . . . ¿qué puede durar? ¿cómo puede durar? No sé cómo vivimos" [What should amaze you is the small number of them. A body as weak as ours . . . What can it last? How can it last? I do not know how we live] (234).[11] What comes into relief in this first sequence is the socially emblematic nature of Tediato and Lorenzo's itinerary. In the city of the dead is a condensed representation—in stone—of the social structure and hierarchies that govern the living, from the aristocracy, to the nouveau riche *indiano* class that was returning from its exploits in America, to the anonymous "everyman" whom Lorenzo tellingly designates with the impersonal, "sujeto"—"qualquier persona indeterminada" [any undetermined person] (*Diccionario de autoridades*, 180). And as Tediato's repeated disavowals accrue it becomes apparent that the object of his vitriolic rejections is not any single member of the social order but rather the social whole itself.

Shortly after this synoptic indictment of society, a second series of questions from Lorenzo focuses more narrowly on the analysis of what eighteenth-century theorists had increasingly posited as the foundation of the social structure: the family.[12] Once more, Tediato's observations manifest themselves as negations of Lorenzo's numerous speculations. While beginning to lift the tombstone that Tediato has designated, Lorenzo muses, "¡si verás en ella [la tumba] a tu padre! Mucho cariño le tienes cuando por verle pasas una noche tan dura" [I wonder if you'll see your father {in the tomb}! You must be very fond of him when you spend such a hard night] (236). Tediato responds:

¡Un padre! ¿por qué? Nos engendran por su gusto, nos crían por obligación, nos educan para que les sirvamos, nos casan para perpetuar sus nombres, nos corrigen por caprichos, nos desheredan por injusticia, nos abandonan por vicios suyos. (236)

[A father! Why? They beget us at their pleasure, they educate us so that we will serve them, they marry us off in order to perpetuate their names, they correct us capriciously, they disinherit us unjustly, they abandon us because of their vices.]

Lorenzo then suggests that, if not a father, perhaps Tediato seeks his mother—"será tu madre . . . mucho debemos a una madre" [it must be your mother . . . we owe a mother much]—to which Tediato counters:

Aun menos que al padre. Nos engendran también por su gusto, tal vez por su incontinencia; nos niegan el alimento de la leche que naturaleza les dio para este único y sagrado fin; nos vician con su mal ejemplo; nos sacrifican a sus intereses; nos hurtan las caricias que nos deben y las depositan en un perro o en un pájaro. (237)

[Even less than to the father. They also beget us at their pleasure, perhaps due to their incontinence; they deny us the nourishment of their milk, which nature gave them for this sole, sacred end; they corrupt us with their bad example; they sacrifice us to their interests; they rob us of the caresses they owe us, and they deposit them on a dog or a bird.]

Lorenzo persists, suggesting that perchance Tediato seeks to visit a recently deceased sibling: "¿Algún hermano te fue tan unido que vienes a visitar los huesos?" [Was a sibling of yours so joined to you that you come to visit his bones?]. Tediato's response undermines the very notion of a familial bond:

> Un año más de edad, algunas letras de diferencia en el nombre, igual esperanza de gozar un bien de dudoso derecho y otras cosas semejantes imprimen tal odio en los hermanos, que parecen fieras de distintas especies y no frutos de un vientre mismo. (237)

> [A year's advantage in age, a few different letters in the name, the identical hope of enjoying a dubious right, and other similar things impress upon siblings such hatred that they seem like wild animals of different species and not fruits of the same womb.]

Finally Lorenzo turns to the only member of the immediate family he has yet to name: "Ya caigo en lo que puede ser. Aquí yace, sin duda, algún hijo que se te moriría en lo más tierno de su edad" [Now I understand what it might be. Without a doubt, here lies a child who must have died on you at the tenderest age]. "¡Hijos! ¡Sucesión!" [Children! Succession!], exclaims Tediato, and then he launches into a lengthy invective against offspring:

> Este, que antes era tesoro con que la naturaleza regalaba a sus favorecidos, es hoy un azote con que no debiera castigar sino a los malvados. ¿Qué es un hijo? Sus primeros años [. . .] un retrato horrendo de la miseria humana. Enfermedad, flaqueza, estupidez, molestia y asco. [. . .] Los siguientes años [. . .] un dechado de los vicios de los brutos, poseídos en más alto grado. [. . .] Lujuria, gula, inobediencia. [. . .] Más adelante, un pozo de horrores infernales [. . .], ambición, soberbia, envidia, codicia, venganza, traición y malignidad. Pasando de ahí [. . .] ya no se mira el hombre como hermano de los otros, sino como a un ente supernumerario en el mundo. (237)

> [What in an earlier time was a treasure with which nature indulged those it favored, is today a scourge with which it should punish only those who are evil. ¿What is a child? Its first years { . . . } a horrible portrait of human misery. Sickness, weakness, stupidity, nuisance, disgust. { . . . } The next years { . . . } a model of the vices of brutes, possessed in the highest degree. { . . . } Luxury, gluttony, disobedience. { . . . } Later on a well of infernal horrors { . . . }, ambition, pride, envy, greed, vengeance, betrayal, malice. Moving on

from there { . . . } man is no longer looked upon as a brother of others, but rather as a superfluous being in the world.]

The social structure, whether examined in toto or in terms of a foundational familial unit, is thus doubly negated. Its various constitutive elements are not what Tediato pursues; at the same time those elements are not what Lorenzo, in his attempt to understand the nature of Tediato's enterprise, has thought them to be. In Tediato's relentless dismantling of Lorenzo's hypotheses it is consequently not difficult to hear the echoes of an older, *desengaño* topos, with its characteristic tension between beguiling false appearances on the one hand—nobility, wealth, the family—and a painful, ugly truth on the other—the fact that they are not what they seem. The baroque genealogy of this leitmotif—which had been reinvigorated by Enlightenment thinkers such as Benito Jérónimo Feijoo in the name of rational demystification—becomes clear when Lorenzo turns to the final possibility he will explore with Tediato.[13] After proposing various representatives of the social strata, and after scrutinizing the family, Lorenzo imagines one last figure as the possible object of Tediato's quest: "No me queda que preguntarte más que una cosa; y es, a saber, si buscas el cadáver de algún amigo" [There is only one more thing left for me to ask you; and it is, to wit, whether you seek the cadaver of some friend]. Tediato's response, echoing an image from Fray Luis de Granada, is consistent with his earlier negations:

> ¿Amigo, eh? ¿Amigo? ¡Qué necio eres! [. . .] ¡Amigos! ¡Amistad! [. . .] Todos quieren parecer amigos, nadie lo es. En los hombres la apariencia de la amistad es lo que en las mujeres el afeite y la compostura . . . nieve que cubre un muladar. . . . Darse las manos y rasgarse los corazones: esta es la amistad que reina. (238)[14]

> [A friend is it? A friend? How dull-witted you are! { . . . } Friends! Friendship! { . . . } Everybody wants to appear to be friends, nobody is. Among men the appearance of friendship is what cosmetics and artifice are among women . . . snow that covers a dunghill. . . . To shake hands while rending each other's hearts: that is the friendship that reigns.]

It is no accident that this final suggestion, the culmination of Lorenzo's litany of inquiries in the "Noche Primera," should focus on what had become one of the privileged categories of enlightenment ethico-civic discourse. With a classical pedigree as authoritative as Plato's *Symposium* and Aristotle's *Nichomachean Ethics,* friendship—almost invariably understood as obtaining among equal *hombres de bien*—had increasingly become *the* model of civic virtue among a generation of neoclassical Spanish writers of the late eighteenth century.[15] In his *Cartas marruecas*, Cadalso had repeatedly displayed this ideal friendship in his representation of the epistolary relationships between the three principal characters—the Spaniard Nuño Nuñez and the Moroccans Gazel Ben-Aly and Ben-Beley—and the author had also made friendship a recurrent theme of the letters themselves. In letter XXXIII of the collection, for example, Nuño—traditionally read as a stand-in for Cadalso—posits enlightened friendship as the very foundation of sociability: "es la madre de todos los bienes sociables" [it is the mother of all social goods] (91). The discourse on male friendship thus represented the idealized public face of sociability, a brotherhood of men that was the public correlate to the affective bonds of the domestic sphere. Male friendship was figured as a source of societal cohesion, as a kind of social glue. "¡Amistad!"—Tediato exclaims in the "Noche Primera"—"Esa virtud sola haría feliz a todo el género humano. [. . .] Su falta es el origen de todas las turbulencias de la sociedad" [Friendship! That virtue alone would make the entire human species happy. { . . . } Its absence is the origin of all of society's upheavals] (238).

In this context Tediato's climactic disavowal of authentic friendship in the "Noche Primera" strikes at the heart of sociability itself. It is the final blow in a series of negations whose cumulative effect is to suggest the impossibility of any social bonds whatsoever, indeed the impossibility of any authentic social life. In terms of the narrative progression of *Noches lúgubres,* it is a key moment inasmuch as it establishes the solipsistic backdrop against which Tediato's identification with Lorenzo's suffering in the "Noche Tercera" will become charged with significance. At the same time, by figuring Tediato's inner life as an alienated self in struggle with the conventions of social life, Cadalso was—perhaps unwittingly—rehearsing a subject position that would become increasingly familiar to a nineteenth-century romantic readership.

The General Confounding and Confusing of All Things

But what is the source of Tediato's alienation to begin with, and how might it be understood in relation to the loss that constitutes his subjectivity? To be sure, the death of his beloved can be read as the catalyst for his initial melancholic withdrawal from social life. It is not difficult to posit, for example, that Tediato's disavowal of all social bonds is simply a case of projection in which the social realm, like nature, becomes an image of his isolation. In this account of things, the atomized social structure that Tediato decries—that is, individuals in utter separation from one another, without the ability to form even the most rudimentary of authentic bonds—would simply be yet another mirror of his own, quasi-solipsistic predicament. And yet projection does not seem to fully account for Tediato's view of social life. His indictment of the social structure—the class hierarchy, family relations, and friendship—seems to be predicated on more than personal loss, for his repeated disavowals also suggest that there is something objectively wrong with social life itself. Behind aristocracy is the image of a morally despicable humanity; *indiano* wealth masks colonial violence and exploitation; misery and disease are the rule for the commoner; fathers, mothers, siblings, and offspring are degraded, grotesque specimens of what they ought to be; and one of the values held most dear by enlightened men, the sacrosanct bond of male friendship based on virtue and goodwill, is but a veil that disguises conflict and competition. In short, while Tediato rather clearly suffers from the effects of a traumatic loss, he repeatedly insinuates that the social organism suffers from an affliction as well.

A brief reexamination of the various invectives that Tediato has directed against his social world confirms this intimation, for the core of his relentless sociocritical impulse in *Noches lúgubres* is a concern with a single, overarching phenomenon that is dialectically linked to his quest for the beloved. The phenomenon in question is an elusive, pervasive force that seems to permeate and debase social life as such, and it is perhaps best summed up by the key term that, in effect, frames the entire exchange between Lorenzo and Tediato in the "Noche Primera"—that is, the word-thought *interés* [interest]. Significantly, both characters utter this word in the initial moments of their first encounter. In response to Lorenzo's request for his wages Tediato scornfully exclaims, "¡Interés! ¡Unico móvil del corazón humano! Aquí tienes el dinero que te prometí" [Interest! Sole motive of the human heart! Here is the money that I promised you] (230). Lorenzo pronounces the word again only a few moments later, when he prefaces the mini-inquisition that will follow with the more basic question that sets the agenda for the dialogue as a whole: "¿Qué interés tan grande te mueve a tanto atrevimiento?" [What great interest moves you to such audacity?] (231).

It is worth noting that for contemporary readers the semantic field of *interés* pertained primarily to a utilitarian, economic, and explicitly monetary sphere. The *Diccionario de autoridades*, for example, renders the following eighteenth-century meanings of the term: "el provecho o utilidad que se saca o se espera de una cosa que se hace [. . .] signfica asimismo lucro o ganancia [. . .] se toma muchas veces por el valor mismo, y precio que merece una cosa" [The benefit or utility that is derived from or is expected of a thing that is done { . . . } it also means lucre or profit { . . . } it is often taken as value itself, and the price that a thing deserves] (*Diccionario,* 291). The decidedly economic valences of *interés* would additionally have been appreciated by educated readers familiar with Adam Smith's *Inquiry into the Nature and Causes of the Wealth of Nations*, which, as Aranguren noted, was at the philosophical core of the eighteenth-century agenda of economic reform in Spain.[16] Indeed, Smith's well-known postulates concerning the centrality of self-interest in economic exchange nicely map the kind of resonance that *interés* would have had for many of Cadalso's readers.

> man has almost constant occasion for the help of his brethren, and it is in vain for him to expect it from their benevolence only. He will be more likely to prevail if he can interest their self-love in his favour, and show them that it is for their own advantage to do for him what he requires of them. Whoever offers to another a bargain of any kind, proposes to do this. [. . .] It is not from the benevolence of the butcher, the brewer, or the baker that we expect our dinner, but from their regard to their own interest. (*Inquiry,* 26–27)

Within such a framework, the socioeconomic dimension of Tediato's alienation can begin to be apprehended more clearly, for the conversation between the two characters is, aside from an attempt to identify Tediato's quest-object, a meditation of sorts on the status of *interés* within the social structure. Tediato's comments are as much a characterization of his social world as they are the reluctant revelation of the object of his pursuit. The ultimate rhetorical effect of the dialogue is, in this regard, to depict social relations thoroughly awash in economic self-interest while hinting at the very different complexion of Tediato's enterprise. Even the realms of family and friendship, Tediato will argue, are entangled in webs of money, power, and exploitation. Fathers and mothers beget children according to selfish interests; siblings vie against one another for their inheritance; offspring grow into the very emblems of ambition and greed; and the bonds of friendship are revealed to be mere platitudes that conceal competition and betrayal. In Tediato's account of things, the realm of affective ties has been thoroughly colonized by relations predicated on the self-interested instrumentalization of others. Monetary *interés*, like the nocturnal setting, seems to reign supreme.

Associating *interés* with the night, however, necessitates a rather disquieting, recoding of the symbolic landscape of *Noches lúgubres*. It effects a scandalous sort of semiosis, a realignment in which the macabre features of the work's gothic registers are suddenly and startlingly indexed, not to Tediato, but to a social order that has been thoroughly debased—that is, "nocturnalized"—by the power of lucre. The stormy night, the city of the dead, the prison—in short, the work's primary symbolic spaces—momentarily become functions of an all-powerful *interés*. And, as if to confirm this troubling state of affairs, when the discussion between the two characters turns explicitly to money—the material representation of *interés* that mediates their very relationship—Tediato's comments yield an uncanny mise en abyme. As he lists the harmful effects generated by an excess of money, Tediato unknowingly names the very psychosymbolic terrain he himself has been inhabiting: "[Mucho dinero] fomenta las pasiones, engendra nuevos vicios y, a fuerza de multiplicar delitos, invierte todo el orden de la naturaleza" [{A lot of money} foments the passions, it begets new vices and, by its power to multiply crimes, it inverts the entire order of nature] (233). Money changes everything.

Tediato's remarks seem to anticipate the well-known comments regarding money that Marx would make more than half a century later in the *Economic and Philosophical Manuscripts of 1844*:

> Money, then, appears as this distorting power both against the individual and against the bonds of society, etc., which claim to be entities in themselves. It transforms fidelity into infidelity, love into hate, hate into love, virtue into vice, vice into virtue, servant into master, master into servant,

idiocy into intelligence, and intelligence into idiocy. Since money, as the existing and active concept of value, confounds and confuses all things, it is the general confounding and confusing of all things—the world upside-down—the confounding and confusing of all natural and human qualities. (140)

Discussion of the functions of money was, of course, an integral part of the burgeoning field of eighteenth-century political economy with which Marx would later dialogue, but it also belonged to an older tradition of classical commentary on chrematistics. It is worth recalling, for example, that in his analysis of the psychology of hoarding in the *Critique of Political Economy*, Marx himself registers numerous classical thinkers—from Xenophon, to Pliny, to Horace—who wrote on the topic of money and its destabilizing effects. At the same time, one need not look very far within the history of medieval and early modern Spanish literature in order to appreciate the degree to which the subject of money had become a well-established literary topos. From the fourteenth-century *Libro de buen amor* [Book of Good Love], with its "Enxiemplo de la propiedat q'el dinero ha" [Example of the power which money possesses]—to Francisco de Quevedo's seventeenth-century "Poderoso caballero es don Dinero" [A Powerful Knight Is Sir Money], the transmutational power of money appears as a common literary theme. Marx's own characterization of money as cited above would famously draw its examples from literary sources—Shakespeare's *Timon of Athens* and Goethe's *Faust*—before arriving at its conclusions. Tediato's claim that money "inverts the entire order of nature" thus belongs to a well-established literary and philosophical tradition. Once again, however, classical antecedents here serve to highlight the distinctively modern—as opposed to early modern—features of the representation of money in *Noches lúgubres*. For the novelty of Cadalso's text is not so much its characterization of the transformative, denaturalizing power of money, but rather its exploration of the affective consequences of living in a social world where lucre and self-interest condition virtually every facet of daily life. To put it more simply, in *Noches lúgubres* money's alchemy is represented as the occasion of human suffering. It is represented as a power that isolates the self by precluding the possibility of noninstrumentalized social bonds.

Even as he decries this situation, however, the negative inflection of virtually all of Tediato's comments in the "Noche Primera" imply a desire to resist this status quo. His pain is intimately linked to a desperate struggle to retain a sense of a decidedly noneconomic *interés*. Indeed, Tediato repeatedly seems to stage this possibility by way of his repeated negations. In this regard, it is useful to think of his declarations to Lorenzo as performative as well as constative utterances; their significance stems not only from the judgments they convey about society, but also from their status as tacit acts of refusal. As negations, each of Tediato's responses to Lorenzo's queries is, in effect, the performance of a "no" to the tacit question of monetary *interés*. They point toward a different understanding of the term. A double movement thus characterizes his declarations in the "Noche Primera": While repeatedly representing all social relations as utterly debased by *interés*, Tediato's negative responses to Lorenzo simultaneously imply that *his interés*—that is, the beloved—is of an entirely different order.

Rhetorically positioned as the negation of economic *interés*, the beloved is in fact imagined as the beyond of the social world against which Tediato rails. As we saw earlier, her characterization in *Noches lúgubres* is remarkably devoid of individuating biographical detail, pointing instead to a diffuse, abstract, socially symbolic entity. She has no name; her presence is known only through the vestiges of her passing; her history is withheld. She is a sort of placeholder, and the symbolic meaning Tediato ascribes to her is made clear when he characterizes her explicitly in relation to the dominion of money. In an apostrophe to money early in the "Noche Primera," Tediato comments: "Ay, dinero, lo que puedes! Un pecho solo se te ha resistido . . . , ya no existe . . . , ya tu dominio es absoluto . . . , ya no existe el solo pecho que se te ha resistido" [Oh, money, the things you can achieve! A sole bosom has resisted you . . . , it no longer exists . . . , now your dominion is absolute . . . , the sole bosom that resisted you no longer exists"] (230). With the death of the beloved, the last soul to remain unconquered by *interés* has disappeared. She symbolizes human relations untainted by the world of money, self-interest, and material gain. Tediato's deeply personal loss is thus revealed to have been fused with a social dimension all along.

An additional facet of Tediato's self-representation can also be grasped more clearly within this context, for the protagonist's melancholic internalization of the beloved—now imagined as the "beyond" of a world dominated by instrumentalized relationships—accounts in part for the spiritual superiority he displays. Even as he represents himself as a wretched, antisocial, corpselike sufferer, Tediato proclaims himself to be above the moral universe he has described. Corresponding to the dualistic (body/spirit) conception of the beloved observed earlier, Tediato's melancholic identification has taken place, it seems, at two different levels. While he has identified physically with the beloved's corpse, he has simultaneously introjected the superiority of a soul that has resisted *interés* into his self-understanding. This logic becomes apparent, for example, when he passionately defends his innocence and moral superiority in the "Noche Segunda." While, as we saw earlier, he is scarcely troubled by incarceration, the prospect of torture, and even an impending bodily death, he is nevertheless extremely sensitive to even the slightest negative ethical judgment directed against him. Thus, when Tediato is accused by his jailers of bearing an evil heart, he responds:

> No injuries a un infeliz; mátame sin afrentarme. Atormenta mi cuerpo en quien tienes dominio; no insultes una alma que tengo más noble . . . , un corazón más puro . . . , sí, más puro, más digna habitación del Ser Supremo que el mismo templo en que yo quería. . . . Ya nada quiero. (245)

> [Do not insult a poor wretch; kill me without affronting me. Torment my body over which you have power; do not insult this soul of mine which is nobler . . . , this heart which is purer . . . , yes, purer, a worthier dwelling place for the Supreme Being than the very temple where I wanted. . . . I no longer want anything.]

Shortly thereafter, he sums up his superior status: "ninguno me ha igualado en lo bueno" [none has equaled me in goodness] (245). Tediato's sense of innocence and moral superiority are, in this regard, the effect of a prior internalization; his imagining himself above his social world is a function of the beyond of *interés* within himself. At this level, the shadow of the lost object that the melancholic internalizes is the shadow of a noble and pure, semidivine soul.

If we return now to the psychoanalytic framework considered earlier, we will be in a position to more fully appreciate the latent social content of the melancholy subject Tediato represents. Earlier we identified a model of subjectivity predicated on loss. Following Freud's *The Ego and the Id*, loss and melancholic identification were understood not as a disorder, but rather as a common feature of psychic life. Furthermore, as Judith Butler observed, in this view the lost love-object became coextensive with the ego itself. The Freudian "character of the ego" was grasped "as the sedimentation of objects loved and lost, the archeological remainder, as it were, of unresolved grief" (133). In Tediato's case, the lost beloved was revealed to be part of the structure of his being, the very occasion for the construction of his subjectivity. What the language of obect-relations psychoanalysis did not contemplate, however, was the beloved's status not only as an object, but also as a sign, a sign of a social world unspoiled by the imperatives of utility and profit. To integrate this socially symbolic dimension of the beloved into our analysis is to invest the representation of subjectivity that unfolds in *Noches lúgubres* with a decidedly historical inflection. For if Cadalso's work represents subjectivity as an inherently melancholic structure, it also suggests that the loss that founds the self—the shadow of the object that the self internalizes—is to be thought of sociohistorically as well as onto-erotically.

In order to apprehend better the historicity of this loss, it will be useful to reconsider *Noches lúgubres* within a series of three progressively widening historical frameworks. The first and most immediate horizon is biographical, and here Tediato's confrontation with a world dominated by relations of self-interest can productively be analogized with Cadalso's own life story. It is well-known, for example, that the author faced pressing financial exigencies throughout his adult life and that he was frequently disillusioned by the slow pace of his military career. He had repeatedly been forced to confront the fact that professional recognition and advancement depended more on wealth and the manipulation of personal contacts that on individual talent or merit. At the same time, Cadalso's experiences with the vagaries of aristocratic favor had taught him painful lessons concerning friendships conditioned by relations of power. To cite a particularly significant example, in 1770 Cadalso managed to garner favor from the Count of Aranda, president of the powerful, governing Consejo de Castilla, only to see that favor abruptly withdrawn when the author had a falling out with the count's adjutant, Joaquín de Oquendo, who had been a close friend. Indeed, it was at this difficult juncture, in the winter of 1770, that Cadalso fell in love with María Ignacia Ibáñez, who would die less than six months later. The genesis of *Noche lúgubres* has traditionally been located in the immediate wake of that death, and it is not difficult to appreciate the ways in which the work might be read as the register of the triple disillusion—professional, social, and amorous—that could be ascribed to Cadalso at this moment in his life. At this level of analysis, Tediato's indictment of the world of *interés* and his loss of the beloved would simply be analogues of authorial experience.[17]

A second horizon of analysis begins to open, however, when one moves from the time of biography to a more expansive temporal framework in which the historicity of the social terrain that Cadalso attempted to navigate comes into view. Of particular interest is the history of the system of social networks that constituted the given of Cadalso's day. As scholars of Spanish economic history have argued, these social networks—with deep roots in the early modern era—were a fundamental facet of political and economic life in the eighteenth century. Drawing on the work of Kagan and Fayard, among others, Ringrose has recently characterized this system of overlapping social webs. He describes the sociopolitical networks as follows:

> The two most familiar are the one created by the state and the intersecting social network of the landed elite, which dominated rural life and staffed the ministries, bureaucracy, and provincial government. In effect we are talking of two networks that were close to being coterminous. [. . .] Provincial notability [. . .] inhabited an immensely sophisticated network of career and marital linkages that moved people all around the country and operated both vertically in elite society and geographically throughout the territory controlled by the Crown. (50)

Akin to these sociopolitical webs was another set of networks characterized by more decidedly economic concerns:

> One can also visualize two overlapping and sometimes intersecting socio-economic networks analogous to the two socio-political ones just mentioned. One of these was a far-flung network of bankers, financiers, and wholesale merchants that operated between the worlds of commerce and politics. [. . .] Behind that network of high finance we find another that is closely related but more local and less well known. [. . .] This network, and the one that produced the bureaucratic nobility, shared virtually the same values, assumptions and techniques for family and clan integration and reproduction. This world of trading families moved managers, trainees, designated spouses, and family investments around the country just as was done in the world of political families. (51)

With such descriptions in view, the sociohistorical reference of Tediato's indictment of a society ruled by *interés* can be identified with considerable precision, and *Noches lúgubres* moves well beyond the realm of coded autobiography. Indeed, it becomes a rather powerful ethical critique of Spain's endogamous eighteenth-century social structure, a structure whose ultimate ground had always been economic self-interest. Despite its drastically different style and tone, the text is in this sense much less distant from reform-driven Enlightenment critique than it initially seems. As we saw earlier, its latent ethos is conversant with the social ideal of the *hombre de bien* that Cadalso had modeled in his *Cartas marruecas*. It is no coincidence, for example, that among the more important qualities that defined the exemplary enlightened man of virtue was his capacity for impartial, *disinterested* social engagement (Haidt *Embodying* 160–71). The difference from one work to the other, however, is the symbolic location of this social ideal. In *Cartas marruecas* the ideal was still a programmatic possibility and a model; in *Noches lúgubres* the ideal is a vestige, a trace of something felt to be irremediably lost. And it is here that the historical dimension of Tediato's pain can begin to be appreciated, for in this context, the beloved represents a lost historical possibility. In a world dominated by exclusionary, self-interested social networks—now understood in their full historical specificity—she represents the lost historical possibility of something different. She is the corpse, as it were, of a sociohistorical *it might have been otherwise*.

There is, however, a final, even broader historical horizon in which to locate Tediato's melancholy. Despite its revealing resonance within the social structure of the late 1700s, the loss represented in *Noches lúgubres* also seems to engage a much vaster historical time. As the mythic overtones of the text suggest, the dead beloved represents an even deeper kind of historical loss, the irreversible forfeiture of a world of social relations free from the dominion of instrumental exchange represented by money. Indeed, a sense of historical bereavement, the feeling of having been dispossessed of classicism's mythic Golden Age, of religion's Paradise, or, mutatis mutandis, of what Marxism would later imagine as primitive communism—seems to mark the inaugural moment of Tediato's constitution as a subject. In this regard, *Noches lúgubres* addresses the remote time of Marx's "general confounding and confusing of all things." It hearkens to that imagined turning point in European social development when rudimentary commodity exchange gave birth to the universal equivalent, money, and money in turn began to go about its business, inverting the order of nature. From this distance, with an immense historical time span in sight, the contours of a lapsarian philosophy of history begin to emerge, suggesting, as we shall see, that the representation of subjectivity we have been considering in *Noches lúgubres* has also been an apologue of the disenchantment of modernity.[18]

Knowing, Feeling, Beginning

Such a reading is possible because money has always been a key trope for narrating the modern. It has been an important part of the nomothetic theorization of modernity—that is, the conception of the modern not as the result of a specific concatenation of singular, historically locatable events, but rather in terms of recurrent conditions, general causes, and general effects.[19] And the monetary has played a decisive role in this broad conception of the modern because, as a social agent, money prefigures at the level of form and practice the very kind of rationality that has tradi- tionally been taken to be the cornerstone of Enlightenment modernity. In *The Philosophy of Money,* for example, Georg Simmel points to the inter- connectedness of money and what he calls human "intellectual functions." At its simplest, his thesis—from a chapter entitled "The Style of Life"—is that money formally propagates a particular kind of rationality. "We have frequently mentioned," he writes, "that intellectual energy is the psychic energy which the specific phenomenon of the money economy produces, in contrast to those energies generally denoted as emotions or sentiments" (429). In Simmel's view the ever-expanding role of instrumental reason in the history of European social life is to be understood as the result of the instrumentalizing power of money itself. To the extent that money increasingly mediates social relations, Simmel argues, the social sphere in fact becomes a rationally intelligible web of connections, not unlike the causally coherent material world that the natural sciences take as their object:

> The crux of the matter is the general fact [. . .] that money is everywhere conceived as purpose, and countless things that are really ends in themselves are thereby degraded to mere means. But since money itself is an omnipres-

ent means, the various elements of our existence are [. . .] placed in an all-embracing teleological nexus in which no element is either the first or the last. Furthermore, since money measures all objects with merciless objectivity [. . .] a web of objective and personal aspects of life emerges which is similar to the natural cosmos with its continuous cohesion and strict causality. (431)

Simmel concludes that as the social structure is progressively monetized, rational calculation simply imposes itself as an everyday fact of life, in effect limiting the emotions to those few areas of existence that do not become pure means: "the conceivable elements of action [. . .] become calculable rational relationships and in so doing progressively eliminate the emotional reactions and decisions, which only attach themselves to the turning points of life, to the final purposes" (431).

A related line of argument is followed by Alfred Sohn-Rethel in his path-breaking *Intellectual and Manual Labor*. Extending Marx's critique of the commodity form into relatively new terrain, the author argues that commodity exchange and money are not only the centerpieces of an analysis of political economy but that they also hold "the key [. . .] to the historical explanation of the abstract conceptual mode of thinking and of the division of intellectual and manual labor which came into existence with it" (33). Zizek has recently condensed the argument as follows:

> Before thought could arrive at the idea of a purely *quantitative* determination, a *sine qua non* of the modern science of nature, pure quantity was already at work in money, that commodity that renders the commensurability of the value of all other commodities notwithstanding their particular qualitative determination. Before physics could articulate the notion of a purely abstract movement going on in a geometric space, independently of all qualitative determinations of the moving objects, the social act of exchange had already realized such a "pure," abstract movement which leaves totally intact the concrete-sensual properties of the object caught in movement: the transference of property. And Sohn-Rethel demonstrated the same about the relationship of substance and its accidents, about the notion of causality operative in Newtonian science—in short, about the whole network of categories of pure reason. (17)

In other words, at the level of form, and prior to its philosophical formulation, money anticipates the framework of scientific rationality. "In the structure of the commodity-form," Zizek observes, "it is possible to find [. . .] the skeleton of the Kantian transcendental subject—that is, the network of categories which constitute the a priori frame of 'objective' scientific knowledge" (16). Money is, in this sense, both a template for and an index of the progressive rationalization of nature and society that—since Weber at least—has traditionally been taken as one of the hallmarks of modernity.

Within this framework it becomes evident that Tediato's sense of loss in *Noches lúgubres* is a response not only to money and self-interest, but also to the kind of rationality money embodies. Indeed, Tediato decries an instrumental rationality much akin to what in the twentieth century Horkheimer and Adorno would critique most thoroughly in their *Dialectic of Enlightenment*. Without approximating the analytic complexity that Frankfurt School thinkers would later achieve, Cadalso's work nevertheless anticipates some of the basic contours of this dialectic. It is an important and relatively early staging within Spanish letters of what might be termed the melancholy of modernity—that is, the experience of an increasingly rationalist, utilitarian present governed by the principle of self-interest as a kind of historical loss. In Weberian terms, the work is a pained response to the disenchantment of the world, and it suggests that modern subjectivity is in a sense constituted by this loss, that the modern self carries within it the traces of lost historical possibility. In more specifically historical terms, *Noches lúgubres* responds to the nodal, networked, and moneyed mercantile modernity of Spain's eighteenth-century elites and their life-world in an emotional register that is qualitatively different from its early modern antecedents. Tediato's emotivity represents something new. It is both an early plaint against the progressive displacement of the emotions as outlined by Simmel, and it is a historically prescient representation of emotional turmoil that is dialectically linked to the empirical certainties of the Enlightenment.

Such observations, however, necessitate further reflection on the respective epistemological status of both reason and the sentiments in *Noches lúgubres*. For if the work can be read as a response to the instrumental reason of modernity, it cannot easily be reduced to a facile sort of sentimentalism. As has often been noted, even while under melancholy's nocturnal spell, Tediato displays considerable rational discernment. In the "Noche Primera," for example, he calmly demystifies Lorenzo's fear of ghosts, explaining that the images the gravedigger sees are mere shadows:

"Lo que te espanta es tu misma sombra con la mía, que nacen de la pos-
tura de nuestros cuerpos respecto de aquella lámpara" [What is frightening
you is your own shadow and mine, which are produced by the position
of our bodies in relation to that lamp over there] (232). Moments later
Tediato also pieces together a rational explanation for the difficult night
that he himself spent several days earlier when he encountered an unknown, frightful creature in the darkness of the cemetery's church. Upon
hearing that Lorenzo's dog had gone astray that same day, Tediato inter-
rupts: "No prosigas. Me basta lo dicho. Aquella tarde [. . .] te fuiste; el
perro se durmió. [. . .] Nos encontramos él y yo en la iglesia (mira qué
causa tan trivial para un miedo tan fundado al parecer)" [Do not continue.
What's said is enough. That afternoon { . . . } you left; the dog fell asleep.
{ . . . } We came upon each other in the church (look what trivial cause for
a fear that seemed so well founded)] (236). With their appeal to the data
of sensory perception and the principle of natural causality, such passages
align themselves rather clearly with the empirical rationality of the new
sciences that had become the vogue among the Spanish educated classes
over the course of the eighteenth century (Sarrailh, 413–72). Thus, while
Tediato expressly decries the rational calculation of *interés*, he himself is
paradoxically also positioned as the voice of empirical reason. How might
one account for the paradox?

The juxtaposition of science and the passions in *Noches lúgubres* has
represented a persistent interpretive challenge to recent readers of the
work. Critics opposed to a romantic account of Cadalso, for example,
have often pointed to Tediato's reason in order to argue that, despite appearances, the work advances a fundamentally empiricist epistemology.
The text's highly successful, nineteenth-century romantic reception, however, suggests that these moments of empiricist analysis were understood
in more complex terms. For while Tediato's intermittent displays of rational lucidity might be taken as uncomplicated evidence of the scientific
spirit of inquiry, one must also consider the rhetorical function of these
passages—that is, their meaning as parts of a larger discursive structure
and their bearing on the central problematic of Tediato's loss. In such a
context, it becomes immediately apparent that Tediato's science can in
the end say nothing regarding what matters to him most. Science is utterly mute on the question of the beloved. While rational scrutiny can
demystify superstitious fears—the work suggests—it is virtually impotent

in the face of the nocturnalized world Tediato inhabits. Scientific excursus in *Noches lúgubres* thus reflects not the tempering effect of reason on a troubled psyche, but rather the limits of scientific inquiry in the face of overwhelming emotional pain. It stages a rather dramatic disjunction between analysis and feeling. The reason for this disjunction becomes evident when one reconsiders the socially symbolic dimension of Tediato's nights. Science is an inadequate remedy for Tediato's isolation and the reified social world he contemplates because science is of a piece with that world; as instrumentalized reason, it belongs to the dominion of *interés*.

Where, then, might one turn for the outline of a solution to Tediato's melancholy? Significantly, the intimations of a remedy to Tediato's dilemma—and they are only intimations—are to be found in the realm of affect, where Tediato has been dwelling all along. Despite its repetitive and seemingly unresolved structure, Cadalso's work is ultimately not the tale of psychological stasis it may seem. Imbedded in Tediato's frustrated attempts to disinter the beloved each night is a rudimentary tale of psychosocial development, and such development—intimately bound up with the way the modern self has been imagined—is predicated on Tediato's capacity to respond emotionally to his surroundings. As we saw earlier, Tediato's exacerbated alienation in the "Noche Primera" cedes to a kind of sociability based on the acknowledgment of universal suffering in the "Noche Tercera." Of particular interest now is that what prompts Tediato's insight to begin with is not rational calculation but rather sympathetic identification with Lorenzo's suffering. To put it more simply, Tediato *is moved* when he learns of Lorenzo's pains, and this sympathetic response marks a significant shift away from the more solipsistic quality of his anguish during the first two nights:

> ¿Qué vi? Un padre de familias pobre, con su mujer moribunda, hijos parvulillos y enfermos; uno perdido, otro muerto aun antes de nacer y que mata a su madre aun antes de que ésta le acabe de producir. [. . .] ¡Qué inhumano si no se partió [el corazón] al ver tal espectáculo! (354)

> [What did I see? A family man in poverty, with his dying wife, sick infant children, one lost, another that dies before being born, killing its mother even before she has finished producing him. { . . . } How inhuman if {my heart} had not broken upon seeing such a spectacle!]

It is the heart, the place of compassion, that begins to reshape what Tediato's science cannot, and in recognizing a suffering other, Tediato also gleans the possibility of reestablishing the very social bonds that earlier seemed out of reach. The virtue of friendship, now predicated on the recognition of shared loss, seems possible once again. Thus, as Tediato waits for Lorenzo at the beginning of the "Noche Tercera," he now beckons to the gravedigger as a newfound brother in suffering:

> ¡Lorenzo, infeliz Lorenzo! Ven, si ya no te detiene la muerte de tu padre, la de tu mujer, la enfermedad de tus hijos, la pérdida de tu hija, tu misma flaqueza. Ven, hallarás en mí un desdichado que padece no sólo sus infortunios propios, sino los de todos los infelices quienes conoce, mirándolos a todos como hermanos. Ninguno lo es más que tú. ¿Qué importa que nacieras tú en la mayor miseria y yo en la cuna más delicada? Hermanos nos hace un superior destino, corrigiendo los caprichos de la suerte, que divide en arbitrarias e inútiles clases los que somos de la misma especie. Todos lloramos . . . , todos enfermamos . . . , todos morimos. (254)

> [Lorenzo, wretched Lorenzo! Come, if you are no longer detained by the death of your father, of your wife, the sickness of your children, the loss of your daughter, your own weakness. Come, you will find in me a poor soul that suffers not only his own misfortunes but those of all of the wretched he meets, looking upon them all as brothers. None is more of one than you. What does it matter that you were born in the greatest abjection and I in the most delicate crib? A higher destiny makes us brothers, correcting the caprices of fate, which divides those of us who are one species into arbitrary and useless classes. We all weep . . . , we all become sick . . . , we all die.]

As it happens, this new bond of compassion is the symbolic antithesis of *interés*, and its appearance in the third and final night marks, if not closure, the beginning of something new. In imaginatively feeling the suffering of another, Tediato seems to have recognized the image of a shared humanity. Compassion—etymologically, "to suffer with"—has led to a form of knowing that reason alone could not. With its exploration of this knowing feeling, *Noches lúgubres* assumes a place within a broader series of eighteenth-century European meditations on the cognitive content of affect and its social functions. In the realm of aesthetics, for example, Kant's *Critique of Judgement*—particularly the third critique—had posed, among other questions, "how affect can indeed count as a form of knowing the world or acting in it" (Cascardi, *Consequences*, 242). Similarly, in the so-called natural theories of sentiment—that is, Shaftesbury, Hume, Smith (*Theory*)—affective sympathy had become one of moral philosophy's central analytic categories as thinkers turned their attentions to understanding "the law of the heart" (Eagleton, *Ideology*, 31–69). At the same time, Rousseauian social theory reflected this growing stress on the affective. Readers of *The Discourse on the Origins of Inequality* will recall that for Rousseau one of the principal shortcomings of the Hobbesian account of individual self-interest in the state of nature had been its failure to acknowledge a natural human propensity for compassionate identification. Indeed, Rousseau would famously contrast the socially deleterious consequences of rational reflection with what he took to be the more natural feeling of compassion:

> It is reason that engenders self-love, and reflection that strengthens it: it is reason which turns man back on himself and that separates him from all that annoys and afflicts him. It is philosophy that isolates him; it is philosophy that allows him to say privately, at the sight of a suffering man: "Perish if you will, I am safe." [. . .] Compassion is a natural sentiment, which, by moderating the activity of self-esteem in each individual, contributes to the mutual preservation of the whole species. [. . .] Although it may be possible for Socrates and minds of that stamp to acquire virtue through reason, the human race would have ceased to exist long ago, if its preservation had depended only on the reasoning of those who compose it. (29)

Tediato's trajectory in *Noches lúgubres*—from the alienated critique of the dominion of *interés* to a rudimentary form of altruistic sympathy—is in many ways an exemplification of this Rousseauian paradigm, and to the extent that such sympathy has been construed as a key feature of modern subjectivity, Cadalso's work once again intersects with one of the macronarratives of modernity. Dipesh Chakrabarty has recently sketched the logic at work in such claims. "The person"—he writes—"[. . .] who has the capacity to become a secondary sufferer through sympathy for a generalized picture of suffering, and who documents this suffering in the interest of eventual social intervention—such a person occupies the position of the modern subject" (119). This is so, in large measure, because the suffering of another becomes an occasion for the abstraction and self-recognition of the modern subject:

> The moment of the modern observation of suffering is a certain moment of self-recognition on the part of an abstract, general human being. It is as though a person who is able to see in himself or herself the general human also recognizes the same figure in the particular sufferer, so that the moment of recognition is a moment when the general human splits into the two mutually recognizing and mutually constitutive figures of the sufferer and the observation of suffering. (Chakrabarty, 120)

Such a process describes the very phenomenon Cadalso has staged toward the end of the work: Tediato's observation of Lorenzo's suffering is at the same time the acknowledgment of an abstracted suffering humanity, and his reference to the arbitrary and useless nature of the social classes hints at the sort of "eventual social intervention" Chakrabarty presumably has in mind. Against this backdrop, *Noches lúgubres* thus renders a compelling image of the modern self that was emerging from eighteenth-century aesthetic, moral, and social philosophy.

In addition to the traditional northern European philosophical genealogy of this modern self, however, it is also important to recall the deeper, early modernity from which this subject emerged. Just as—against the presumption of an agrarian, backward Spain—we found a disenchanted modernity within the socioeconomic networks that were distinctive to Spain's historical development, so too the modern self described above can be linked to distinctively southern intellectual traditions that have all too often been overlooked by a hegemonic northern European account of modernity. The notion of the moral equivalence of individuals, which subtends eighteenth-century conceptions of sympathetic identification, for example, has deep roots in Christian theology. At the same time, Spain's history of conquest and colonization had placed the image of the suffering other—in this case the Amerindian—at the center of ethical and political debate long before eighteenth-century moral philosophy took up the question of sympathetic identification. Indeed, the basic questions and contours of the Rousseauian system are already identifiable in Bartolomé de Las Casas's sixteenth-century defense of the indigenous peoples of the Americas (Waltz, 5; Maravall, *Antiguos*, 447). Additionally, Spanish Enlightenment writers themselves—from Feijoo, to Campomanes, to Cadalso—had repeatedly grappled with the problems of colonialism (Mesa, 55–88). To contemplate the modern in *Noches lúgubres* is thus to recall that the modernity traditionally imagined as radiating from an eighteenth-century north also has an older southern (Hispano-Italian, humanist) genealogy. A full account of the modern in *Noches lúgubres* thus makes clearer the ways in which the Enlightenment modernity of the north is perhaps best conceived of as a palimpsest written over the histories and analytic categories of early modern thought.[20]

This is not to minimize in any way the profound significance of the most visible features of the modernity of Enlightenment in *Noches lúgubres*. Indeed, the text rather eloquently bears witness to the eighteenth-century transition from a religiously inflected conception of compassionate identification to an entirely secular one. In Cadalso's text, ethical critique and sympathetic identification are decidedly secular affairs. The brotherhood that Tediato affirms is a worldly one, and even his quasi-messianic promise to take on the suffering of all those he encounters is devoid of any explicit metaphysical reference. Moreover, in light of the historical location of Cadalso's text—written in the early 1770s and published for the first time in 1789—the political implications of both the abstracted human equality Tediato evokes and the classless brotherhood he espouses cannot be overlooked. Given the socially symbolic meanings of friendship considered earlier, Tediato's compassionate breakthrough at the end of the work figures nothing less than the template for a new form of sociability. For an eighteenth-century Spanish reading public, the image of a refined gentleman asserting his brotherhood with a miserably impoverished gravedigger—and in this world rather than in the next—would certainly have been a shocking if not overtly revolutionary gesture, and the initial censorship of the text confirms the threatening quality of its political content.[21]

We are thus in a position to understand more fully the claims of *Noches lúgubres* on Spain's nineteenth-century romantic reading public, for the representation of subjectivity in this work announced what might be best described, following Raymond Williams, as an emergent structure of feeling.[22] The self-marginalizing, alienated, morally superior, expressly antisocial, quasi-messianic, passionate subject represented by Tediato was a beginning of sorts. To be sure, the kind of subjectivity represented in the work initially occupied a subordinate position within the field of eighteenth-century Spanish literary production. It would be difficult to argue, for example, that Tediato represented the dominant zeitgeist of Spain in the 1770s. The work was, however, what Pierre Bourdieu would call a significant *prise de position*, or literary position taking within the field of literary writing. Moreover, as the field itself slowly changed over the course of the 1820s, 1830s, and 1840s, increasing amounts of symbolic capital—that is, literary prestige—accrued to this position until it became the new dominant. Indeed, as the Spanish Ancien Régime slowly crumbled and an inchoate nineteenth-century liberalism began to restructure the Spanish social order by placing private property and self-interest at the center of its economic agenda, Cadalso's melancholy of modernity was imbued with an increasing sociohistoric relevance. The passage of time paradoxically made the text more rather than less contemporary.

The emergent structure of feeling that *Noches lúgubres* represents, however, also reflects the early stirrings of a thoroughly modern problematic, for the universal humanity announced at the end of the work conspicuously manifests the contradictions of modernity that contemporary cultural theory (marxian, feminist, postmodern, subaltern) has insistently taken up in its general, ongoing quarrel with the legacy of Enlightenment. Indeed, a solely redemptive reading of Tediato's sympathetic breakthrough runs the risk of reinforcing rather than exposing what have by now become a familiar set of ideological problems. If, for example, the beloved represents a utopian space beyond *interés*, she also belongs to a long history of representation of the feminine—that is, disembodied, voiceless, devoid of agency, and symbolically divorced from the economic—that in the nineteenth century would be subsumed into the ideology of domesticity known as the "angel del hogar" [angel of the hearth/home] (Aldaraca, Charnon-Deutch, Jagoe, Blanco, Labanyi). Similarly, if the bond between Tediato and Lorenzo can be read as vaguely analogous to the equality championed by the political revolutions that had been fed by Enlightenment philosophy, the gendering of this bond, which takes place exclusively between men, against the backdrop of conveniently dead women, speaks to the male homosocial limit that would historically circumscribe this initial conception of equality to men of property (Kirkpatrick, "Constituting").

Even more striking is the class mystification that Tediato's declaration of brotherhood engages by deftly analogizing his emotional pain with Lorenzo's abject poverty and material immiseration. Behind its initial appeal, Tediato's rhetorical transformation of both characters into emblems of universal human suffering—Chakrabarty's telltale sign of the modern self—paradoxically serves to efface the utterly different sources, conditions, and qualities of each character's pain. At the same time, despite Tediato's discovery of a newfound brotherhood, the initial asymmetrical power relations between the two characters remain curiously unaltered. Tediato's altruistic sympathy is an entirely unidirectional proclamation. It persists, even at the end of the work, as the pronouncement of an employer to his worker. Indeed, one of the more profound ironies throughout *Noches lúgubres* is that the entire trajectory we have charted—from alienation to sympathetic identification—unfolds in a conversation between a moneyed gentleman and an impoverished wage laborer whose economic subordination does not change. While the brotherhood-in-misery that Tediato discovers may symbolically announce a new form of sociability, this new friendship does not modify in the least the economic basis of the relationship. The closing lines of the work in fact bear witness to the irony that, for all of his clamoring against *interés*, Tediato has been, at best, oblivious to his own instrumentalization of Lorenzo's labor. In his pursuit of the beloved—the symbolic beyond of *interés*—Tediato remains blind to the gravedigger's material misery. He seems to see only the utility of Lorenzo's labor: "No te deseo con corona y cetro para mi bien"—he comments at the end of the work—"Más contribuirás a mi dicha con ese pico, ese azadón" [I do not want you with a crown and scepter in order to pursue my good. { . . . } You will contribute more to my happiness with that pickaxe, that mattock] (255).

One is in this sense forced to confront the disquieting fact that Tediato's melancholy, his compassionate identification, and the modern subject they seem to inaugurate are far more self-serving than the rhetoric of universal suffering initially suggests. Significantly, this ideological structure— the masking of the particular within an appealing universal—was also destined to make a special claim on the largely bourgeois Spanish public that in the early nineteenth century was still struggling against a weakened but recalcitrant Ancien Régime. The universalizing gesture in *Noches lúgubres*—its fleeting ideal of a classless brotherhood—was an attractive symbolic negation of the entrenched social hierarchies that this public was in the process of changing. At the same time, Tediato's invocation of the universal also subtly satisfied bourgeois liberalism's need to represent its own rather narrow class interests in the more appealing categories of a common humanity. As Marx and Engels observed, "each new class which puts itself in the place of one ruling before it is compelled, merely in order to carry through its aim, to present its interest as the common interest of society [. . .]: it has to give its ideas the form of universality" (*German*, 68). *Noches lúgubres* anticipated this need for universality not by way of the universal reason of Enlightenment, but rather by way of an equally capacious Rousseauian affect. Its brotherhood-in-suffering was in many ways the affective analogue to the universal rights of man, and it was particularly suited to a Spanish cultural and religious apparatus otherwise suspicious of philosophe rationality. As an emergent structure of feeling, the work's representation of melancholic suffering thus announced what would later become one of the fundamental contradictions of the emancipatory impulse in Spanish romantic discourse. While recoiling from the instrumental rationality of Spanish modernity and while deriding a corrupt social status quo, romantic discourse would at the same time mystify its own class interests. Indeed, as we shall see in subsequent chapters, the painful desire of the bourgeois romantic subject would, like Tediato, repeatedly co-opt the suffering of its laboring other by transmuting it into the image of its own condition.

CHAPTER 3

Rethinking the Modern
in Saavedra's *Don Alvaro*

—*Madrid, 1835.* Days of liberal revolution and reform. Several decades have elapsed since Cadalso's *Noches lúgubres* first began circulating. Ferdinand VII, the despot, bastion of absolutism, has been dead for almost two years. Political exiles have returned to Spain under a general amnesty, and debate in the capital—*moderados* versus *progresistas*—openly dialogues with the tenets of the Constitution of 1812, the touchstone of nineteenth-century Spanish liberalism. In the countryside, especially in the north, a dynastic dispute has erupted into civil war. The forces of reaction have rallied around Ferdinand's brother, Carlos, under the motto of "Dios, Patria, Fueros y Rey" [God, Country, Privileges, and King].[1] María Cristina, queen-regent for her three-year-old daughter Isabella, has made a pact with the forces of liberalism in order to counter the threat posed to her reign by Carlism. In the newspapers of the day, columnists regularly refer to the tumultuous uncertainty of the times. As Lukàcs would later observe of the early 1800s, across Europe the Era of Revolution has prompted an acute historical consciousness, the sense of living in decidedly historical times (*Historical*, 23–24).

Among those who have returned to the capital is a prominent liberal aristocrat, Angel de Saavedra, soon to be known as the Duke of Rivas.[2] While in exile in France he composed a play, a historical drama originally written in prose. Translated into French by his friend Antonio Alcalá Galiano, the work was originally intended for the Paris stage, but the course of events overtakes such plans, and the play does not debut north of the Pyrenees. In Spain once again, Saavedra revises the original, rewriting substantial portions in verse. The result is a markedly innovative, hybrid text. It is a play set in the late eighteenth century, during the reign of the Enlightenment reformer, Carlos III, and it stages the tale of a mestizo of noble Inca and Spanish lineage who aspires to marry Leonor, daughter of a tradition-bound aristocrat, the Marqués de Calatrava. Indifferent to his daughter's feelings, the marquis disdains the wealthy newcomer from America, and when the young mestizo's attempt to steal Leonor away is foiled, a freak accident leads to her father's death: The pretender throws down his revolver in order to submit to the will of the marquis, but upon hitting the ground the gun goes off and his beloved's father is fatally wounded. Fortune's die is cast.

Over a total of five acts spanning some five years and multiple geographical localities, the young man will be persecuted relentlessly by an adverse fate rooted in this first misfortune. A series of uncanny coincidences, the feeling that a cosmic ill will works to thwart him, and a vendetta sworn against him by Leonor's brothers, Carlos and Alfonso, slowly close in on the protagonist until his sense of life possibility is undermined. Although he attempts to flee from the world by seeking refuge first in military life and then in religious seclusion, before the play's end he will witness his beloved's murder, and he will have killed not only her father but both brothers as well. The hero's last, desperate act—either a final affirmation of his free will, or the ultimate capitulation to his destiny, or both—is to hurl himself off of a mountainous precipice, cursing humanity before falling to his death. The protagonist's name is Don Alvaro; the play is *Don Alvaro o la fuerza del sino* [Don Alvaro or the Force of Destiny], and its radical formal and thematic novelty immediately accord it a shocking, even revolutionary quality in the eyes of Madrid theatergoers.[3] Within Spanish literary historiography, the opening of the Duke of Rivas's *Don Alvaro* quickly becomes an emblematic moment—for many, *the* emblematic moment—of romantic rebellion on the Spanish stage.[4]

—*Somewhere in the Atlantic Ocean, 1560.* Gómez Suárez de Figueroa, a mestizo of noble Inca and Spanish lineage, is on a ship bound to Spain. He is the son of a prominent Spanish captain, Sebastián Garcilaso de la Vega y Vargas. The young man's mother, Isabel Suárez Chimpu Ocllo, is an Inca princess, niece of Inca Huaina Capac, and concubine to Sebastián. Fluent in Quechua and Castilian, the young noble has been educated in the cultural traditions of Old and New World alike. Upon his arrival in Seville, he is received by paternal relatives. He soon learns, however, that his integration into Spanish Renaissance society will not be a seamless affair, for his father has fallen out of favor with the crown. Reports on Sebastián's activities in the early chronicles of the Indies have called his loyalty into question, and Gómez regularly travels to Madrid attempting to rehabilitate his family name. He serves in the military against a Morisco uprising, hoping to garner recognition from the court, but the royal favor he seeks is never forthcoming, and his integration into sixteenth-century Spain is never fully achieved.

Turning away from a career at arms, he settles in Montilla, a village on the outskirts of Córdoba, where he begins to pen the works that will constitute his legacy in the world of letters. These include a highly influential translation of Leon Hebreo's neo-Platonic *Dialoghi de amore* (*Diálogos de amor*, Madrid 1590), an epic chronicle of De Soto's expedition to the present-day southeastern United States (*La Florida del Inca*, Madrid 1605), and his *opus magnum*, a chronicle of the history and conquest of the Incan Empire (*Comentarios reales de los Incas*, Madrid 1609; the continuation, *Historia general del Perú*, appears posthumously in Madrid in 1617). During his later years, Gómez will turn to religious life, taking minor orders and working at a charitable hospital. Posterity will come to know him by the name he proudly adopts in his written work: el Inca Garcilaso de la Vega. In the twentieth century, his *Comentarios reales* will circulate as one of the most canonical texts within Spanish American colonial studies, and as the first American writer to self-consciously celebrate—and even tout—his dual heritage, he will become the very emblem of Euro-American mestizaje. He dies on 23 April 1616 and is buried in the cathedral at Córdoba, a cathedral that, over two hundred years later, a young Angel Saavedra, future Duke of Rivas, will come to know well.[5]

—*St. Petersburg, The Imperial Theater, 1862.* Giuseppe Verdi has traveled to Russia to attend the debut of his newest opera, *La Forza del Destino.* It is the culmination of a circuitous series of events. Originally approached by the tenor Enrico Tamberlick with a proposal that he develop a project for the famed Russian opera house, Verdi first offers to write an opera based on Victor Hugo's *Ruy Blas.* When imperial censors respond negatively, the composer turns for inspiration to Saavedra's now well-known *Don Alvaro.* Francesco Maria Piave writes the libretto, adapting its plot to the new formal exigencies of the genre.[6] The opera belongs to Verdi's rich middle period, and the theme of destiny readily lends itself to his musical imagination. He figures fate by means of a series of haunting, recurring musical phrases; even the overture's traditional announcement of things to come is imbued with fateful significance. The opera opens successfully, garnering the czar's attendance shortly after its debut. One year later, in 1863, the production opens to wide acclaim in Madrid's Teatro Real. The seventy-one-year-old Duke of Rivas is in attendance.

Verdi, however, remains dissatisfied with the libretto, particularly with the final act's disheartening accumulation of death and suicide, and in the years that follow he turns to Antonio Ghislanzoni, who revises the libretto and rewrites the last act. In the newer version, Don Alvaro no longer kills himself. Instead, as the opera comes to its end, the protagonist dolefully mourns Leonora's death, awaiting the time when he will join her in the afterlife. Gone too is the disquieting curse that Saavedra's Don Alvaro had directed at humanity, the curse that implied the spectators of the work. The new treatment of Saavedra's play successfully opens in Milan's La Scala theater in 1869, and it quickly becomes the standard rendering of what is widely acknowledged as an operatic classic. To this day it remains the version most often performed in opera houses across the world.

Three beginnings; three representations; three historical moments. To approach Don Alvaro as a distinctively modern figure is to encounter the phenomenon that came into view in the preceding analysis of *Noches lúgubres*; that is, the multiple temporalities (from punctual event to *longue durée*) and histories (from the colonial encounter to liberal revolution) that invariably impinge on the concept of the modern. If as we have seen, modernity's ruptural gesture is in some sense always a palimpsest, this is not only because it is necessarily written over earlier moments which can themselves be construed as important historical shifts, but also because insofar as it seeks historical authority, the concept of the modern necessarily participates in the aporetic structure—identity and difference, continuity and change—that characterizes historical time itself. Much as the rhetoric of the modern relentlessly attempts to banish its conceptual antitheses—that is, the first terms in each of the preceding oppositions—it cannot help but carry them within.[7] My intention in bringing the three preceding narratives into proximity, however, has not been merely to emphasize once more the basic tension that obtains between the idea of the modern as a transformative threshold on one hand, and the idea of history as a multilayered or deep structure on the other. I have also brought these tales together in order to recall those various histories that so often subtend artworks that, through circumstance or design, have been raised to representative dominance.

Arguably, if the story of Don Alvaro's adverse fortune is known internationally today, it is primarily through Verdi rather than through the Duke of Rivas or the Inca Garcilaso de la Vega's biography; and in this sense the three stories I have evoked are also meant to draw attention to those curious silences that have tended to accompany the formation of modern classics such as *La Forza del Destino*. A funny thing happened on the way to the opera, for as one moves from the figure of the Inca Garcilaso de la Vega, to Saavedra's *Don Alvaro*, to Verdi's *Forza*, an intriguing kind of historical hygiene seems to take place. A subject initially rooted within colonial social, political, and ethnographic narratives gives way to a figure of romantic rebellion, and this figure in turn seems to be distilled into a lyrical-philosophical meditation on the universal problems of destiny, free will, and the meaning of human life.[8] In many regards the process mirrors the kind of historical housecleaning that we considered in the chapter 1, and it recalls the traces of empire that so often lie just below the surface of many of Europe's more prized cultural artifacts (Said, *Culture*). At the same time, the very fact that the figure of Don Alvaro has come to be known internationally through non-Spanish mediation—in this case Verdi, Piave, and Ghislanzoni—speaks again to the manner in which, throughout much of the modern era, Spanish culture tended to circulate primarily by means of the representation of others.[9]

The work I will consider in the pages that follow, Saavedra's *Don Alvaro o la fuerza del sino*, occupies a fascinating midpoint of sorts within the rudimentary trajectory I have sketched, and in turning to this play I hope to elucidate the plural histories with which the text dialogues. More specifically my aims will be to offer a new framework for thinking about the relationship between *Don Alvaro*'s intriguing formal features and the historical moment of its initial staging (1835), to reconsider the meanings of the play within the framework of Spain's waning colonialism, and to examine the way in which each of these phenomena intersects with the idea of the modern. Saavedra's *Don Alvaro* represents an intriguing moment in an oft-overlooked history that links the story of the Inca

Garcilaso de la Vega to Verdi's *La Forza del Destino*. And, as we shall see, the Duke of Rivas's play still has much to tell us about romanticism in Spain, about the idea of modernity, and about the ways in which we continue to imagine both.

The Poetry and Prose of the World

Among *Don Alvaro*'s many departures from the classicist poetics that had been losing authority over the Spanish stage of the 1830s, the work's formal rebellion—that is, its clear disregard for the neo-Aristotelian conception of dramatic illusion and the much-discussed unities of time, place, and action—is perhaps the most striking. From the moment of its debut to the present, the formal novelty of Saavedra's play has been a habitual locus of critical inquiry and debate, and among those who have analyzed the play's structure—Azorín (*Rivas*), Peers ("Angel"), Casalduero, Shaw ("Acerca"), and Rey Hazas, for example—a consensus seems to have emerged in recent years concerning the extraordinary care with which Saavedra organized his material. While the play clearly produced an exciting sense of disorientation among its viewers, the Duke of Rivas appears to have engaged in a rather calculated kind of chaos.[10]

Jarring scenic juxtapositions, brusque transitions, and the interaction of characters from widely ranging social strata seemed to tacitly reaffirm a national tradition that had embraced the generically hybrid *tragicomedia* as one of its distinctive forms. But *Don Alvaro,* like Spanish romantic drama more generally, engaged in a radical reappropriation of this form by investing it with a series of sociohistorical, political, and philosophical meanings that could scarcely be more distant from the baroque Weltanschauung of Spain's early modern theater.[11] The telltale signature of much of Spain's classic dramaturgy—the reestablishment of order and a sense of poetic justice (Parker)—was pointedly absent. In addition, disregard for classicist conceptions of unity seemed to have migrated into the realm of language itself in *Don Alvaro.* The play's alternating use of prose and verse represented a departure not only from neoclassical standards, but also from the common practices of contemporary romantic dramaturgy. Even on the French stage of the mid-1830s, romantic plays were written in prose or in verse, but not in both.[12]

Analysis of the oscillation of prose and verse in *Don Alvaro* has tended to approach this phenomenon in one of three ways: as a reflection of the complex history of the play's various redactions (Blecua), as a manifestation of Saavedra's rebellious romantic "free spirit" (Picoche), or as a compositional device designed to heighten dramatic impact by means of systematic stylistic contrasts (Casalduero). They are analyses that have lead to a precise mapping of Saavedras's aesthetic choices: The use of prose is largely driven by content, and the passages in verse similarly reflect a refined, thematically motivated selection from among the myriad meters that Spanish dramaturgy had historically adopted.[13] For most analysts of the work today, it is design rather than romantic caprice that best accounts for the play's unique features:

> Dada la preocupación de Rivas por las capacidades expresivas de uno u otro tipo de versificación y la conciencia de estar escribiendo algo radicalmente nuevo [. . .] es impensable imaginar que la transformación o reescritura en verso de algunas partes de Don Alvaro [. . .] fuese dictada por el azar o con el solo fin de embellecer mediante un *ornatus* meramente efectista y decorativo, una pieza de profundas implicaciones filosóficas, morales y psicológicas. (Busquets, 435–36; cited by Lama, *Prólogo*, 62–63)

> [Given Rivas's preoccupation with the expressive capacities of one or another kind of versification and his awareness of writing something radically new { . . . } it is unthinkable to imagine that the transformation or rewriting in verse of some of the parts of *Don Alvaro* { . . . } was dictated randomly or with the sole goal of beautifying by means of a merely effect-seeking and decorative *ornatus*, a play of profound philosophical, moral, and psychological implications.]

While such work has served as a useful reminder that *Don Alvaro* is a keenly crafted dramatic composition, it is a line of inquiry that has tended to circumscribe its questions to the domain of form. It is worth asking, however, whether form in this play might not itself be historicized more fully. One of the fundamental issues that subtends *Don Alvaro*'s innovative shifts between prose and verse is the sociohistorical meaning of these modes of representation. What had poetry and prose respectively come to signify, even before Saavedra began to wield one against the other for dramatic effect? Natural as it may seem, the very opposition between the two modes is suffused with history, and, as we shall see shortly, the split between them is intimately linked in the romantic era to the idea of the modern. In what follows, I will consequently aim to foreground the latent historical content of *Don Alvaro*'s celebrated formal juxtapositions. My purpose will be to recall the array of basic symbolic meanings that prose and poetry had attained by the 1830s in order to examine how such meanings inform the oscillation between the two in *Don Alvaro*.

A brief review of the significant shifts that took place within the semantic field of the word "poetry" during the late eighteenth and early nineteenth centuries provides a revealing point of departure. The following two entries for the word *poesía*—separated by the span of some forty-two years—are from two editions of the dictionary of the Spanish Royal Academy.

1780

> Poesía. Ciencia que enseña a componer versos, y a escribir y representar con ellas las cosas al vivo, excogitando y fingiendo lo que se quiere. *Poetica*.
> Poesía. La misma obra, o escrito compuesto en verso. *Opus poeticum, poema, poesis.* (734)

> [Poetry. The science that teaches to compose verses and to write and represent things with them in a lively manner, excogitating and feigning what one wants. *Poetica*.
> Poetry. The work itself, or a writing composed in verse. *Opus poeticum, poema, poesis.*]

1822

> POESÍA. El arte, ciencia o facultad de hacer composiciones en verso con invención y entusiasmo, imitando a la naturaleza. *Ars Poëtica*
> POESÍA. La misma composición hecha en verso con invención y entusiasmo, en la que se imita a la nuturaleza. *Poësis.*
> POESÍA. El fuego y viveza de las imágenes de la poesía; así se dice: esta obra, aunque tiene buenos versos, carece de POESÍA. *OEstrum.*
> POESÍA. Cualquiera obra o parte de ella que abunda de figuras, imágenes y ficciones. En este sentido se aplica también este nombre a la prosa escrita en estilo poético, como es el de algunas novelas. *Poësis.*
> POESÍAS. Las obras de los poetas, en especial hablando de los modernos, como las poesías de Garcilaso, de los Argensolas. *Poëmata.* (647)

[Poetry. The art, science, or faculty of making compositions in verse with invention and enthusiasm, imitating nature. *Ars Poetica.*

Poetry. The composition itself, made in verse with invention and enthusiasm, in which nature is imitated. *Poësis.*

Poetry. The fire and liveliness of poetry's images; thus it is said: this work, although it has good verses, lacks poetry. *OEstrum.*

Poetry. Any work or part thereof that abounds in figures, images, and fictions. In this sense this name is also applied to prose written in a poetic style, as is the style of some novels. *Poësis.*

Poetry. Works of the poets, especially in speaking of the moderns, like the poetry of Garcilaso, of the Argensolas. *Poëmata.*]

Even a merely quantitative perusal of the two entries attests to the burgeoning of meaning—the semantic efflorescence—that marked the concept of poetry within Spain's emergent romantic culture. In the span of the years separating these two entries, definitional restriction and acuity seem to have yielded to a proliferation of meaning. In contrast to the eighteenth century's "art of verse-composition and its products," *poesía* for the romantic era is clearly a more plural, inherently multifaceted phenomenon, and the fact that the shift should be as apparent as it is in a dictionary as linguistically conservative as the academy's is a testament to the importance of the phenomenon within nineteenth-century Spanish culture.

Beyond this semantic expansion, a series of fundamental qualitative changes come into view over this time period as well. Even as it repeats the classical definition of poetry as *ars poetica*, for example, the 1822 entry significantly adds the adverbial qualifiers "con invención y entusiasmo," registering those spheres of poetic creation—imagination and feeling—that had increasingly come to be privileged by romantic aesthetics. In addition, the term *poesía* is no longer applied to all verse making—as it had been throughout most of the 1700s—but rather to a particular kind of *poesis*. Indeed, by the early nineteenth century, the poetic is no longer conceived as entirely coextensive with language. This suggestion of poetry's relative autonomy from its linguistic vehicle becomes clear by the third definition in the entry, where one finds that poetry dwells more in the subjective quality of its images—"fuego y viveza de las imágenes"—than in its particular form. The autonomization of the poetic, the idea that the poetic is somehow present but irreducible to its particular linguistic manifestations, thus makes possible a paradox that would have been unthinkable within a classicist framework: If sufficiently lacking in imagination, feeling, or liveliness, a poem may in fact not be poetry at all.

Significantly, the Latin word that appears at the end of this definition is *oestrum* (Sp. estro, Eng. estrus), which in nineteenth-century poetics designated "aquel estímulo que siente interiormente el poeta para hacer sus versos, y se finge provenir de cierto numen que lo agita e inflama" [that stimulus to make his verses which the poet feels internally and pictures to himself as arising from a certain spirit that stirs and inflames him] (*DRAE*, 1822 ed., 868). Poetry here becomes roughly synonymous with inspiration itself, and it is precisely this change in emphasis—from *poesis* to *oestrus*—that attests to the well-known shift to an expressive poetics during the romantic era. Moreover, as the expression of *estro* took center stage within the rhetoric of romanticism, it became natural to find the phenomenon not only within verse compositions but in other discursive contexts as well. The fourth definition of the 1822 entry thus makes clear that a certain figurative and imaginative density could qualify prose and even novelistic passages, for example, as a kind of *poesía*. The common denominator of these shifts and their key terms—"invención, entusiasmo, fuego, viveza, and estímulo"—is the suggestion of creative, subjective agency itself. *Poesía* by 1822 had increasingly come to be equated with the realm of the subject and the enchanted qualities of experience, hence the fundamentally lyrical understanding of the poetic during the romantic era.

The symbolic meanings of prose were also dramatically recoded during these years. If *poesía* became a sign of creative subjectivity, prose and the prosaic—*lo prosaico*—increasingly came to be conceived antithetically, as the marker of a dreary objectivity. And just as the category of the poetic was increasingly conceptualized as a phenomenon that was relatively independent of its linguistic vehicle, the concept of the prosaic also began to signify much more than a particular mode of language. Throughout most of the eighteenth century the adjective *prosaico* had been restricted primarily to the discourse of poetics, where it indicated passages within verse compositions that where rhetorically stale, flat, or otherwise lacking. The playwright Leandro Fernández Moratín uses the term in this common *setecentista* sense, for example, when he appraises a play in his *Viage a Italia* as follows: "El estilo, aunque algunas veces degenera en prosaico, tiene buenos pedazos de versificación" [The style, although it degenerates into the prosaic at times, has good pieces of versification] (478). Well into the nineteenth century, dictionaries would continue to document this usage: "Prosáico, ca. adj. Lo que pertenece a la prosa o está escrito en ella. *Prosaicus.* El verso o el poema que por falta de armonía o por la llaneza de su lenguaje parece prosa" [Prosaic. adj. That which pertains to prose or is written in it. *Prosaicus.* Verse or poem that for lack of harmony or due to the flatness of its language is like prose] (*DRAE,* 1843 ed., 593).

Over the course of the first decades of the 1800s, however, the uses of *prosaico,* like *poesía* and *poético,* clearly begin to move beyond of the domain of poetics. The prosaic is increasingly conceived as an attribute of the world itself. As the following examples demonstrate, Spanish romantic writers repeatedly describe not only verses but also people, places, and entire ways of life with the term *prosaico*:

Manuel Bretón de los Herreros, *Marcela, o ¿cuál de los tres?* 1831

Mi corazón sólo anhela
ver a la hermosa Marcela;
y no viéndola, mi amor,
ese prosaico señor
me cansa, no me consuela. (48)

[My heart only desires
to see beautiful Marcela;
and without seeing her, my love,
that prosaic man
tires me, he does not console me.]

Ramón de Mesonero Romanos, "Madrid a la Luna," 1837

No se puede negar que la persona de un sereno considerada poéticamente tiene algo de ideal y romancesco, que no es de despreciar en nuestro prosaico, material y positivo Madrid, tan desnudo de edad media, de góticos monumentos y de ruinas sublimes. (320)

[It cannot be denied that the person of the sereno, considered poetically, has something ideal and romantic, which is not to be disdained in our prosaic, material, and positive Madrid, so stripped of a Middle Ages, of gothic monuments, and of sublime ruins.]

Nicomedes Pastor Díaz, "Los Problemas del Socialismo," 1848

> Nuestro problema no era la felicidad individual, la dicha del corazón. Ese no es problema de los hombres, ni el objeto de las sociedades. Es el secreto de Dios; es el destino y el misterio del hombre.
>
> Nuestro problema es más humilde, más prosaico, más exterior. Es un problema económico; es un problema político; es una cuestión social. (789)

> [Our problem was not individual happiness, the joy of the heart. That is not the problem of men, nor is it the objective of societies. It is God's secret; it is man's destiny and mystery.
>
> Our problem is more humble, more prosaic, more exterior. It is an economic problem, a political problem; it is a social question.]

Wenceslao Ayguals de Izco, *La bruja de Madrid*, 1850

> Tú hablas como poetisa, Enriqueta, pero el mundo es desgraciadamente muy prosaico y no hay en él más que un ídolo ante cuyos altares se tribute incienso. Este ídolo es el oro. (301)

> [You speak as a poetess, Enriqueta, but the world is unfortunately very prosaic and in it there is only one idol before whose altars incense is offered. That idol is gold.]

This romantic vision of daily life as *prosaico* still conveys the sense of insufficiency that had informed earlier uses of the term; but whereas the eighteenth-century notion designates *language* that does not measure up, by the 1800s it is the social world itself that is found to be lacking. The everyday is increasingly experienced as stale, dissatisfying, inadequate. To speak of the world as prosaic in this sense is to conceive the status quo of social existence as inherently deficient; it is to decry common life as something fundamentally paltry.

Lo prosaico, however, is also consistently associated by these writers with a different set of categories, a series of terms that evinces the links between the romantic sense of an impoverished reality and the social and economic changes that Spanish culture had been undergoing over the course of the 1830s, 1840s, and 1850s. As the preceding examples make clear, the prose of the world is conceptually linked to the positive knowledge of the sciences, to materialism, to political calculation, and to the realm of the monetary. In short, the romantic conceptualization of the prosaic is intimately related to the agenda that Spanish liberalism had slowly begun to implement as it dismantled the social and economic structures of the Ancien Régime. Central to that modernizing agenda, it is worth recalling, was the rationalization of politics (i.e., constitutionalism) and economics (i.e., market-driven reform) in the name of increased national efficiency, productivity, and wealth. Although Spanish historians have, until recently, tended to point to the disappointing results of liberalism in Spain—its piecemeal implementation, its unevenness, and its transformation into authoritarian bourgeois oligarchy—romantic writers who experienced this process clearly attest to its generation of an increasingly rationalized, prosaic world.

Indeed, there is a striking gap between the image of the world these writers convey and those accounts of Spanish romantic culture that have been informed by the metageography of modernity that we considered in chapter 1. Even as Spanish writers were lamenting the progressively prosaic quality of their social world, the historical imagination of modern Europe—well into the twentieth century—saw only a poetic culture replete with backward enchantments. The dominance of this second paradigm, regardless of what the Spaniards themselves might write, speaks rather eloquently to the power of northern European cultural imperialism in creating the image of romantic Spain. For those willing to acknowledge that Spanish modernity has a deeper history than it has traditionally been accorded, however, the elements of a different story are also clearly on display. As we considered in the preceding chapter, already by the late eighteenth century writers such as Cadalso had begun to decry the nocent effects of instrumental reason within their social world. Indeed, the liberal revolutions of the early 1800s were themselves not ex nihilo historical phenomena, but rather particularly intense moments within a much longer, ongoing process of secularization in Spain, and as the pace of change intensified, it prompted pained and often ambivalent responses from an increasing number of Spanish writers.

If Cadalso had offered an early articulation of the melancholy of Spain's mercantile modernity in *Noches lúgubres*, however, by the mid-1830s the effects of a decidedly liberal modernity were becoming increasingly clear. In demystifying the enchanted auras of the aristocracy and the church, in codifying the legal foundations of private property, and in fomenting the values of an emergent market economy, Spanish liberalism had heightened the conceptual separation between the poetic and the prosaic at the level of political practice. The antithetical values attributed to the two concepts in the early nineteenth century can thus be seen as a reflection of the more general, compartmentalizing rationality that has frequently been taken as one of the hallmarks of modernity. It is precisely an awareness of this rift within language itself, for example, that Frankfurt School thinkers would subsequently take as an index of the modern: "As a system of signs," Horkheimer and Adorno write in *Dialectic of Enlightenment*, "language is required to resign itself to calculation in order to know nature. As image, it is required to resign itself to copying nature in order to be nature entire, and must discard the claim to know nature" (17–18). Behind the romantic opposition of the prosaic and the poetic there is a more fundamental split that speaks to divorce of the language of art from the language of science in the modern era.

The Purging of Possibility

Within the context outlined in the preceding pages, the oscillation of prose and verse-poetry in *Don Alvaro* can begin to be grasped not only as a daring technical innovation—the definitive affront to neoclassical norms—but also as a phenomenon that resonated in fundamental ways with an important rift that was opening within Spanish social life itself. Saavedra's play speaks to the chasm that was widening between the sense of a progressively rationalized, prosaic world on one hand, and intuitions of a waning, enchanted realm of poetic experience on the other. It reflects the tension between two separate epistemological modes that, by the 1830s, were increasingly perceived to be irreconcilable with one another. Only a year before the play's opening, in a well-known prologue to Saavedra's 1834 narrative poem, *El moro expósito*, Antonio Alcalá Galiano had defended his friend's stylistic unevenness, arguing that the reality of the times could no longer be accurately conveyed within a single system of representation:

> Ha mezclado [. . .] retazos de apariencia pobre con otros de contextura brillante, páginas en estilo elevado con otras en estilo llano, imágenes triviales con otras nobles, y pinturas de la vida real con otras ideales. Tal vez con

ello escandalizará a no pocos de sus lectores, pero no es culpa suya que en la naturaleza anden revueltos lo serio y tierno con lo ridículo y extravagante; y él quiere tener a la naturaleza por guía y describir las cosas como pasan. (Saavedra, *Moro*, 30–31)

[He has mixed { . . . } snippets of poor appearance with others of brilliant contexture, pages in elevated style with others in plain style, trivial images with others that are noble, and portraits of real life with others that are ideal. Perhaps with this he will scandalize not a few of his readers, but it is not his fault that in nature the serious and the tender are mixed together with the ridiculous and the extravagant; he wants to have nature as a guide and to describe things the way they happen.]

The passage is a useful reminder that much of the "romantic revolution"— like virtually all modern aesthetic rebellions—was made in the name of a purportedly *more* authentic, "realistic" system of representation.[14] The same can be said for the mix of verse and prose in *Don Alvaro*: To the extent that it registered a collective sense that life experience itself was increasingly characterized by a schism between the poetic and the prosaic, it was driven by a realist impulse.

In turn, attention to the socially symbolic dimensions of each of these two forms affords relatively new insights into *Don Alvaro*, for the tension between prose and poetry is, among other things, a way of figuring at the level of linguistic style the dramatic conflict that takes place between Don Alvaro and his world at the level of plot. By this I mean that the reprieve from the world that Don Alvaro pursues, either through love (Act I), an imagined death (Acts III and IV) or religious seclusion (Act V), belongs for the most part to the order of "poetry" as commonly understood within Spanish romantic rhetoric. The turn to the world of affect, a suicidal dissatisfaction with existence as it is, and the quasi-religious search for nonworldly values correspond to the realm for which *poesía* had increasingly become a kind of shorthand. This is so because, in focusing on the realm of the subjective, the romantic conception of the poetic also began to function as an imagined site of refuge from the strictures of modern life. The strategies of coping with rationalized life that Freud famously discusses in "Civilization and Its Discontents," for example, echo those values that increasingly came to be considered poetic within romantic culture. "Against the dreaded external world"—Freud writes—"one can only defend oneself by some kind of turning away" (*Freud*, 730). Not by coincidence, several of Freud's methods of turning away name the paths Alvaro pursues in his own struggle against the external world:

> One procedure [. . .] clings to the objects belonging to that world and obtains happiness from an emotional relationship to them. [. . .] I am, of course, speaking of the way of life which makes love the centre of everything, which looks for satisfaction in loving and being loved. (733)

> The hermit turns his back on the world in which its most unbearable features are eliminated and replaced by others that are in conformity with one's own wishes. (732)

> Religion succeeds in sparing many people an individual neurosis. But hardly anything more. [. . .] If the believer finally sees himself obliged to speak of God's "inscrutable decrees," he is admitting that all that is left to him as a last possible consolation is an unconditional submission. (735)

Alvaro's final method of turning away—that is, his climactic suicide—also finds its analogue in psychoanalytic terms, for Alvaro's death wish is of a piece with the destructive principle that Freud would ultimately name Thanatos.[15] Inasmuch as each of these strategies came to be regarded by romantic culture as inherently "poetic," the plot of Saavedra's play can aptly be described as a doomed struggle to establish a measure of poetry in the world.

In such a context, it is not surprising to find that a considerable portion of the adverse fate that pursues Alvaro and Leonor manifests itself, quite literally, in a prosaic mode. This is so because, in addition to suggesting the realm of the objective, prose is also the mode of representation that Saavedra consistently chooses for the portrayal of collective life. Whereas the play's principal characters (i.e., Alvaro, Leonor, the Calatrava family, etc.) tend to be individuated by means of a lyrical voice expressed in verse form, the social backdrop for these characters is evoked primarily in the mode of prose, by means of the *costumbrista* sketches with which most acts open.[16] In addition, such backdrops are more than the neutral spaces of commentary they might initially seem to be. While they have been recognized for performing several of the functions of the classical chorus—they provide background information, they summarize events that may have taken place offstage, and they offer an image of the social reception of the protagonists' actions—these prose representations of collective life also subtly participate in the workings of the destiny that pursues Don Alvaro.

A brief review of several such scenes will help to illustrate that Saavedra's *costumbrismo* is, among other things, a prose that persecutes. The opening of the play is exemplary in this regard. At a freshwater stand on the outskirts of Seville, a military official, a colorful street-dweller or *majo*, a Cervantine gypsy girl, a canon, and several other inhabitants of the city chat with one another while Tío Paco, the owner of the establishment, serves them their afternoon refreshments. Replete with familiar social types, local color, and colloquial linguistic registers, these emblematic scenes have a decidedly popular, quotidian air. As the characters informally narrate the prehistory of the protagonist's amorous plight, they thus also offer viewers an initial representation of the everyday, a staging of the habitual against which Don Alvaro's first appearance is thrown into dramatic relief. Indeed, his entry (Act I, Scene III) is marked by the suspension of speech, as if to underscore that his poetic presence is antithetical to commonplace language. It is a scene that has often been heralded for is masterful theatricality. A shift in lighting, coupled with dramatic quietude, charges the simple act of walking across the stage with poetic meaning:

> Empieza a anochecer, y se va oscureciendo el teatro. DON ALVARO sale embozado en una capa de seda, con un gran sombrero blanco, botines y espuelas; cruza lentamente la escena, mirando con dignidad y melancolía a todos lados, y se va por el puente. Todos le observan en gran silencio. (87)

> [Night begins to fall, and the theater slowly darkens. DON ALVARO enters cloaked in a silk cape, with a great white hat, riding boots, and spurs; he slowly crosses the stage, looking everywhere with dignity and melancholy, and he leaves by the bridge. Everyone observes him with great silence.]

As soon as Alvaro disappears, however, the play quickly returns to the realm of the ordinary. Characters begin to comment on what they have witnessed, and the silent, mysterious, poetic figure they have contemplated is rapidly recontained within the narrative structures of their gossip.

There is thus a subtle but unequivocal tension between Don Alvaro as the emblem of a poetic, subjective mystery on one hand, and the customary discourses of collective life as represented by the *costumbrista* sketches on the other. The antagonistic quality of this relationship becomes apparent when one reconsiders the plot function of these initial scenes, for they do not simply update spectators with the stories of Alvaro's difficult courtship, of the marquis' resistance to the mestizo interloper, and of Leonor's removal to outskirts of Seville. These *costumbrista* scenes also participate in that narrative by effectively setting in motion the series of events that will thwart the protagonist's attempt to elope with his beloved.

In Act I, Scene IV, Tío Paco notes that for several days he has observed Alvaro exit the city each evening to meet with a servant who goes before him with two horses. A townsperson adds that he has seen the two returning to Seville with exhausted horses during the early morning hours. On the day of the play's opening scenes, the water vendor announces that he has witnessed the servant pass with not two, but three horses. Upon hearing this comment, the canon departs to warn the marquis of Don Alvaro's plans. In short, a clear causal chain links the apparently ordinary, even mundane dialogue of these *costumbrista* characters to the tragedy that awaits Don Alvaro at the end of Act I: Alerted by the canon, the marquis will interrupt Alvaro's attempt to take Leonor away; Alvaro's gun will accidentally fire; Leonor's brothers will swear vengeance. The force of destiny that pursues Don Alvaro throughout the rest of the play is thus in fact launched in a sketch of manners, by minor characters, and in prose.

To the extent that the structure of *Don Alvaro* is characterized by repetition (Shaw, "Acerca"), the play's opening scenes announce a paradigm that spectators will witness at the beginning of subsequent acts. The opening of Act II, for example, reaffirms the persecutory quality of *costumbrista* prose. It begins with a series of scenes set in a roadside inn on the outskirts of Hornachuelos, a provincial town. A year has elapsed since the first act, and Leonor, who is fleeing from her vengeful brothers, arrives at the inn on her way to the monastery of Los Angeles, where she will enter a life of religious seclusion. She has traveled disguised as a young man, and, as the opening scenes unfold, spectators learn that she has shut herself in her room for the evening. Like Alvaro at the beginning of Act I, she remains offstage, the subject of discussion for secondary characters who dialogue in the kitchen. These characters include the innkeeper, his wife, a university student, a serving girl, the town mayor, several additional travelers and villagers, and a muleteer—Tío Trabuco—who has provided Leonor transport. A typically picturesque, *costumbrista* grouping, the characters' banter seems innocent enough, but as the conversation progresses, the student takes increasing interest in the mysterious guest who has not joined them. He presses Tío Trabuco for information concerning his passenger, but the muleteer prudently says very little. When the other characters take interest in the student himself, he reveals that he is in fact implicated in the drama that has unfolded in Act I:

> Soy bachiller Pereda, graduado por Salamanca, "in utroque," y hace ocho años que curso sus escuelas. [. . .] Salí de allí hace más de un año acompañado de mi amigo y protector el señor licenciado Vargas, y fuimos a Sevilla a vengar la muerte de su padre el Marqués de Calatrava y a indagar el paradero de su hermana. [. . .] Pero no la hallamos. [. . .] Y yo me vuelvo a mi universidad a desquitar el tiempo perdido. (108)

> [I am Bachelor Pereda, graduate of Salamanca, "in utroque" {in canon and civil law}, and I have studied in its colleges for eight years. { . . . } I left over a year ago accompanied by my good friend and protector, Licenciate Vargas, and we went to Sevilla to avenge the death of his father the Marquis of Calatrava and to look into the whereabouts of his sister { . . . } but we didn't find her. { . . . } And I am returning to the university to make up for lost time.]

Minutes later, the innkeeper's wife will find Leonor's room empty. Money has been left, and a window that opens to the surrounding fields is suggestively still open. It becomes clear that, having overheard the *costumbrista* scene in the kitchen, Leonor has had to flee suddenly from the inn. She has been expelled, as it were, by a prose conversation that was about to overtake her.

The dangerous edges of *cotumbrista* prose can similarly be seen in the play's final act, which opens with a sketch of rural poverty. The crippled, the maimed, and the poor of all ages gather around the lower cloister of the monastery of Los Angeles. Brother Melitón serves soup as part of the Franciscan's regular charitable activities, while the monastery director, Padre Guardián, slowly paces. The initial dialogue is banal enough; Melitón talks to the poor he is feeding. As the scene progresses, however, spectators learn that a mysterious priest has joined the religious community, taking his vows under the name of Padre Rafael, and that over the course of his four years there he has become highly popular among the people. Weary of some of his companion's darker moods, Melitón suspects that Rafael is not as saintly as he appears. Indeed, the Franciscan wonders aloud whether Rafael might not be in league with the devil. He confesses to Padre Guardián that, "la verdad, siempre que le miro me acuerdo de aquello que vuestra reverendísima nos ha contado muchas veces, [. . .] de cuando se hizo fraile de nuestra Orden el demonio." [The truth is that every time I look at him I remember what your reverence has told us many times { . . . } about the time the devil became a monk in our Order] (172). By this point, spectators deduce that Rafael is in fact Don Alvaro, who has sought monastic seclusion after returning from the wars in Italy (Acts III and IV). Although he is attempting to hide from the world, Don Alvaro is once again exposed by *costumbrista* prose. He is the object of the narrative of bystanders, and just as his silent, poetic presence was transmuted into prose by gossiping characters at the beginning of Act I, here at the end of the play the secret of his identity—the seemingly inscrutable nature of Padre Rafael—prompts a speculative narrative concerning demonic possession.

Prose again acquires a social dimension as well, for the story to which Melitón refers is collective in more than one sense: It circulates as a well-known tale within the religious community of the monastery, and it is also a narrative that would have been familiar to many of the play's spectators.[17] Its function is akin to earlier *costumbrista* narrative acts. By inscribing Alvaro into narrative, Melitón's seemingly innocent, superstitious story inadvertently becomes part of the former's persecution. When Don Alfonso, the final agent of Calatrava vengeance, arrives at the monastery in search of a Padre Rafael, Melitón tells him that more than one priest has the name. "¿Con cuál queréis hablar vos?" [With which one do you wish to speak?]—he asks—to which Don Alfonso uncannily responds "el del infierno" [the one from hell]. Only then does Melitón confess, "pues ahora caigo en quién es" [now I realize who it is], and he proceeds to lead him to his fateful encounter with Alvaro (174). The demonic identity ascribed to Alvaro by Melitón's musings in the *costumbrista* scenes becomes the basis for his subsequent recognition. Once more, Alvaro is identified because he has already been narrated, in prose, by a secondary character.

If *costumbrista* prose can be described as part of *Don Alvaro*'s persecutory apparatus, this is because one of the epistemological functions of such prose in the play is to bring the mystery of Don Alvaro into collective regimes of knowledge. Insofar as Alvaro is represented as an exoticized, poetic unknown—he is racially other, and his origins remain unclear throughout much of the work—the task of making him intelligible is indeed an antagonistic one.[18] Within the world of *Don Alvaro*, transparency and intelligibility consistently augur danger. To be known, for Don Alvaro at least, is to be in peril. Recognition—in the etymological sense of being brought back into cognition—is marked as an act of symbolic violence. For this reason, the identification that classical poetics would have called *anagnorisis* is almost always shadowed by death. Each of Don Alvaro's clashes with the Calatrava house is in fact preceded by a moment of fatal recognition: Alvaro will accidentally kill the marquis in Act I because he has been recognized on the way to the house; he is forced to kill Don Carlos in Act IV because the friendship they have formed dissipates into deadly recognition; and in Act V, the dazzling multiplication of recognition—between Don Alfonso and Don Alvaro, between Leonor and Don Alfonso, between Don Alvaro and Leonor—is a prelude to death for all. A characteristically romantic inversion has been at work throughout: The conceptual centerpieces of the celebratory tale of modernity—lucidity, discovery, the power of recognition, and the rational unveiling of mystery—are represented as instruments of symbolic persecution.

And yet, if one turns to the verse passages of *Don Alvaro* that for viewers would have been coded as the domain of the poetic, one finds that this mode of representation is itself not an unproblematic alternative to prosaic recognition. Don Alvaro and Leonor are not the only figures disproportionately accorded expression in verse. In symbolic terms, the primary engine of antagonism in the work, the house of Calatrava, also belongs to the realm of the poetic. The marquis, Don Carlos, and Don Alfonso also speak in verse. There is, to be sure, a socially motivated reason. Verse had long functioned as a sign of social elevation, and in this sense by according the principal agonists similar treatment the play tacitly affirms at the level of language what the Calatrava house seeks to deny: the fact that Don Alvaro is—or could be—one of them. In addition, the use of verse by both parties subtly speaks to the historical conjunctures that Spain's social structure was undergoing under liberalism—as the Ancien Régime was dismantled, an ascendant bourgeoisie increasingly came to dialogue with the world of waning aristocratic power. Over the course of the century each class would famously exert considerable influence on the other. The life-world of the aristocracy—especially when it came to economics—was progressively informed by bourgeois values, while bourgeois social customs—particularly the idea of social refinement—were increasingly modeled on the aristocracy. Within this context, the fact that a wealthy American newcomer "speaks the same language" as an aristocratic family that has seen better days evinces the social proximity of the two classes that was being wrought by the modern liberal world.

Shared expression in verse, however, does not simply suggest the historical convergence of aristocratic and bourgeois life-worlds, for there is a sense of the poetic in *Don Alvaro* that is not reducible to class. In according poetic expression to the protagonist and his primary persecutors, the play also establishes qualitative differences between the two. The category of the poetic itself is effectively bisected, as if to call attention to two very different, competing models of poetry. While Alvaro's poetic nature is initially linked to subjective mystery, the poetry of the Calatrava house is known all too well. It is the poetry of parental authority, familial honor, and vengeance. Echoing the conventions of Spain's baroque honor plays, Calatrava poetry, like the decaying coat of arms that presides over the house in Act I, is overtly marked as the poetry of the past. It is a poetry that attempts to foreclose the emergence of the new. Predictable and even formulaic in its rigidity, Calatrava poetry is, among other things, a vehicle of refusal. The marquis, Don Carlos, and Don Alfonso act out of an unwavering, a priori rejection of Don Alvaro, and in this regard their poetry represents the past's "no" to the present.

In contrast, it becomes clear that Don Alvaro's poetic nature stems not only from his mystery, or from the "poetic" nature of his pursuits, but also from the way he comes to represent possibility itself. As the antithesis to Calatrava intransigence, Don Alvaro throughout the play repeatedly performs the poetry of "what might be." Indeed, the play draws much of its pathos not from the longstanding philosophical problem of destiny and freedom, but rather from the particular way it poignantly stages possibility itself and its tragic evanescence. A fascinating paradox informs the representation of fate in *Don Alvaro*: It is only because the play so consistently flirts with *possibility* that the force of destiny is ultimately conveyed so successfully. To put it more concretely, it is only because Don Alvaro actively pursues one possibility after another—love, death in war, religious seclusion—that the failure of each becomes part of the image of fate. The extinction of possibility is one of the play's key rhetorical gestures, and the death of possibility—a romantic motif to which we shall return in the next chapter on Larra—is in fact a prelude to each of the deaths that ensue in Alvaro's clashes with the house of Calatrava. Death and the refusal of possibility are repeatedly linked to one another.

In Act I, it is the marquis' refusal to accept Alvaro's offer of surrender that leads to the accidental firing of the gun. Alvaro first kneels in capitulation before Leonor's father; he draws his gun only when the Marquis insults him by ordering servants to apprehend him (101). Similarly, before dueling with Don Carlos in Act IV, Don Alvaro argues that their friendship—a heartfelt bond established under false names in Act III—holds the very real possibility of a different future:

> Pues trataron las estrellas / por raros modos de hacernos / amigos, ¿a que oponernos / a lo que buscaron ellas? / Si nos quisieron unir / de mutuos y altos servicios / con los vínculos propicios, /no fue, no, para reñir. (152)

> [Since the stars tried / by rare means to make us / friends, why oppose ourselves / to what they sought? / If they wanted to join us / with propitious ties / of mutual high service, / it was not, no, not to fight.]

It is only after Don Carlos refuses to acknowledge the potential within their friendship that the two characters proceed to fight. Carlos's rejection of possibility prefaces his death.

In the last act, the image of a possibility other than persecution, violence, and death is intentionally dangled before Alvaro's eyes by Don Alfonso as part of the latter's act of final vengeance. Having traveled to Perú, the youngest member of the Calatrava house has discovered that Alvaro is the son of a Spanish viceroy and an Inca princess. He has also learned that Alvaro's parents, who had been incarcerated for rebellion, have been pardoned. Alvaro's name has been restored. Coupled with the intimation that Leonor is not dead, as Alvaro believed her to be, Alfonso's words are expressly designed to evoke the very sense of possibility he intends to crush. In the play's penultimate scenes, all impediments to Alvaro's initial desire have seemingly vanished: He is revealed to be, in fact, an equal in class and stature to the Calatrava house; he belongs to one of the wealthiest Peruvian families; and his beloved is alive. Alfonso conveys this information to Alvaro, however, precisely because he wants to relish the effect of refusing the possibilities that inhere in the news. "Un sol hermoso y radiante / te he descubierto," Alfonso gloats, "y de un soplo / luego he sabido apagarle" [A beautiful and radiant sun / have I uncovered for you, and in a puff of air / I have then been able to put it out] (186). While Alfonso's reference to the sun mocks Alvaro's Inca heritage, as many have noted, these words also sum up the logic at work throughout the play, where the repeated staging of possibility has been the precondition for the representation of destiny's power. As the progression from the marquis, to Don Carlos, to Don Alfonso suggests, in *Don Alvaro* the force of destiny is proportional to the magnitude of the possibility it ultimately extinguishes. In the end, the very scale of the possible happiness Alfonso sketches is the measure of fate's power.

With the preceding interpretive frameworks in view, it becomes apparent that both the symbolic opposition between the poetic and the prosaic, and the rift within the poetic world itself—that is, refusal versus possibility—encode an intriguing, rudimentary allegory of social history. As poetic mystery, Don Alvaro is pursued in an epistemological sense, by a prosaic *costumbrista* world "from below;" and as poetic possibility, he is pursued "from above" by a poetry of aristocracy that is grounded in the refusal of the new. Caught between an aristocratic rock and a modern, prosaic hard place, Alvaro's position succinctly captures the tensions that an emergent bourgeoisie, torn between the utilitarian imperatives of liberalism and a desire for the enchantments of a crumbling Ancien Régime, would experience throughout much of Spain's nineteenth-century history. In this regard, *Don Alvaro* reflects not only the difficult emergence of the new, but also the painful consequences of the modern itself.

To the extent that, as we have seen, the prose of the world can be indexed to processes of liberal modernization, the force of destiny in the play has both a modern and a traditionalist face. In its traditionalist guise, it comes to be understood as the weight of the past on the present; but in its more contemporary, prosaic, *costumbrista* visage, destiny also represents the exorcizing of the unknown from an increasingly modern, secular world. Don Alvaro's leap into the abyss at the end of the play is a result of both forms of destiny, and it is not easily reducible to a tale of tradition's triumph over the present. Whether one reads his suicide as the final affirmation of his will (Navas Ruiz, *Don Alvaro*, lvi) or as the expression of its negation, Alvaro's death marks the painful purging of mystery, possibility, and hope from a violently conflicted, modernizing social order.[19] Insofar as such poetic values are associated with subjectivity itself by romantics—or with what psychology would later call self-realization—*Don Alvaro* stages a parable of sorts concerning the modern diminishment and delimitation of subjective agency. Even as the play decries the intransigence of the reactionary, nonmodern strata of Spain's social structure, it also subtly records a pained sense that the mystery, possibility, and poetry of the self were losing ground within Spain's emergent, modern liberal world.[20]

Modernity's Amnesia

While the death of poetic possibility in *Don Alvaro* can productively be linked to the painful processes of social change that Spanish culture was experiencing under liberalism, this is not the only historical matrix in which the play is embedded. We have already seen that the play also dialogues rather openly with an older, vaster historical structure than liberalism in the 1830s; that is, Spanish colonialism and its legacies. It is a history that has often remained on the margins of research dedicated to eighteenth- and nineteenth-century Spanish culture. While analyses of the literary culture of Spain's early modern era have taken empire and colonialism to be central analytic categories, these terms seem to have had far less purchase on critical engagement with the country's modern era. Within the traditional literary historiography of modern Spain, the topic of empire in fact makes little or no appearance until the Spanish-American War and the so-called Generation of 1898, and even then the focus falls primarily on the crisis of national identity that Spain's defeat engendered among artists and intellectuals. If one were to judge by the standard progression of literary movements alone—that is, the late baroque, neoclassicism and rococo, romanticism, realism, modernism—one might be left with the impression that the two centuries of Spanish letters preceding 1898 had elapsed with little or no literary trace of the colonial enterprise.

Indeed, in lieu of empire, the basic narrative that has typically structured literary-historical discourse on Spanish letters from the eighteenth century forward is the very tale we examined in chapter 1, the story of Spain's seemingly sui generis relationship to modernity. This shift in organizational concepts—from empire to the problem of modernity—is fascinating if one recalls that modern Europe remained thoroughly imperial throughout the eighteenth and nineteenth centuries. The Spanish Empire witnessed a dramatic diminishment of its power in relation to other European empires, to be sure, but it did not vanish. The rhetorical effacement of empire from the conceptual map of the historiography of eighteenth- and nineteenth-century Spanish literature cannot be explained by a weakening of imperial agendas; instead it speaks to the Hegelian "History" of modern Europe and exemplifies its erasure of imperialism from the story of the modern. Spain's hegemonic moment is automatically coded as imperial, while the imperial powers of northern Europe are simply modern. Although such thinking operated across Europe, as we considered earlier, it was also clearly at work within nation-states. In short, the conceptual apparatus that effaced the Iberoamerican Atlantic from the history of modernity in Europe also worked within Spanish historiography to segregate Spanish America from the history of modern Spain.

The effects of this thought-structure have had a profound impact on literary and cultural studies by subtly circumscribing the range of meanings imagined for modern Spanish texts and modern Spanish aesthetic movements. If, as we considered in chapter 1, it has been difficult for the literature of posthegemonic Spain to break into the hallowed halls of "modern European literature," it is also the case that until recently "Peninsular studies" have kept Spanish America in the figurative margins of the story of modern Spanish cultural production. Critical debates concerning Spanish romanticism, for example, have rarely if ever explored its links to Spanish colonialism, despite the fact that liberalism and South American decolonization were inextricably linked to one another.[21] Spanish romanticism flourishes in the years immediately following the first important wave of decolonization within the Hispanic world. By the mid-1820s, and especially in the wake of the Battle of Ayacucho (1824), South America had in effect ensured the political autonomy of its nascent republics. Spain's imperial identity had been dealt an extraordinary blow. It had lost an entire continent, yet few theoretical formulations have attempted to relate such events to Spanish romanticism in explicit ways.[22]

Even in a canonically romantic text such as *Don Alvaro*, which engages the topic of Spanish America in a fairly obvious manner, critical discussion of the work has tended to focus on its more abstract, philosophical implications—that is, the problem of destiny—rather than on those decidedly "American" issues of race, ethnicity, and identity. Within the bourgeoning critical bibliography on this play, analyses that deal with

Spanish America at length are few and far between, and, as we shall see in a few moments, the standard reading of Don Alvaro's Peruvian origins typically posits a conventional romantic topos that obviates the need for further historical analysis. Similarly, despite the striking parallels between *Don Alvaro* and the life story of *the* paradigmatic mestizo, the Inca Garcilaso de la Vega (Alonso Seaone), critical introductions to Saavedra's work treat this information as, at best, one more datum to add to the list of the author's sources. A structural forgetting of imperialism/colonialism seems to have shaped not only inquiry into *Don Alvaro,* but also Spanish romantic studies grosso modo.[23] In order to better understand this process, I would like to focus on the representation of Alvaro's American identity. More specifically, I hope to explore the relationship between Don Alvaro's mestizo identity and broader questions concerning empire and colonialism. By empire, however, I will be invoking two very different frameworks of analysis, for I mean to name not only the Spanish colonial world I have just described, but also the northern European cultural imperialism that we have considered in earlier chapters. Saavedra's play, like Spanish romanticism more generally, unfolds within the complex overlapping of both forms of imperial power.

I

In turning to the first framework—Spanish empire, and more specifically the massive decolonization that had taken place during the 1820s—one of the more immediate questions raised by *Don Alvaro* concerns the kind of ideological work the play realized as it was first performed for a Madrid audience in 1835. What are the implications of *Don Alvaro*'s representation of the death not just of possibility qua possibility, but of a decidedly American poetic possibility? The work stages a rather straightforward tale of failed social integration, but what is to be made of the fact that it is specifically an American, colonial subject who experiences this failure? If we briefly reconsider each of Alvaro's encounters with the house of Calatrava—particularly each antagonist's repudiation of the hero—a series of shifting justifications for refusing the protagonist comes into view. It is a series that will help to illuminate the question of Spanish America's symbolic status in the play.

In Act I, the canon defends the marquis' right to refuse Don Alvaro's amorous pretensions as follows:

> Don Alvaro llegó hace dos meses; y nadie sabe quién es. Ha pedido en casamiento a doña Leonor, y el marqués, no juzgándolo buen partido para su hija, se la ha negado. [. . .] En todo lo cual el señor marqués se ha comportado como persona prudente. (86)

> [Don Alvaro arrived two months ago; and nobody knows who he is. He has asked for doña Leonor in marriage, and the marquis, not judging it a good match for his daughter, has denied her to him. { . . . } In all of this the marquis has acted as a prudent person.]

Don Alvaro's rejection is, at this stage, predicated on his status as a newcomer. The canon intimates that he is simply not known enough to the community, and the marquis is described as an agent of judicious communal reticence before an outsider. As the dramatic conflict progresses, however, it becomes apparent that the marquis' rebuff is not merely a function of prudence, but in fact stems from his judgment that Alvaro is a social inferior. The exchanges between the two in Act I, Scene VIII, as Alvaro attempts to surrender to the marquis, leave little doubt about the matter:

> Alvaro: Vuestra hija es inocente. [. . .] Yo soy el culpado. [. . .]
> Atravesadme el pecho. (Hinca una rodilla).
> Marqués: Tu actitud suplicante manifiesta lo bajo de tu condición. . . .
> (101)

> [Alvaro: Your daughter is innocent. { . . . } I am to be blamed. { . . . }
> Pierce my chest. (He drops to one knee).
> Marquis: Your supplicant attitude manifests the base nature of your
> condition. . . .]

Moments later, as the marquis orders his servants to apprehend Alvaro, the class basis of the aristocrat's repudiation becomes explicit:

> Alvaro: ¡Ay de vuestros criados si se mueven! Vos solo tenéis derecho para
> atravesarme el corazón.
> Marqués: ¿Tú morir a manos de un caballero? No; morirás a las del
> verdugo. (101)

[Alvaro: Woe to the sevants if they move! Only you have the right to pierce
my heart.
Marquis: For you to die at the hands of gentleman? No; you shall die at the
hands of an executioner.]

Similarly, Alvaro's duel with Carlos in Act IV is preceded by declarations from the latter that, as the protagonist himself notes, repeat the class
judgments his father had expressed in Act I:

Alvaro: ¿Teméis que vuestro valor / se disminuya y se asombre / si halla en
su contrario un hombre / de nobleza y pundonor?
Carlos: ¡Nobleza un aventurero! / ¡Honor un desconocido! / Sin padre, sin
apellido, / advenedizo, altanero!
Alvaro: ¡Ay, que ese error a la muerte, / por más que lo evité yo, / a vuestro
padre arrastró! . . . (152)

[Alvaro: Do you fear that your valor / will diminish and be overshadowed /
if it finds in its adversary a man / of nobility and honor?
Carlos: Nobility in an adventurer! / Honor in a stranger! / Without a
father, without a surname, / a haughty upstart!]
Alvaro: Oh, that very error, / dragged your father to death, / avoid it
though I tried.]

The irony throughout these exchanges, of course, is that Alvaro is in fact a
noble by birth, and it is precisely this information that, as we considered
earlier, Alfonso tauntingly reveals in the last act. Even as he communicates
to Alvaro that the fundamental obstacles to his social integration have
vanished, however, Alfonso also gives voice to a new, final basis for refusing him. It is no longer a question of class differences, but rather a repudiation of the protagonist because of his racial identity: "Soy un hombre
rencoroso / que tomar venganza sabe"—Alfonso declares—"y porque sea
más completa, / te digo que no te jactes de noble. [. . .] / Eres un mestizo
/ fruto de traiciones." [I am a spiteful man / who knows how to take vengeance, / and to make it more complete, / I tell you not to pride yourself a
noble. { . . . } / You are a mestizo / the fruit of treasons.] (187). Such is the
final affront that prompts Alvaro to cross swords with Alfonso. Alvaro's
final duel, which will lead to Leonor's death and to his own suicide, is
precipitated by an overtly racist rejection.

To the extent that Alvaro's encounters cumulatively figure not only the persistence of destiny but also the progressive amplification of its power, the fact that this culminating refusal—the refusal that will literally send Alvaro over the edge—is predicated on race is especially significant. In the proliferation of excuses for refusing Alvaro, the play subtly captures the face of modern racism and its subterfuge: Audience members first hear that it is not Alvaro's race but the fact that he is a stranger that makes his integration difficult; then they learn that it is the difference of class. It is only when the fallacious nature of these excuses is exposed that racial animus—subtly there all along—makes itself seen without equivocation. The effect of this progressive revelation is to suggest that, as a mestizo, Alvaro would never have been accepted as an equal, despite his wealth and class status. Destiny in *Don Alvaro* is sociohistorical, cosmic (Cardwell), and astrological (Caldera, Introducción), to be sure. In the end, however, it is literally race and racial prejudice that mark the insurmountable obstacle to Alvaro's integration into Spanish society.

In turn, this final emphasis on racial alterity helps to elucidate the question of Alvaro's symbolic status more clearly. Don Alvaro is not just any racial other; his racial identity bespeaks the history of Spanish conquest and colonization in no uncertain terms. He is a paradigmatic example of Euro-American miscegenation, and the parallels between his story and the life story of the Inca Garcilaso de la Vega—the first mestizo writer—subtly accord a quasi-foundational dimension to this identity. His identity and his destiny clearly have an emblematic quality. It is consequently not difficult to see in *Don Alvaro* a meditation on the status not simply of one man besieged by fortune, but of Spanish America's fortune within the collective imagination of Spain's emergent liberal order. In its initial stages (1808–1814) Spanish liberalism had expressly attempted to address the grievances of colonial Spanish America, and during the years of the Liberal Triennium (1820–1823) liberals had actively pursued a policy of reconciliation:

> Restoration of constitutional government brought with it a return to earlier efforts to effect a peaceful solution of the vexing colonial dilemma. Once again there were distinct schools of thought on the question. One group continued to place its faith in the former policy of negotiation and persuasion, based particularly on the supposed advantages of the liberal constitution of 1812. Others felt that the time had come for a bolder conciliatory approach

and contemplated the creation of semi-independent, constitutional monarchies in America. (Van Aken, 8)

The Fernandine years that followed (1823–1833) represented a hiatus from such projects, but during the resurgence of liberalism that followed Ferdinand's death—that is, precisely the historical moment in which *Don Alvaro* would be staged in Madrid for the first time—the question of America had returned to public debate with considerable intensity. In the capital, pamphlets circulated calling for rapprochement, repeated legislative resolutions were passed in favor of policies that would bring the colonies back into political unity with Spain, and diplomatic and commercial missions were established to explore such possibilities. Recognition of most of the South American republics would proceed haltingly over the next several decades, but the climate of public opinion in the early 1830s was clear:

> An overwhelming majority of influential Spaniards desired reconciliation with the lost colonies. In choosing to acknowledge the independence of the new states Spaniards hoped to promote the economic recovery of their own nation and to perpetuate its primacy in the New World. Accordingly they fashioned a new image of empire to be based upon commerce and the ties of religion, language, and customs. Herein was the beginning of the Pan-Hispanic movement. (Van Aken, 29)

For decades after its definitive military defeats in South America, Spanish governments firmly believed that the colonies would one day return to Spain, and at the time of *Don Alvaro*'s opening in 1835, the dream of a reunited, transatlantic Spanish polity based on a model of constitutional federalism was not a distant one. The play's tale of failed South American integration would consequently have sounded an especially contemporary note for Madrid viewers; and in *Don Alvaro*'s plot it is not difficult to discern a vaguely allegorical lament over Spain's failure to integrate South America into its emergent political order. As imperial nostalgia increasingly manifested itself in the form of Pan-Hispanic sentiment, the play's symbolic critique of the impossibility of reintegration and the final image of a mestizo cursing humanity—and with it, the Spanish viewing public—would surely have had a powerful effect on contemporary audiences.[24]

Even as it allegorically laments the impossibility of Spanish America, however, the play also offers a subtle rewriting of decolonization from a Spanish perspective. In place of the image of colonies vanquishing the empire in order to achieve their autonomy, the play develops the figure of an Alvaro/America that repeatedly seeks integration but is spurned by a sociopolitically myopic motherland. Similarly, *Don Alvaro* decries Spanish society for its social inertia and for its racial prejudice, thus simultaneously marking Spanish American nonintegration as a tragedy that is largely of Spain's own making. As a symbolic response to decolonization, the work rehearses a series of powerful fantasies that characterized nineteenth-century Spanish imperialism more generally: the idea that Spain had lost South America rather than that the colonies had won it; the idea that to seek independence was a kind of suicide; the idea that colonial South America would one day return to Spain; and finally, the idea that facilitating such a process was in Spain's hands. Following Fredric Jameson, one could claim that this tragedy symbolically rewrites and resolves decolonization within the political unconscious of Spanish imperialism (*Political*, 79).

Don Alvaro's symbolic engagement with decolonization is also an intriguing example, however, of the way in which the purportedly "backward" culture of nineteenth-century Spain was in many regards historically prescient. In staging a European society's relentless refusal to incorporate its paradigmatic, colonial other into the imagined community of the nation, the play announced a phenomenon that would haunt modern Europe in the wake of its own twentieth-century experiences of decolonization. It is worth asking, for example, how distant fortune's refusal of the mestizo in *Don Alvaro* is from those more contemporary refusals, real and symbolic, that so often circumscribe the idea of national identity within postcolonial Europe today—that is, the symbolic denial of the Arab and the Indian, for example, as constitutive parts of French and British national identity respectively. Similarly, the imperial point of view that subtly remains at work within *Don Alvaro's* critique raises the question of the extent to which modern Europe itself—now on the margins of a very different colossus—has been capable of mounting a critique of its own imperial history.

II

In the preceding reading of *Don Alvaro*, I have intentionally placed the protagonist's mestizo status in dialogue with the histories of colonialism and liberalism in nineteenth-century Spain and Spanish America; I call attention to this gesture because, in contrast, the second imperial framework we shall consider—the cultural empire of modern Europe—has largely entailed a turn away from such concerns. Indeed, from the time of the play's first staging to the present, the dominant interpretive template for discussion of Don Alvaro's American identity has not been Spain's colonial and postcolonial history, but rather a mode of understanding summed up by a single name: Jean-Jacques Rousseau. Even today, for most critics Don Alvaro's status as a non-European and his function as a placeholder for poetic possibility remit to the paradigm of the noble savage, a figure whose romantic lineage is almost invariably traced to Rousseau.[25]

Miguel Angel Lama has noted, for example, that in the immediate reception of *Don Alvaro*'s debut, the work was already understood in terms of a Rousseau-like conflict between nature and civilization. Writing in the pages of *Revista Española* in 1835, shortly after the play's opening, a reviewer offered the following analysis:

> a mis ojos don Alvaro es una explicación de la lucha entre un hombre, que entre bárbaros creció como él propio dice, cuyos afectos, hijos de una educación salvaje, son todos violentos, todos extremos, cuyas pasiones se han afilado, y aún no gastado por un ligero roce con la sociedad; y esta misma sociedad con sus preocupaciones y sus pasiones frías y raciocinadas e inmudables. Y esta contienda entre pasiones semejantes en su esencia, pero diferentes en su forma, conduce, como una fatalidad invencible, todos los agentes en la acción a su ruina. (cited by Lama, Prólogo, 52)

> [To my eyes don Alvaro is an explanation of the struggle between a man who grew up among barbarians, as he himself says, a man whose feelings, children of a savage education, are all violent, all extremes, whose passions have been sharpened and not yet worn down by his light contact with society; and on the other hand that same society, with its preoccupations and its cold, reasoned, immutable passions. And like an invincible fatality this struggle between passions that are similar in essence but different in form leads all agents of the action to their ruin.]

Lama goes on to note that many of the standard twentieth-century critical interpretations of the play—Pattison, Cardwell, Navas Ruiz (*Don Alvaro*), Shaw ("Acerca")—have been structured along similar lines, and he himself concludes that the work's ultimate thesis concerns the impossibility of the fusion of nature and civilization, the impossibility of nature/Alvaro's integration into society (Prólogo, 52–53, 61).

My intention in recalling this line of interpretation is not to argue against a Rousseauian understanding of *Don Alvaro*, but rather to reframe the question of Rousseau in order to observe its relationship to the geopolitics of culture that we considered in chapter 1. More specifically, I would like to focus on the way in which what I shall call the "Rousseau-effect" can be grasped as a historical and ideological event in its own right. The symbolic construction of racial and cultural others as more "natural" than Europeans belongs to a long history that begins much earlier than Rousseau's eighteenth century. In the previous chapter it became clear, for example, that the key features of the "Rousseauian" paradigm were already in place in the sixteenth-century work of Fray Bartolomé de las Casas. Similarly, any protracted engagement with Spanish chronicles of the colonial era makes clear that, as early as Columbus himself, the European gaze projected the image of its own utopian desire onto the foreign peoples and places it subjugated. The links between European colonialism and the figure of the noble savage are clear enough, and within this broader historical framework the question of Rousseau can itself begin to be grasped more precisely.[26] Indeed, against the backdrop of centuries of mystifying representations of the savage, the Rousseau-effect begins to look like a rather curious phenomenon.

Simply put, it represents a moment in which *one* European discourse concerning the noble savage suddenly attains unprecedented, unquestioned representative value. Throughout most of the twentieth century few critical and theoretical discussions of the romantic mystification of non-Europeans seem to have proceeded without turning to this model, and modern anthropology continues work under its shadow (Ellingson, 1–8). The phenomenon thus bears witness to the cultural power that modern Europe—in this case a tradition of Anglo-French commentary—successfully exerted in constituting its categories of analysis and representation as transnational standards. One need only contemplate the historical irony of Spanish writers turning to Rousseau in order to represent the peoples of

South America to appreciate the extent of such cultural power during the romantic era. Indeed, it is one more example of the structural shift away from Iberoamerican coloniality that accompanied the consolidation of the field of "modern European culture" and its theorization; even today, the story of Europe's mystification of the savage typically privileges Rousseau over early modern Spanish writers.[27]

Modernity's amnesia is not limited, however, to the displacement of interest from the Hispanic colonial Atlantic to northern Europe; it is also embedded within the noble savage paradigm itself insofar as the image effectively erases non-European history. The noble savage can function as a stand-in for nature only because a prior conceptual evacuation of history has already taken place. To see the noble savage as primarily "natural" is to foreclose the possibility of a non-European historicity; it is to abstract non-Europeans into a people without history.[28] The Rousseauian paradigm is distinctively modern then, in that like the Hegelian model of History—with a capital H—it was written over the Hispanic colonial Atlantic. To the extent that *Don Alvaro* has been read within a Rousseauian framework, interpretations of the work continue to participate in this thought-structure. Such readings rightly engage an important stratum of meaning, to be sure; but in doing so without reflecting on the cultural geopolitics of Rousseau's dominance or without recognizing the deeply ideological nature of the figure of the noble savage itself, they inadvertently replicate the ideology of modern European colonialism within contemporary critical discourse. One cannot make Alvaro a marker of nature without noting the way in which such a positioning erases colonial history. To read *Don Alvaro* primarily through Rousseau is to mark it as "modern" and "European" rather than "colonial" and "Hispanic"; it is also to mute the other intertext we have considered—the Inca Garcilaso de Vega—a personage who not by coincidence is known precisely for having transmitted indigenous history to European readers. Indeed, if the noble savage is a figure for the evacuation of history from the non-European, the Inca Garcilaso is a figure of its inscription. To the extent that one figure has eclipsed the other in contemporary analyses, the historical expulsion of coloniality from the concept of modernity continues to structure critical inquiry to this day.

It is worth noting, however, that in contrast to this interpretive legacy, *Don Alvaro* may in fact contain a largely unheeded invitation to embrace a more hybridized conception of the modern. The issues we considered at the beginning of this chapter—liberal modernization, prosaic disenchantment, and the sense of diminished subjective possibility—are inextricably linked in this work to those questions we have taken up in the latter portions—that is, Alvaro's racial identity, historical meanings, and his symbolic resonance in the context of decolonization. Significantly, spheres of inquiry that have tended to be separated analytically are fused to one another in Saavedra's work: The protagonist is both a Rousseauian noble savage *and* an echo of the Inca Garcilaso de la Vega, and in this regard the play brings into visibility what more traditional narratives of the modern have tended to occlude. Rather than separating modernity and coloniality, it represents them as two sides of the same coin. As a sign of romantic subjectivity, Alvaro is a harbinger of modern sensibilities; as a mestizo indiano, he is a reminder of modernity's roots in empire and colonialism. In short, he is an example of the plural histories that necessarily impinge on the modern subject.

Strange Liberties

The overlapping frameworks of liberal modernity, empire, and coloniality that we have considered also help to make clearer the ideological parameters within which the more attractive, utopian impulses of Don Alvaro operate. Although easily overlooked in discussions of the problem of destiny, *Don Alvaro* was for its day a powerful vehicle of social critique. The play scandalized audiences, not only because of its formal innovations but also because of the latent political content of its indictment of Spanish society. At the heart of Saavedra's critical project is the tacit affirmation of two key values of nineteenth-century liberalism: freedom and equality. Indeed, the force of destiny in this work is often simply another name for the denial of such ideals. As we have already seen, what the Calatravas insistently refuse is Alvaro's equality, and his freedom—his sense of possibility—is progressively muffled over the course of the play. Freedom and equality are in this regard the affirmative underside of Saavedra's ethico-political denunciation; they are the assumed values from which his trenchant critique of Spanish society is launched. Closer scrutiny of the articulation of these ideals in the play, however, reveals that their scope is narrower than might initially be imagined. Just as Tediato's compassionate identification with Lorenzo in Cadalso's *Noches lúgubres* was ideologically conditioned, freedom and equality in *Don Alvaro* are also conditioned by the ideological limits of nineteenth-century liberalism.

Such limits become apparent if one begins to consider the representation of Alvaro's pain in relation to the suffering of those around him. A review of Leonor's trajectory over the course of the play, for example, makes clear that she is as much a victim of fortune's injustice as her beloved is. A witness to her father's death at the hands of her beloved (Act I), she is disowned by her family and persecuted by her brothers. She turns to a life of harsh, ascetic reclusion in the hermitage at Los Angeles (Act II), but before the play's end, circumstances force her to break her vow of isolation. She rushes out of the hermitage to aid a dying man whom she recognizes as her brother. In response to her aid, the moribund Alfonso curses her and then fatally wounds her; she dies with her beloved Alvaro in sight (Act V). Despite these myriad torments, however, Leonor's suffering is made a mere correlate to the story of Alvaro's pain. While the parallels between her trajectory and Alvaro's are clear, her story is accorded far less stage time than his: After the second act she literally vanishes from the play until her brief appearance at the end of Act V, and in accordance with a longstanding history of representation, even when she is on stage she is never represented as a fully autonomous subject (Kirkpatrick, *Las Románticas*, 118–19). In addition, her death is ultimately indexed not to her own experience but to Alvaro's tragedy. Her murder is positioned as fate's culminating blow against *him*. If injustice manifests itself as the denial of freedom and equality, *Don Alvaro* reflects the extent to which historically these key liberal values were accorded almost exclusively to men. Leonor's suffering, like her life, is represented as a supplement to Alvaro's.[29]

The scope of freedom and equality, however, was also curtailed by means of the institution of private property itself. Throughout the nineteenth century, even the most liberal constitutions limited their conception of legal subjects to property-holding men.[30] Property was a precondition for full participation in national life, and the traces of this ideological structure are not difficult to identify in *Don Alvaro*. Indeed, property seems to underpin Alvaro's claim to equality all along; his wealth and nobility, although initially unrecognized, are intimated throughout the play, and Alfonso's final rebuff of the protagonist is set up as the most egregious of insults precisely because it takes place as audience members discover what they have suspected all along: that Alvaro is in fact a wealthy noble. The height of injustice in *Don Alvaro*—the intolerable affront—is thus to deny freedom and equality to another man of property and stature. In order to appreciate the ideological maneuver at work here, one need only note that Saavedra's ending would have had far less power if Alfonso had discovered, for example, that Alvaro was in fact a commoner. Insofar as property was often synonymous with happiness itself within liberal ideology, it is no coincidence that the ultimate affront to Don Alvaro should be linked to his material wealth. For nineteenth-century audiences Alfonso's racist repudiation of Alvaro would most likely have been an outrage not in and of itself but because it violated the tacit equality presumed to correspond to honorable men of property.

Analysis of the symbolic status of property in *Don Alvaro*, however, is not fully exhausted by noting that the protagonist is in fact wealthy and noble. There is also another category of property that makes a fleeting appearance in this play. It is a class of property that was common to imperialism, colonialism, and modern liberalism, a form of property that was also forgotten by the traditional, celebratory tale of the modern. I am referring to that habitual form of nineteenth-century property that happened to be a human being: the slave. To be sure, the evocation of the historical institution of slavery in the context of *Don Alvaro* may initially seem puzzling, for it is not an explicit object of reflection in the play. Its presence in the work, however, offers an additional, fascinating glimpse at the ideological limits within which freedom and equality were conceived by most Spanish nineteenth-century liberals. Before turning to the textual marker of this presence in the play, it will be useful to recall several of the key moments in the history of slavery in Spain.

At the time of *Don Alvaro*'s debut in 1835 slavery remained legal throughout Spain and its colonies. Debates within Spanish liberalism had focused on the subject from the time of the Cortes at Cádiz, but abolitionist voices remained in the minority.[31] The Fernandine years witnessed an 1817 treaty with Britain that began to restrict Spanish participation in the African slave trade, but for the most part the absolutist crown allied itself with slave interests. As liberalism took firmer root in the 1830s, the question of slavery was fused with a foreign policy designed to protect Spain's remaining colonial possessions, particularly the revenues flowing from a booming slave economy in Cuba and Puerto Rico. Spanish governments generally pursued a course of incremental change as part of a strategy to delay outright abolition. Spain would outlaw slavery within its European territory—but not the colonies—in 1837. An additional law approved in 1845 outlawed the African slave trade definitively while protecting the institution—and its perpetuation via offspring—in the colonies. Abolitionist pressure did not gain significant social traction within Spain until the 1860s, with the creation of the Sociedad Abolicionista Española in 1865 and the subsequent establishment of newspapers such as *El Abolucionista* (1866). Nevertheless, bolstered by powerful colonial interests, slavery in the Spanish colonies would remain legal well after the Revolution of 1868. It was abolished in Puerto Rico under the first republic, in 1873; it was not dismantled in Cuba until 1880–1886.[32] For most of *Don Alvaro's* 1835 viewers, African slavery, while perhaps debated in certain intellectual circles, would still have belonged to the realm of the ordinary.

It is with this sense of the historically ordinary that I would like to return briefly to the *costumbrista* scenes with which the play opens. The stage represents a watering stand on the outskirts of Seville; a military official, a colorful street-dweller or *majo*, a Cervantine gypsy girl, a canon, and several other inhabitants of the city chat with one another while Tío Paco, the owner of the establishment, serves them their afternoon refreshments. They are about to make a discovery that will set fortune's wheel in motion on its inexorable course to Alavaro's suicide. Tío Paco notes that for several days he has observed Alvaro exit the city each evening to meet with a servant who goes before him with two horses. A townsperson adds that he has seen the two returning to Seville with exhausted horses during the early morning hours. The water vendor then announces that on that very afternoon he has witnessed the servant pass with not two, but three horses. The canon departs to warn the marquis of Don Alvaro's plans. A causal chain leading to Alvaro's death has begun, and its first link has been the image of a servant, a servant who as Tío Paco's words make clear, is of African descent:

> Hace tres días que a media tarde pasa [. . .] un negro con dos caballos. [. . .]
> Esta tarde ya ha pasado el negro, y hoy no llevaba dos caballos sino tres. (88)

> [For three days a black man has passed in the middle of the afternoon { . . . }
> with two horses. { . . . } The black man has already passed this afternoon, and
> today he was not leading two but three horses.]

Saavedra does not of course feel the need to indicate the status of this black servant any further. He belongs to the realm of the ordinary, and in both the Madrid of 1835 and the play's fictional setting in the late eighteenth century, what was ordinary was for this man to be a slave.

We suddenly confront a profound historical irony. Don Alvaro, emblem of subjective mystery in an increasingly prosaic world, symbol of poetic possibility, the paradigmatic mestizo, noble savage, Inca Garcilaso de la Vega, image of colonial Spanish America, quintessential victim of injustice, vehicle of impassioned social critique; this Don Alvaro is also in all likelihood a slaveholder. To confront this contradiction is not only to recall that the practice of slavery did not disappear with the advent of liberal modernity; it is also to grapple once more with a modern structure of feeling not unlike Tediato's in *Noches lúgubres*. It is to note how, just beyond the modern subject's own alienated pain, there is often a laboring other whose suffering is eclipsed by the more visible anguishes of the self, in this case Alvaro's romantic self.

In Cadalso's work it became apparent that Tediato had transmuted Lorenzo's very different, material suffering into the image of his own emotional pain. Suffering in Saavedra's play maintains a similar relationship to the figure of the slave. For if destiny represents the denial of individual freedom in an abstract, philosophical sense, slavery is the de facto legal and social mechanism that materially realized such a denial in practice. It is the history, as it were, that underlies *Don Alvaro*'s more philosophical meditations on the possibilities of freedom. Even if the slave did not make an appearance in Saavedra's play, as a historical institution that was contemporary to the play's debut, slavery would nevertheless haunt the work's interrogation of freedom and equality. To juxtapose liberal freedom with the institution of slavery is thus not only to come to terms with yet another historical thread that comprises the tapestry of the modern, it is also to grasp the profoundly contradictory nature of modernity as an historical formation. It is to find historical oppression still palpitating within the heart of freedom's ideal. As we shall see in the following chapter, the experience of such contradictions—an acute awareness of the historical limits within which ideals such as freedom and equality are in fact realized—is itself one of the properties of romantic discourse in Spain.

CHAPTER 4

Late Larra, or Death as Critique

On the evening of 13 February 1837—not quite two years after the opening of *Don Alvaro*—Mariano José de Larra, one the most noted essayists of Madrid's burgeoning newspaper world, put a revolver to his head, pulled the trigger, and successfully committed what would become the most famous suicide in Spanish literary history. The representation of suicide—from Tediato's macabre ideations in *Noches lúgubres* to the climactic, recriminating leap into the abyss of *Don Alvaro*—seemed to have crossed the notoriously porous romantic threshold between art and life, putting an end to both for Larra. Two days later, the journalist's burial, a secular funeral charged with political significance, drew some of the most celebrated romantic figures of the day. Among them, a young José Zorrilla, the future author of *Don Juan Tenorio*, made his literary debut in Madrid by reciting an elegy at Larra's tomb: "A la desgraciada memoria del joven literato Mariano José de Larra" [To the tragic memory of the young man of letters Mariano José de Larra].[1]

Following the rhetorical conventions of elegiac poetry, Zorrilla attempted to come to terms with sudden loss by offering a rudimentary narrative interpretation of Larra's final act. He thus imagined that the essayist "miró en el tiempo el porvenir vacío / vacío ya de ensueños y de gloria / y se entregó a ese sueño sin memoria / que nos lleva a otro mundo a despertar" [gazed through time at the empty future, / empty of dreams and of glory, / and he delivered himself to that dream without memory / that takes us to another world to awaken] (Urrutia, 401). The press too attempted to understand the suicide by situating it within the broader context of a debased, culpable world. Jacinto de Salas y Quiroga, for example, wrote of Larra in the 15 February issue of the *Revista Nacional* that "esa flor no pudo arraigarse en un mundo corrompido" [that flower was unable to take root in a corrupted world] (cited by Escobar, "Canonización"). Although more conservative pens would counter by reading the suicide as a moral lesson on the dangers of passionate romantic excesses, the lasting legacy of Larra's death would be a narrative of liberal martyrdom.[2] If the famous journalist had pulled the trigger—the story would come to suggest—it was Spain that had loaded the gun and guided his hand. More specifically, it was the forces of reaction, tradition, and cultural stagnation—in short, Spanish backwardness—that had extinguished Larra's sense of a future. The preeminent romantic cultural critic had died, one might conclude, because Spain had not been modern enough.

The fact that Larra's suicide was immediately imbued with this broader social significance, even if its most immediate cause had been the definitive end to a love affair, speaks to the power of suicide as a signifying act that paradoxically transcends its notoriously individual locus of action.[3] Perhaps because its finality carries within it the threatening image of the end of meaning, death is rarely allowed to be itself by those left in the wake of its passing. As the existentialist philosophical tradition has repeatedly taught—from Heidegger, to Blanchot, to Agamben, for example—significance swirls around death's black hole with a desperate density rivaled only perhaps by the life-affirming energy that the mature Freud would come to call Eros. For the living, it seems, death and the imperative to create meaning have never been far apart. As the preceding paragraphs suggest by recalling the narratives that Larra's suicide immediately engendered, and as the same paragraphs themselves exemplify by in effect retelling the story of Larra's suicide, the potential nothingness of death is one of the more powerful progenitors of that particular kind of meaning-making we call narrative.[4]

If death and narrative have long been bound by an uneasy sort of intimacy, however, what is particularly striking about those narratives that grapple with suicide is how often they turn for answers to the social world that the deceased has left behind. Because the fabric of the self is in part woven with social and historical threads, suicide has a paradoxically collective resonance, despite its initial guise as a compellingly individual, even solipsistic, act. As Emile Durkheim observed, "the victim's acts which at first seem to express only his personal temperament are really the supplement and prolongation of a social condition which they express externally" (299). In this passage Durkheim makes explicit what Tediato had already intimated and what the spectacle of Don Alvaro's death had staged, for he suggests that selfhood is, in the end, not quite as autonomous an affair as liberal modernity would have one believe.[5] The ostensibly closed circuit of self turning on self is revealed to be deeply social after all, for suicide is an act whose very realization signals that something is wrong with the social world it renounces. As we have observed in previous chapters, suicide is an exit that indicts.

The object of suicidal recrimination in Larra, however, is far more complex than the image of an intransigent, traditionalist Spain posited by the martyrdom narrative and the "two Spains" framework that long sustained it. As such thinking has slowly been displaced by less Manichean conceptions of nineteenth-century Spanish culture, the story of liberalism-as-victim that has so often attached itself to the image of Larra has begun to yield to a more nuanced tale. It is a narrative in which not only reactionary traditionalism but also the modern liberal world—a world that had clearly begun to emerge over the course of the 1830s—stand equally accused by Larra's death. In the wake of studies by Escobar (*Orígenes*) and Kirkpatrick (*Larra*), among others, the image of a highly self-conscious, ideologically complex, and deeply contradictory writer now competes with the earlier, mystified Larra of liberal political hagiography. Consequently, if Larra's work and untimely death have been read as a condemnation of Spanish political and cultural inertia, they have also begun to be understood as one of the more perspicacious Spanish romantic critiques of liberal modernity itself. To read Larra in this light involves dispelling the aura of self-sacrificing liberal heroism that has historically accompanied his image, and it requires entertaining the notion that the very modernity Larra is reputed to have championed may have had as much of a role in the author's death as did the forces of reaction and tradition. Similarly, lest it merely replicate the terms of Larra's critique, analysis of his late writing ought to remain attuned to the ideological parameters that circumscribed his thought. While Larra crafted one of the more powerful demystifications of nineteenth-century modernity in Spain, his thinking, as we shall see, was itself subject to a series of ideological limits, limits related to participating in the very structures of modernity he would decry.[6]

This chapter will attempt to make the case for such a reading by focusing on the so-called "tetralogy of Larra's pessimistic articles" (Ullman, 34). These are "Necrología. Exequias del Conde de Campo Alange" [Obituary.

Obsequies for the Count of Campo Alange], "Horas de Invierno" [Winter Hours], "El Día de Difuntos de 1836" [All Souls' Day, 1836], and "La Noche Buena de 1836" [Christmas Eve, 1836]. Among Larra's most famous pieces, these essays have aptly been understood as representing a kind of labyrinthine dead end in the well-known trajectory of Larra's psycho-political development. In them, the author's enlightenment faith in the liberal project—evident in earlier essays such as "Literatura"—gives way to concern and uncertainty about the means and ends of liberalism, and this skepticism in turn cedes to a highly subjective, quasi-solipsistic, mal du siècle pessimism that intensifies over the course of 1836 (Kirkpatrick, *Larra*, 285–88, "Spanish Romanticism" 459–71). In addition, as Larra's satirical gaze turns inward, the social reality that was the object of his famously acerbic commentary appears to be subsumed into an everexpansive self. To recall Paul Ilie's words, "insofar as social reality corresponded to or mirrored his inner incongruities, it produced an integrated political nightmare whose center was an anguished, modern liberal" ("Larra's," 166). The articles consequently bear witness, as many have noted, to a crisis of bourgeois liberal conscience, and it is the realm of conscience and subjectivity that will once more be a fundamental object of analysis.

At the same time, I will pay particular attention to Larra's representation of the dead and the dying. The image of death is a key rhetorical device in Larra's late articles, and much of the force of the critique Larra mounts stems from the uncanny power with which the invocation of death in his writing became invested following his suicide. By means of a fascinating, posthumous semiosis, the trope of death in these essays and the fact of Larra's subsequent suicide were seemingly fused. Death in his essays was retroactively accorded psycho-biographical significance, while the act of suicide was imbued with a quasi-essayistic, tropological quality. In effect, the images of death in Larra's late writing prepared the way for his suicide itself to be understood as a socially symbolic act; that is, as a kind of writing. Even today, one cannot return to his late work without noting its eerily adumbrative overtones. Similarly, the biographical fact of Larra's suicide has accorded such weight to the images of death that preside over the most famous essays of 1836 that it has become difficult to read them as a merely thematic concern. They are commonly understood as the chronicle of a death foretold (Romero Tobar, "Estudio," x). The analyses that follow will consequently explore the ways in which death signifies in Larra's late work. While keeping this double status of death in view, I hope to make clearer the cultural and sociopolitical meanings of the representation of death in each of these essays in order to bring into focus the relationship between lifelessness and modernity in Larra's writings. If death encodes a critique of modernity, the aim of the pages that follow will be to make the terms and ideological limits of Larra's pained cultural analyses clearer.

An Obituary for Transcendence

Just over a year before the news of Larra's death echoed through the pages of Madrid's newspapers, Larra himself would publicly grapple with a sense of loss not unlike the feeling his own passing was destined to provoke among his peers. A close friend, José Negrete, Count of Campo Alange, was dead at the age of twenty-four. A member of the segment of Spain's aristocracy that had embraced liberalism, Negrete had volunteered his services in the Ejército del Norte, which the national government had organized in order to break the Carlist siege of Bilbao. The count was wounded in the chest during the initial skirmishes that preceded the battle, and he expired on 12 December 1835. His death was commemorated in Madrid, at the church of Santo Tomás, on 15 January 1836, and Larra's "Necrología. Exequias del Conde de Campo Alange" [Necrology. Obsequies for the Count of Campo Alange] appeared in the pages of *El Español* the following day.

Steeped in the rhetoric of romantic obituary, Larra's essay initially appears to carry out several of the conventional functions of the form: It openly mourns Negrete's death, it sketches his biography, and it attempts to ascribe meaning to his life and his passing. As is so often the case with Larra's writing, however, the author does not long remain within the bounds of generic convention, for from the outset he signals that the article will be more than a meditation on the death of the Count of Campo Alange. The essay opens with an epigraph that symbolically announces that the ways of the world will be as much an object of reflection for Larra as the death of his friend. Adapted from a poem by Nicasio Alvarez Cienfuegos, the epigraph reads: "Vive el malvado, atormentado, y vive, / y un siglo entero de maldad completa / y el honrado mortal [. . .] / nace y deja de ser" [The evil man lives, tormented, and he lives, / and an entire century of evil he completes, / and the honorable mortal { . . . } / is born and ceases to be] (620).[7] In effect, these verses and the moral contrast they posit chart the two poles between which Larra's essay will subsequently oscillate. Commentary on the passing of an "honorable mortal" and critical engagement with the "century of evil" will be two sides of the same mournful coin; obituary—Larra seems to announce—will at the same time be a vehicle for sociopolitical critique.

To the extent that, as readers of Nietzsche will recall, the question of power never lurks far beyond the rhetoric of good and evil, one might reasonably suspect that the moral dichotomy that Larra initially draws from Cienfuego's verses is rooted in a more fundamental political conflict. It is not difficult to surmise, for example, that Negrete, who died fighting for the liberal state, is the implied referent of the "honorable man" in Larra's citation; and it would consequently stand to reason that the "century of evil" might correspond to the count's historical antagonists, the forces of unmodern, reactionary Spain as represented by the Carlists. Yet one need not read very long in order to realize that the terrain Larra traverses in the essay does not correspond to the map he appears to offer readers in the epigraph. It is not the death of liberalism that Larra grafts onto the figure of Negrete, nor is it the traditionalism of Carlist Spain that the essay ultimately decries. As we shall see shortly, the death of the Count of Campo Alange represents the disappearance of something more fundamental, something that for Larra is ultimately even more heart-wrenching than the death of his friend.

In order to comprehend more fully the nature of this void, which will be our primary object of inquiry in what follows, it will be useful to review the article with a view to identifying the socially symbolic dimensions of the representations of the count and of the world of his survivors. Already in the first lines that follow the epigraph, Larra marks the latter domain as a place of unremitting pain. "Hace días ya"—he writes—"que se consumó el infausto acontecimiento que nos pone la pluma en la mano; pero por una parte el sentimiento ha apagado nuestra voz, y por otra no temíamos que el tiempo, pasando, amortiguase nuestro dolor" [Days have passed since the ill-fated event that puts the pen in our hand took place; but on one hand sentiment has extinguished our voice, and on the other we did not fear that time, in passing, would diminish our pain] (620). If this initial formulation can readily be understood in terms of those early moments of grief, when the intensity of suffering eclipses language and with it any sense of a future, Larra's certainty concerning the permanence of pain also seems to hint at the external presence of suffering as an immutable feature of his social world's landscape. As was the case with Tediato in *Noches lúgubres*, while pain is clearly indexed to the loss of a loved one, it cannot be fully explained within such a framework. The *in valle lacrimarum* topos with which the essay initially seems to flirt quickly takes on additional, more novel meanings.

Indeed, as Larra begins to describe the ritual commemoration of the count, the social dimensions of his pain become apparent. Behind the tribute to the deceased, he finds the image of an everyday world of vain indifference: "sus deudos y sus amigos, y la patria con ellos, han tributado al amigo y al valiente el último homenaje que la vanidad humana rinde después de muerto al mérito, que en vida suele para oprobio suyo desconocer" [his relatives and his friends, and the nation with them, have paid their friend, the valiant one, the last homage that human vanity posthumously renders merit, which to its shame, it tends to overlook in life] (620). The homage, while deeply moving, is thus at the same time a reminder of an everyday world remarkably devoid of such concerns. Recognition of the extraordinary is itself revealed as the exception to a more ordinary, secular, morally suspect state of affairs, and this contrast is accentuated as Larra begins to reflect on the religious context of the commemoration.

Just as the tribute to Negrete brings quotidian indifference to the extraordinary into view by way of contrast, for Larra the invocation of the sacred during the ceremony remits to an increasingly nonreligious weltanschauung in which the metaphysical is no longer capable of assuaging earthly anguish:

> En buena hora el ánimo que se aturde en las alegrías del mundo, en buena hora no crea en Dios y en otra vida el que en los hombres cree, y en esta vida que le forjan; empero mil veces desdichado sobre toda desdicha quien no viendo nada aquí sino caos y mentira, agotó en su corazón la fuente de la esperanza, porque para ése no hay cielo en ninguna parte y hay infierno en cuanto le rodea. (620)

> [Happy is the soul that is bedazzled by the joys of the world, may he who believes in men and in this life that is forged for him happily not believe in

God and the other life; but a thousand times wretched above all wretched-
ness is he who, seeing nothing here but chaos and lies, has exhausted the font
of hope in his heart, because for him there is no heaven anywhere and there
is hell in everything that surrounds him.]

In such a world, the rituals of the older religious tradition are heard with
either a lingering sense of regret or with a fearful sense of foreboding:

El rumor compasado y misterioso del cántico que la religión eleva al Criador
en preces por el que fue, el melancólico son del instrumento de cien voces
que atruena el templo llenándole de santo terror, el angustioso y sublime
De profundis [. . .] son algo al oído del desgraciado cuando, devueltos los
sublimes ecos por las paredes de la casa del Señor, vienen a retumbar en el
corazón, como suena el remordimiento en la conciencia, como retumba en
el pecho del miedoso la señal del próximo peligro. (621)

[The mysterious rhythmic sound of the canticle that religion lifts up to the
Creator in prayers for he who passed; the melancholy sound of the hundred-
voiced instrument that thunders through the temple, filling it with holy
terror; the anguished and sublime *De profundis* { . . . } are something to the
ear of the wretched listener when, reverberating along the walls of the house
of the Lord, their sublime echoes resound through his heart, as regret rever-
berates through conscience, as the sign of impending danger resounds in the
fearful man's breast.]

At the same time, religious doubt leaves Larra with a disquieting existential question concerning Negrete's—and implicitly, his own—destiny. "A
los pies del Altísimo"—he writes—"no es ya la opinión de los hombres a
quien recurre el alma en juicio. [. . .] ¿Y no ha de haber un Dios y un
refugio para aquellos pocos que el mundo arroja de sí como arroja los
cadáveres el mar?" [At the feet of the Highest, it is no longer to the opinion of men that the soul in judgment turns. { . . . } And shouldn't there be
a God and a refuge for those few that the world hurls away from itself as
the sea hurls out cadavers?] (621).

But what could account for such an open expression of religious
doubt from the capital of "Catholic Spain" in the 1830s? For readers ac-
quainted with the traditional macrohistorical narrative of secularization,
the relationship of such passages to the idea of the modern is not especially difficult to apprehend, for these examples participate in the telltale

dialectic of disenchantment/reenchantment that since Weber's work have habitually been taken to characterize Western rationalization. In Larra's article, a rationally disenchanted world plagued by metaphysical doubt agonizes next to a world of new secular deities—that is, the quasi-religious, "humanist sublime" experienced by Larra's hypothetical happy believer in mankind—and an exacerbated sense of anguish ensues when even the new gods and their attendant cults begin to wither away.[8]

Over the course of its five opening paragraphs, Larra's essay thus moves almost seamlessly from the death of the count to the troubling image of a modern landscape haunted by the death of God. The void with which the essay grapples is inextricably linked to those displacements that accompany the secular world of liberal modernity:

> The shift from primary preoccupation with the superempirical to the empirical; from transcendent entities to naturalism; from other-worldly goals to this-worldly possibilities; [. . .] from speculative and "revealed" knowledge to practical concerns [. . .]; from an acceptance of [. . .] charismatic manifestations of the divine to the systematic, structured, planned and routinized management of the human. (Wilson, 14)

To the extent that Larra's essay can be positioned *within* such a history, we once more confront the shortcomings of the metageography that would posit an absent, defective, or merely imported modernity in Spain. To a presumed "not modern enough," Larra's "Exequias" seems to counter with "see what the modern has already done." Indeed, an oft-quoted passage from another article, "Un periódico nuevo" [A new newspaper], makes clear the extent to which Larra was aware of the modernity of contemporary times:

> Los adelantos materiales han ahogado de un siglo a esta parte las disertaciones metafísicas, las divagaciones científicas; y la razón, como se clama por todas partes, ha conquistado la imaginación. [. . .] Los hechos han desterrado las ideas. Los periódicos, los libros. La prisa, la rapidez, diré mejor, es el alma de nuestra existencia. [. . .] Las diligencias y el vapor han reunido a los hombres de todas las distancias; desde que el espacio ha desaparecido en el tiempo, ha desaparecido tembién en el terreno. (293)

> [In the span of a century, material advances have drowned metaphysical dissertations, academic rambling; and as people shout everywhere, reason

has conquered imagination. { . . . } Facts have exiled ideas. Newspapers have displaced books. Rushing, or better said, speed, is the soul of our existence. { . . . } Stagecoaches and steamboats have brought men together from all distances; from the moment space has disappeared into time, it has also disappeared in the land.]

Larra's work is, in this sense, a useful reminder of those insights we considered in previous chapters: that the rational "disenchantment of the world" had deep roots within Spanish history itself, from imperial Spain's bureaucratic management of the world-system during the early modern era, to the achievements of its own Enlightenment, to the impact of its liberal revolution and reform. His work makes clear that the perception of more accelerated processes of modernization elsewhere did not by any means hinder Spaniards from feeling the full effects of the modern at home. Among the romantics of his generation Larra was arguably the writer most keenly aware of the differences between Spain and modern Europe; and yet as we have begun to see, he was also extraordinarily attuned to the alienating effects that modernity itself had begun to wreak within Spain. The drama of "Spanish difference" did not by any means inhibit responses to the drama of Spanish modernity itself.

Moreover, if one passes from the still relatively abstract, macrohistorical terrain of rationalization and disenchantment to consideration of the more local geotemporal scale of Spain in the 1830s, the immediacy of the question of modernization within Spanish culture becomes apparent. More than a problem within the philosophy of history, secularization was, for Larra and his readers, a very specific, decidedly contemporary political, social, and economic agenda. The post-Fernandine years (1833–1843) were characterized by a fundamental restructuring of the relationship between church and state:

> Between the death of Ferdinand VII on September 1833 and the departure into exile in July 1843 of General Espartero [. . .] a battered ecclesiastical organization collapsed before a final liberal assault. Institutions, functions, and intellectual assumptions that had long sustained the Church disappeared before a new wave of reforms. [. . .] The kingdom remained officially Catholic even in the most radical phase of the extended liberal revolution. [. . .] But in this still confessional State, monks and friars were murdered, priests assaulted, churches and monasteries sacked, and dioceses left without bish-

ops. [. . .] The issue between 1833 and 1843 was not Catholicism or anti-Catholicism. No politician suggested the separation of Church and State. [. . .] [But] liberal opinion demanded that the Church adjust to the needs of a changing society dominated by an emerging bourgeoisie, a society secular in its concerns and committed to the doctrines of economic individualism and human progress. (Callahan, 146)

And it was precisely between September 1835 and May 1836, under the government of Juan Alvarez Mendizábal, that one of the more famous liberal disentailments of church properties in Spain was executed:

[Mendizábal's government] proceeded to complete the process initiated under Carlos IV and then accelerated by the Bonaparte regime and the liberal triennium of 1820–1823 by almost completely suppressing the male orders in Spain, opening the way to thoroughgoing *desamortización*—government confiscation and sale—of their properties. This virtually ended the life of these orders in Spain for the next fifteen years. (Payne, 83)

While *secularizar* retained its etymological meaning—"to make worldly"—by the mid-1830s the term also reflected the emergent economic basis of "worldliness" as understood by liberal reformers: When it came to ecclesiastic property, to secularize became synonymous with "to make salable, to transform into private property." The profound nature of this legal and economic recoding of the land as *private property*, which was underway as Larra was writing, cannot be overstated, for it was one of the pillars of the ideology of market-oriented economic change that accompanied liberal revolution and reform in Spain.[9] From the perspective of the culture of a waning Ancien Régime, it was as fundamental and radical a transformation as, for example, the legal construction of property as *anything else* would seem to be for the world of globalized capitalism today. It is consequently not difficult to appreciate just how pressing the question of religion and, more specifically, the question of its claims on public life would have been to the readers of Larra's "Exequias," for the spiritual anemia that comes into view in the essay is inextricable from the secularizing cultural machinery that accompanied liberal political economy. It is worth recalling that, only eleven years after Larra's death, Marx and Engels would famously characterize the emergent world of bourgeois modernity in the following terms: "[It] has drowned out the most heavenly ecstasies of religious fervour, of chivalrous enthusiasm, of philistine sentimentalism, in the icy water of egotistical calculation. It has resolved personal worth into exchange value" (*Economic*, 211). The crisis of faith on display in the "Exequias" is thus not simply a function of the individual religious doubts Larra may have entertained. It also is an index of the degree to which the authority of the Christian deity as the ultimate, traditional legitimizer of land tenure under the Ancien Régime was being structurally displaced by liberal economic reform. Catholic as the country might have remained officially, and riddled with shortcomings as its reforms were, when it came to economics, and particularly to the question of unproductive property controlled by the church, God was slowly ushered offstage.[10]

It was not simply religious authority, however, that was being modified by the emergent life-world of liberal modernity. As Marx and Engels suggest, it was also those modes of human comportment—chivalry, enthusiasm, sentimentalism—that aimed beyond the material contingencies of the everyday. Just as the disentailment of church properties dispelled ecclesiastic authority over the land, liberalism's emphasis on commerce and exchange—particularly in Spanish cities—began restructuring late-feudal social relations. From a vestigial world of titular obligations and allegiances slowly emerged a social order increasingly governed by relationships of economic interest. Liberal modernity thus ushered in, at the level of economic practice, a diminishment within human affairs of what might be termed the will to transcend, and it is precisely the decline of such modes of comportment that Larra laments in the death of the Count of Campo Alange. A correlate to the death of God, the death of heroism thus becomes a dominant motif throughout the essay, as Larra attempts to ascribe meaning to the count's passing. Refusing to call Negrete a hero because the word "hero" itself has, for Larra, become debased by its indiscriminate use in an unheroic age, he characterizes the count as follows:

> Era un joven que hizo por principios y por afición, por virtud y por nobleza de carácter, algo más que su deber; dio su vida y su hacienda por aquello por que otros se contentan en dar escándalo y voces. Amaba la libertad, porque él, noble y generoso, creyó que todos eran como él nobles y generosos; y amaba la igualdad, porque igual él al mejor, creía de buena fe que eran todos iguales a él. (622)

[He was a young man who, because of principles and inclination, because of virtue and nobility of character, did something more than his duty; he gave his life and his property for that to which others are happy to contribute scandals and argument. He loved liberty, because he, noble and generous, thought that like him others were noble and generous; and he loved liberty because, an equal to the best, he thought in good faith that all were equal to him.]

The series of abstract moral ideals incarnated in the count, along with the "algo más que" [something more than] that characterizes his actions, function as the image of everything that an increasingly modern, practical liberal world of 1830s Spain is not, and after reviewing key moments of Negrete's biography, Larra makes the socially symbolic meaning of the count's life explicit. In a characteristically sarcastic conclusion, the author observes:

Pero era justo; Campo Alange debía morir. ¿Qué le esperaba en la sociedad? Militar, no era insubordinado; a haberlo sido, las balas le hubieran respetado. Hombre de talento, no era intrigante. Liberal, no era vocinglero; literato, no era pedante; escritor, la razón y la imparcialidad presidían a sus escritos. ¡Qué papel podía haber hecho en tal caos y degradación! (623)

[But it was just; Campo Alange had to die. ¿What awaited him in society? Although a soldier, he wasn't insubordinate; had he been, the bullets would have spared him. Although a man of talent, he wasn't a schemer. Although a liberal, he was not loud-mouthed; although a man of letters, he was not a pedant; although a writer, reason and impartiality presided over his writing. What role could he have played in such chaos and degradation!]

Within this degraded chaotic world, physical death paradoxically becomes for Larra a refuge of sorts, and those who, like the count, die without seeing their liberal humanist hopes dissipate are imagined to have been spared from something far worse. In the closing lines of the essay he writes thus of Negrete:

En la vida le esperaba el desengaño, ¡la fortuna le ha ofrecido antes la muerte! Eso es morir viviendo todavía: pero ¡ay de los que le lloran, que entre ellos hay muchos a quienes no es dado elegir, y que entre la muerte y el desengaño tienen antes que pasar por éste que por aquella, que esos viven muertos y le envidian! (624)

[In life disillusion awaited him; fortune has offered him death first! That is to die while still living: but woe to those who grieve him, for among them are many who are not given a choice and who, between death and disillusion, must go through the latter before the former, for they are living dead and they envy him!]

This final image of the living dead is reminiscent of the earlier evocation of life-as-hell, and both images speak to the disenchantment—indeed the despair—that accompanied the emergence of a modern, increasingly secular, liberal world. As was the case with Tediato's beloved and Don Alvaro's various pursuits, death in this essay symbolically becomes a space of reprieve from a social milieu increasingly informed by the liberal principles of economic self-interest, calculation, and exchange. In addition to the vilified Carlist traditionalism readers might have expected, liberal modernity itself is also an object of Larra's mournful critique. The painful void figured by the count's passing is the result of the modern world.

If this is the case, however, an intriguing contradiction emerges from Larra's representation of the Count of Campo Alange, for readers cannot help but conclude that, as a combatant for the liberal state, Negrete sacrificed his life to the very sociopolitical and economic order that would undermine the values he heroically incarnated. Similarly, while Larra decries an increasingly postmetaphysical, disenchanted world as a kind of living hell, the disentailment of church properties—the practice that, perhaps more than any other, systematically stripped away the "godly" claims to the land by effectively turning church property into merchandise—paradoxically made the struggle against Carlism materially possible. It was largely with revenues from the *desamortización* that Mendizábal financed the war in which Negrete lost his life (Payne, 83). In this regard, Larra's critique of the emergent world of modern liberalism seems to be at odds with his defense of liberalism in the struggle against Carlism. As is often the case with Larra's late essays, readers confront a rather daunting conceptual impasse.

One might attempt to understand such contradictions as symptoms of fundamental ideological inconsistencies within Larra himself. If the heroism to which the author remains attached in the essay is in fact a marker of Negrete's privilege as a noble, and if the concept of the heroic, with its roots in the demiurgic, is unavoidably tangled up in the history of aristocratic life-worlds, the "Exequias" may reflect an unresolved ambivalence in Larra concerning the changing class structure that accompanied Spanish liberal revolution and reform. One might even interpret the essay as an example of an aristocratic sensibility within Larra that was ultimately incommensurable with his more egalitarian commitments. In such a reading, the contradictions in the "Exequias" would stem from Larra's inability to bid farewell fully to the aristocratic order.[11] His difficulty in imagining that part of Negrete's heroism could indeed have been a struggle for the obsolescence of his own heroic privilege would mark the ideological limit of Larra's liberalism.

Such an account, however, runs the risk of forgetting that by the 1830s "heroic idealism" and "crass materialism" could not easily be reduced to mere functions of class positions. Heroism was more than a simple placeholder for aristocracy, and the world of material interests was certainly not bound exclusively to a growing bourgeoisie. Negrete himself, an aristocrat fighting for liberalism, exemplifies the degree to which the categories of aristocracy and bourgeoisie do not ever fully account for the lived complexities of any given class position. Similarly, the nineteenth-century bourgeoisie's well-known imitations of aristocratic culture, along with the Spanish aristocracy's successful, almost seamless transition into the world of entrepreneurial capital, bear witness to the hybridized social identities that were created as bourgeois hegemony was slowly consolidated.[12] Against such a backdrop it is difficult to dismiss Larra's lament over the death of heroism as merely a case of more-or-less conflicted nostalgia for the waning life-worlds of the aristocracy. The count in Larra's "Exequias," like the beloved in *Noches lúgubres* or Inés in *Don Alvaro*, seems to represent something more complex, as does the contradiction he embodies.

To the extent that he is characterized precisely by his ability to see and act beyond determinate contingencies, the Count of Campo Alange reflects a kind of subjectivity that—to recall a formulation by Herbert Marcuse—"steps out of the network of exchange relationships and exchange values" and resists such values "by shifting the locus of the individual's realization from the domain of the performance principle and the profit motive to that of the inner resources of the human being: passion, imagination, conscience" (4). What Larra laments in the count's passing is, among other things, the diminishment of the realm of *subjective possibility* within the modern liberal world. Despite its emphasis on the individual, the model of the self that was promoted by liberal ideology was rather narrowly construed. "Liberal individualism," Nancy Rosenblum reminds, "is typically calculating, or accommodating, or it rests on rights; it is not heroic. Even when individualism becomes politicized and liberalism supports popular revolution or civil disobedience, the end in view is securing conditions for the regular pursuit of private happiness" (103).[13] It is for this reason perhaps that, even as the liberal state was struggling against a reactionary foe that he himself opposed, Larra could nevertheless mourn the symbolic death of the heroic under liberalism.

For numerous romantic sensibilities "even self-legislation and autonomous choice are cruelly limiting. Something is lost, not exhibited or gained, when infinite possibility gives way to the limitations of actuality" (Rosenblum, 50). While Larra's representation of Negrete does not fully replicate this sense of "infinite possibility," his characterization of the count as an "algo más que" [something more than], unbound by the contingencies of the actual—that is, the chaotic, corrupted world of Spanish liberalism in the 1830s—participates in a similar pattern of thinking. The figure of the count is in the end far closer to the "empty infinity" that Schiller saw as the basis of personality, for example, or to the "beautiful soul" of Hegel's *Phenomenology*, than one might initially suspect.[14] Thus, while there are undoubtedly traces of aristocratic privilege in the heroism whose passing Larra laments, there is also the latent, utopian image of a self that belongs neither to the symbolic order of the Ancien Régime nor to the discourses of liberal modernity, a self whose very ground is to be and act beyond the given.

Within such a framework, the contradiction that manifests itself in the "Exequias"—a liberal lament for the death of the transcendent—can be understood as belonging to liberal modernity as much as it does to Larra. And, contrary to a long interpretive history that would suggest otherwise, there is nothing essentially Spanish about this. It is the contradiction inherent in the notion of "liberal freedom" itself, a freedom that by the mid-1830s—in Spain and elsewhere—had already begun to be experienced as restrictive. Indeed, it is the sense that liberal freedom is *not free enough* that often lies just below the surface of those common antagonisms—the poetic versus the prosaic, the spiritual versus the material, the heroic versus the ordinary—that characterize much romantic rhetoric. Ultimately, such tensions reflect the more fundamental contradiction of a project of emancipation (from the Ancien Régime) that was already understood by many writers of Larra's generation as a new form of servitude (to the emergent modern bourgeois order). Each of Larra's late essays confronts this aporetic structure of the modernity of the early 1800s, and in each case, as we shall see, Larra's sense of profound loss, coupled with despair over the future, transforms his present into a kind of living death.

Dead Culture: Spain's Winter Hours

The next of the four essays we shall consider is perhaps the most anomalous, for unlike the articles with which it is usually coupled, its subject is not drawn from the world of religious ritual traditionally associated with Larra's late essays. For readers encountering the article for the first time in the pages of the 25 December 1836 edition of *El Español*, the essay's title, "Horas de invierno" [Winter Hours] would have immediately signaled something ostensibly less weighty: a book review. *Horas de invierno* was the title of a short-story anthology that had successfully been launched via subscription by the Madrid publisher Sancha earlier in the year.[15] Such collections were a relatively common, commercially successful form of publication, and this particular anthology had gathered together the work of some of the more popular short-fiction writers of the day, including Hoffman, Scott, Soulié, Victor Hugo, and Washington Irving. The editor and translator for the project was Eugenio de Ochoa, a well-known figure within Madrid's literary circles for his work as the director of the romantic periodical, *El Artista*.

Within this context, the assumption that Larra would evaluate Ochoa's work would not have been an unreasonable one, and the first lines of the essay, which begins with characteristically mixed praise, initially seem to confirm the expectation. "El editor de esta colección"—Larra writes— "tiene harto acreditado su buen gusto para que su publicación pudiera confundirse en el sinnúmero de otras del mismo género y que con títulos semejantes duermen en nuestras librerías" [The editor of this collection has had his good taste amply accredited for his publication to be confused with the countless others of the same genre and similar titles that sleep away in our bookstores] (599). Almost immediately after this observation, however, "Horas de invierno" and the pretense of a book review dissolve into a series of more general considerations. They are thoughts that range from the politics of translation, to power relations within Europe, to the problem of literary culture in Spain.[16] The shift takes place by the third sentence of the essay, in which translation, the activity into which Ochoa "se ha lanzado cuerpo y alma" [has thrown himself body and soul], is deftly transformed into a collective, national problematic. As a widely practiced phenomenon, translation of the literature of modern Europe is for Larra a symptom of national decline: "Esto es un efecto natural de nuestra decadencia, del poco premio, del ningún estímulo, del peligro, del escalón que ocupa, en fin, en las jerarquías europeas la sociedad española" [This is a natural effect of our decadence, of the scarce esteem, of the null encouragement, of the danger, in short, of the rung that Spanish society occupies within the European hierarchies] (599). With this gesture, the translation of northern European culture becomes for Larra a trope of Spain's creative impotence, the image of its subordination to modern Europe; and with the exception of a brief return to Ochoa at the end of the article, "Horas de invierno" will become an extended meditation on the very subject that was our point of departure in the opening chapter of this book; that is, the implications of Spain's peripheral status within the cultural politics of modern Europe.

Although the article has traditionally been marshaled as *the* emblematic nineteenth-century lament over Spanish nonmodernity—it is frequently positioned as a precursor of sorts to the so-called Generation of 1898—analysis of several of the essay's key passages suggests that Larra's famous plaint is in fact part of a much more complex response to modern Europe's cultural geopolitics. Before reaching Larra's climactic conclusion that "escribir en Madrid es llorar" [to write in Madrid is to weep] (602), the essay moves rather deliberately through (a) an overview of recent historical events in Spain, (b) a rudimentary philosophy of history, and (c) a thesis about the relationship between power and culture. While the trope of writing-as-weeping has arguably become the most famous and highly reproduced image associated with Larra's oeuvre, the discursive context from which the image emerges has received considerably less scrutiny. It will consequently be useful to review several of the essay's earlier moments in order to grasp more fully the oft-overlooked meanings that accompany writing/weeping in "Horas de invierno." As was the case with the "Exequias," we shall see that Larra's mournful plaint is much more than the straightforward lament it appears to be.

Following the essay's introductory comments, Larra dwells on Spain's imperial past and on its history since the late eighteenth century. He observes that, dispossessed of its power, the only treasures to which Spain can lay claim in the modern age are the ruins of its former splendor. Larra notes, however, that even such vestiges are scarcely recognized by a public for whom ruins have taken on the invisible colors of everyday life:

> Nada nos queda nuestro sino el polvo de nuestros antepasados, que hollamos con planta indiferente; segunda Roma en recuerdos antiguos y en nulidad presente, tropezamos en nuestra marcha adondequiera que nos volvamos con rastros de grandeza pasada, con ruinas gloriosas, si puede haber ruinas que hagan honor a un pueblo; pero así tropezamos con ellas como tropieza el imbécil moscardón con el diáfano cristal, que no acierta a distinguir de la atmósfera que le rodea. (599)

> [Nothing of ours is left but the dust of our forebears, which we trample with an indifferent sole; a second Rome in ancient memories and in current nullity, wherever we turn on our march we stumble upon traces of past greatness, upon glorious ruins, if there can be ruins that honor a people; but we stumble upon them as the stupid fly crashes into diaphanous crystal, which it is unable to distinguish from the atmosphere that surrounds it.]

Decadence, the dust of ancestors, rubble, and even the fly, with its latent association to carrion, suggest that, viewed from an impassive present, Spain's past is dead, not only in the sense that it is irretrievable but also—and perhaps more importantly—because its relation to contemporary times is scarcely recognizable. The past is lifeless in the sense that it no longer informs a present that has been left to buzz about, seemingly bereft of any mooring. Significantly, this image of an inert past is the very antithesis of the vitalizing power of the past that is one of history's primary functions.[17] In addition, Larra notes that national pride—for him the catalyst of historical action—has also died: "Es demasiado cierto que sólo el orgullo nacional hace emprender y llevar a cabo cosas grandes a las naciones, y ese orgullo ha debido morir en nuestros pechos" [It is too true that only national pride makes nations take up and realize great things, and that pride must have died in our breasts] (599). Shorn of authentic historical life, for Larra Spain is both the plaything of greater powers—"juguete desde hace años de la intriga extranjera" [for many years a toy of foreign intrigue]—and the passive stage for others' conflicts—"aquí vienen los principios encontrados a darse el combate" [principles in conflict come here to battle it out] (599). A symbolically dead country has become the ground for the history of others.

The essay proceeds with three examples of the way that Spain has come to be what Larra calls "el *Bois de Boulogne* de los desafíos europeos" [the *Bois de Boulogne* of European duels] (599). The first is drawn from the Napoleonic Wars:

La Inglaterra, el gran cetáceo, el coloso del mar, necesitó medir sus fuerzas con el grande hombre, con el coloso de la tierra, y uno y otro exclamaron: "Nos falta terreno, ¿dónde reñiremos?." Y se citaron para España. Ventilada la cuestión, aniquilado el vencido, acudieron los amigos del vencedor y reclamaron la parte en el despojo. El huesped que había prestado su casa para la acerba entrevista reclamó siquiera el premio de su cooperación; y ¿qué le quedó? Lo que puede quedarle al campo de batalla: los cadáveres, el espectáculo de los buitres, y un letrero encima: "Aquí fue la riña." (599)

[England, the great cetacean, the colossus of the sea, had to measure its strengths against the great man, against the colossus of the land, and one and the other exclaimed: "We need terrain. Where shall we quarrel?" And they agreed to meet in Spain. Once the question had been settled and the vanquished had been annihilated, the friends of the victor came by and they demanded their part in the spoils. The host who had lent his house for the bitter meeting demanded some reward for his cooperation; and what was left for him? What might remain on a battle field: the cadavers, the spectacle of the vultures, and above it a sign reading "Here was the fight."]

The second example refers to the 1823 invasion of Spain by the "Hundred Thousand Sons of Saint Louis" in order to put an end to the Liberal Triennium and restore Fernandine absolutism:

El Norte [. . .] lanzó contra el principio democrático el credo de la Santa Alianza. Pero ¿dónde pelearemos?, se dijeron. Nuestras campiñas son fértiles, nuestros pueblos están llenos: ¿dónde hay un palenque vacío para la disputa?

Y también se citaron para España. Pero esta vez no hubo necesidad de combate: los buitres, citados por el rumor de la próxima pelea, vinieron, y no pudiendo repartirse los muertos, se repartieron los vivos. (600)

[The North { . . . } hurled the credo of the Holy Alliance against democratic principle. But where shall we fight?, they said to one another. Our countrysides are fertile, our towns are full: Where is there an empty arena for the dispute? And they also agreed to meet in Spain. But this time there was no need for combat: The vultures came, called by the rumor of the impending fight, and as they could not divvy up the dead, they divided the living.]

The final example is drawn from the second Carlist Wars, the confrontation—ongoing at the time of the essay's publication—between Spain's liberal state and the remaining bastion of monarchical reaction:

Más tarde, el derecho divino y la legitimidad por la gracia de Dios han necesitado reunir sus últimas fuerzas para dar combate al derecho del hombre y a la legitimidad por la gracia del pueblo, y esta última vez no ha sido necesario ya traer los principios al palenque: ellos han nacido en su terreno [. . .] las provincias vírgenes de España han visto su velo desgarrado, y profanado su seno [. . .] por las sangrientas manos de los liberales y de los carlistas. (600)

[Later, divine right and legitimacy by the grace of God have had to gather their remaining forces to give combat to the right of man and legitimacy by the grace of the people, and this last time it has no longer been necessary to bring principles to the arena: They have been born within its territory { . . . } the virgin provinces of Spain have seen their veil torn and their bosom profaned by the bloodstained hands of Liberals and Carlists.]

A consistent logic of political abjection subtends the representation of each historical episode. Next to the active force of other nations, Spain in the modern age is represented as passive terrain, host, house, arena, or countryside. In each case, the nation is portrayed as an entity devoid of historical agency; it is no longer conceived as a subject of history—in Larra's terms, a colossus—but merely as an empty place where History chooses to go at its convenience. Such images in effect reproduce—albeit from the viewpoint of the subordinate—the standard rhetorical maneuver of Western imperialist historiography that we considered in chapter 1: The subjugated are imagined as a people without history. Indeed, the generalized Hegelian logic by which the "Spirit" of history could only radiate outward from northern Europe is replicated in these passages by northern European historical protagonists who repeatedly decide to meet in Spain. Similarly, the progression from one passage to another manifests the telltale signs of colonization: Direct military intervention cedes to a model in which the colonized themselves are performing a script drafted for them by the ideological conflicts of modern Europe.

The "imperial difference" that transected the European continent from the eighteenth century forward is clearly on display (Mignolo, "Rethinking," 165). But what is Larra's relationship to this cartography? If "Horas de invierno" initially replicates the northern European symbolic map of modernity, it is not simply an internalization of this paradigm, for the essay also rewrites some of its key terms. While Larra clearly entertains a diffusionist model of history—it issues forth from the north— he also carries out a powerful reversal of the content of the traditional story that accompanied modern Europe's exploits. Whereas the dominant nineteenth-century historical narrative had envisioned History, Civilization, and Progress as the symbolic goods that modern Europe was destined to distribute to the rest of the world, in Larra's essay such ideals have been displaced by a far less appealing array of European exports. In this account, it is violence, destruction, the naked exercise of power, and, ultimately, death that radiate into Spain from a mythical north. A fascinating paradox thus begins to emerge in "Horas de invierno," for if the essay has been widely acknowledged as the quintessential canonical lament over Spain's distance from modern Europe, it is at the same time a powerful demystification of modern Europe's tale of enlightened progress. What binds the series of conflicts that Larra summarizes—Britain versus France, the Holy Alliance versus secular democracy, Carlists versus Liberals—is the legacy of blood they leave behind, the cadavers that pile up un their wake, and the flock of vultures that follows them, ready to feed on the living and the dead. Moreover, in the shared propensity to kill of *all* parties to the conflict is the disquieting suggestion that, despite the profoundest of ideological differences, the forces of modernity and those of reaction are in fact mirror images of each other, mere variations on a single, unwavering paradigm of power.

Such is the conclusion that Larra himself seems to draw as he moves from the question of recent Spanish history to the more philosophical field of history's first principles. Attempting to come to terms with the historical landscape he has described, Larra posits the following fundamental historical "law":

> Es una verdad eterna: [. . .] las naciones como los individuos, sujetos a la gran ley del egoísmo, viven más que de su vida propia de la vida ajena que consumen, y ¡ay del pueblo que no desgasta diariamente con su roce superior y violento los pueblos inmediatos, porque será desgastado por ellos! O atraer, o ser atraído. Ley implacable de la naturaleza: o devorar, o ser devorado. Pueblos e individuos, o víctimas o verdugos. Y hasta en la paz, quimérica utopía no realizada todavía en la continua lucha de los seres, hasta en la paz devoran los pueblos, como el agua mansa socava su cauce, con más seguridad, si no con tanto estruendo como el torrente. (600–1)

> [It is an eternal truth: { . . . } nations like individuals, subjected to the great law of selfishness, live from the life of the others they consume more than from their own life; and woe to the country that does not wear down neighboring countries daily with its superior and violent friction, because it will be worn down by them! To attract or be attracted. The implacable law of nature: to devour or be devoured. Countries and individuals, either victims or executioners. And even in peace, a chimerical utopia that has yet to be realized in the ongoing battle among beings, even in peace countries devour, just as calm water hollows out its riverbed, with more assurance, if not with as much noise as the torrent.]

The passage is a fascinating synthesis of Larra's late thinking on the history of European politics, and for readers who recall that Darwin's *On the Origins of Species* would not be published until 1859, or that Social Darwinism would not crystallize as a political philosophy until the 1870s, this dog-eat-dog vision may initially seem strangely prescient. It is worth noting, however, that Darwinian thinking itself emerged from a deeper history of evolutionary theory, a tradition to which Larra clearly bears witness. As Raymond Williams notes, "the popular application of the biological idea to social thought comes not so much from Darwin as from the whole tradition of evolutionary thought, which is much older than Charles Darwin [. . .], and which in the first half of the nineteenth century, is already a well-founded system" (*Problems*, 87). Engels would similarly point to the relationship between Darwin's conception of natural history and an older, Hobbesian/Mathusian tradition of political theory:

> The whole Darwinist teaching of the struggle for existence is simply a transference from society to living nature of Hobbes's doctrine of bellum omnium contra omnes and of the bourgeois-economic doctrine of competition together with Malthus's theory of population. ("Engels to Pyotor")

The naturalization of conquest in Larra—that is, the "eternal law"—is in this sense not an especially new formulation. Appeals to "the nature of things" had long been attached to imperial agendas, for "in the case of imperialism"—Williams recalls—"it was perfectly possible to argue, and many did, that the strongest [nation] [. . .] had a duty to humanity to continue to assert itself, not to limit its competition with weaker peoples out of some false ethical consideration for them or out of some legalistic notion of rights" (*Problems*, 93). What is relatively novel in Larra's formulation, however, is the way the older Hobbesian logic of imperial domination and the newer "bourgeois-economic doctrine of competition" to which Engels would refer begin to converge.

Such a fusion is evident in the analogy Larra establishes between the struggle for national existence and the competitive struggle among individuals. Indeed, his account of national struggle eerily approximates the model of competing, self-interested agents that was at the core of the political economy of liberalism. For Larra, the principle governing both nations and individuals is the very same force that Tediato had earlier identified as *interés* in *Noches lúgubres*; that is, the principle of self-interest, now rendered as "la gran ley del egoísmo" [the great law of selfishness]. But while Tediato's melancholy of modernity had initially addressed the rationalizing principles of the culture of Spain's late eighteenth-century mercantilism, Larra's reference to the law of selfishness was now speaking to an era in which Smith's principles of self-interest, private property, and market exchange were not only being championed by Spain's liberal economists but were also in fact being codified into law.

Alvaro Flórez Estrada's *Curso de economía política,* one of the touchstones of economic reform in Spain during the 1830s, is illustrative of the economic valences that Larra's *egoísmo* would have had within the culture of Spain's emergent liberalism.[18] For liberal political economy, self-interested calculation is the very basis for the legal institutionalization and defense of private property as a natural right. In a chapter entitled "De la inviolabilidad de la propiedad" [Of the inviolability of property], Flórez Estrada thus articulates the classical liberal credo that self-interest is the ultimate source of economic value. While human labor transforms the natural world into wealth, for Flórez Estrada labor itself is in the end merely a function of self-interest:

> Nadie trabaja por solo el placer de trabajar, sino por el beneficio que espera reportar del producto de su trabajo. Jamás el hombre perseverará en reproducir espontáneamente objetos de riqueza, si no tiene esperanzas fundadas de disponer a su árbitro del fruto de su industria. [. . .] Para hacer a un pueblo activo e industrioso, esta confianza es absolutamente necesaria. (89)

> [Nobody works only for the pleasure of working, but rather for the benefit he expects to gain from his work. Never will man persevere in spontaneously reproducing objects of wealth, if he does not have well-founded hopes of disposing of the fruit of his industry according to his will. { . . . } To make a people active and industrious, this confidence is absolutely necessary.]

It was precisely with a view to fomenting confidence in the self-interested pursuit of wealth that liberal reform in Spain had systematically begun to dismantle the late-feudal economic structures of the Ancien Régime.

Larra's identification of "la gran ley del egoismo" as the engine of history in "Horas de invierno" would consequently have had a particularly contemporary, economic resonance for many of Larra's readers. Similarly, while the logic of devouring that informs his vision of history can be linked to an older tradition of representing political conflict, it too would have struck a chord with readers who had become increasingly familiar with the importance of the newer category of consumption within liberal political economy. Flórez Estrada dedicates no fewer than four chapters of his *Curso* to the analysis of consumption: "De los diferentes modos de consumir la riqueza" [Of the Different Ways of Consuming Wealth], "De los efectos del consumo productivo" [Of the Effects of Productive Consumption], "De los efectos del consumo improductivo" [Of the Effects of Nonproductive Consumption], "De los consumos públicos" [Of Public Consumption]. He also makes clear that persistent, rapid consumption is essential to economic well-being: "Todos los productos de la industria son consumibles, y desde que se hallan en estado de ser consumidos, cuanto más tardío es el consumo, tanto más sufre la industria" [All of industry's products are consumible, and from the moment they find themselves ready to be consumed, the later the consumption, the more industry suffers] (772–73). When Larra refers to the way nations consume the life of others, his comments again seem to take on a contemporary economic connotation as well as a political one.

With such a backdrop in view, it becomes evident that, while internalizing contemporary paradigms of thought, Larra inverts the symbolic meanings conventionally accorded these terms within the narrative of enlightened modernity. Whereas liberal political economy held that the promotion of self-interest and consumption would lead to collective good by increasing the wealth of nations, Larra's account offers a far less sanguine version of the consequences of unleashing such forces. His words suggest that rather than promoting the general welfare, self-interest and consumption are in fact part of a machinery of domination that can only produce one of two equally unjust results: "o devorar o ser devorado. Pueblos e individuos, o víctimas o verdugos" [to devour or be devoured. Countries and individuals, either victims or executioners] (601). The shadow of death returns once more here, and history is for Larra simply a question of the particular position nations happen to occupy within this macabre paradigm at a given moment in time. War is merely the overt manifestation of a struggle for survival that structures socioeconomic relations—within nations and among them—during peacetime as well. Without approximating the systematic dimensions of the Hegelian master/slave dialectic or of its adaptation into the Marxist theory of class struggle, Larra's abbreviated philosophy of history thus bears witness to the suspicion, already in 1836, that modernity's narrative of historical progress was simply the mythic mask of a more brutal historical process. Whether considered at the level of imperial subjugation or, more subtly, at the level of the economic implications of Larra's rhetoric, the modern in "Horas de invierno" is figured as an agent of death.

After establishing this view of history, the essay shifts to consider the cultural consequences of Spain's position as a devoured, historically abject, symbolically dead nation. Larra posits a direct correspondence between military and cultural power: "El pueblo que no abruma [. . .] a los pueblos vecinos"—he writes—"está condenado a la oscuridad; y donde no llegan sus armas, no llegarán sus letras; donde su espada no deje rasgo de sangre, no imprimirá tampoco su pluma ni un carácter solo, ni una frase, ni una letra" [The country that does not crush neighboring countries is condemned to darkness; and where its arms do not reach, its letters will not reach; where its sword does not leave a stroke of blood, its pen will imprint neither a single character, nor a sentence, nor a letter] (601). In accordance with this logic, only a return to imperial power would assure Spanish culture international stature and recognition. Larra thus engages openly in an imperial nostalgia that has often been overlooked by those critics who have wanted to cultivate the image of Larra as a liberal martyr:

> Volvieran, si posible fuese, nuestras banderas a tremolar sobre las torres de Amberes y las siete colinas de la ciudad espiritual, dominara de nuevo el pabellón español el golfo de México y las sierras de Arauco, y tornáramos los españoles a dar leyes, a hacer Papas, a componer comedias y a encontrar traductores. (601)

> [Would that our flags waved once more, if it were possible, over the towers of Antwerp and the seven hills of the spiritual city, would that once more the Spanish flag dominated the Gulf of Mexico and the mountains of Arauco, and we Spaniards would again impose laws, make popes, write plays, and find translators.]

To be sure, Larra's sense of postimperial abjection, along with his hope that Spanish culture might one day be renewed, help to explain the purchase his writing would later have on those writers who, in the wake of the Spanish-American War, were jarred into a similar sense of historical loss. What is most striking in Larra's formulation of the problem, however, is the stark conclusion that culture—particularly cultural prestige—is in the end merely a function of power. Creativity, the very force that romantic poetics had privileged as the fount of artistic production, is represented as a mere corollary to the law of domination. In the absence of a return to imperial supremacy, the attempt to create original works of literature is in Larra's view a futile one: "[R]enunciemos a crear"—he writes—"y despojémonos de las glorias literarias como de la preponderancia política y militar nos ha desnudado la sucesión de los tiempos" [Let us renounce creating, and let us strip ourselves of literary glories, just as the passage of time has stripped us of political and military preponderance] (601). He proceeds to make explicit the reason for such a renunciation:

> El genio, como el cedro del Líbano, nace en las alturas, y crece y se hace fuerte a los embates de la tempestad, no en los bajos ni en las vertientes cenagosas que se desprenden a inundarlos de la montaña. El genio ha

> menester del laurel para coronarse; y ¿dónde ha quedado entre nosotros un
> vástago de laurel para coronar una frente? El genio ha menester del eco, y no
> se produce eco entre las tumbas. (601)

> [Genius, like Lebanon's cedar, is born in the heights, and it grows and
> strengthens itself exposed to the blows of the tempest, not in the lowlands
> nor in the muddy streams that come off of the mountain to flood them.
> Genius is in need of laurel to crown itself; and where among us has a sprout
> of laurel remained? Genius is in need of an echo, and no echo is produced
> among tombs.]

The image of death appears once more as a sign of Spain's cultural abjection. If the nation had been a symbolically empty space awaiting the arrival of History, the same emptiness now characterizes the arena required
by genius in order to thrive. Genius is only at home, it would seem, where
Hegel had placed the Spirit of History, and it is Larra's pained awareness
of the ways in which Spanish culture in the 1830s does not belong to
that "modern world" that leads to the most famous passage of "Horas de
invierno":

> Escribir y crear en el centro de la civilización y de la publicidad, como Hugo
> y Lherminier, es escribir. [. . .] Escribir como Chateaubriand y Lamartine
> en la capital del mundo moderno es escribir para la humanidad; digno y
> noble fin de la palabra del hombre, que es dicha para ser oída. Escribir como
> escribimos en Madrid es tomar una apuntación, es escribir en un libro de
> memorias, es realizar un monólogo desesperante y triste para uno solo. Es-
> cribir en Madrid es llorar, es buscar una voz sin encontrarla, como en una
> pesadilla abrumadora y violenta. (601–2)

> [To write and to create in the center of civilization and publicity, like Hugo
> and Lherminier, is to write. { . . . } To write like Chateaubriand and Lamar-
> tine in the capital of the modern world is to write for humanity, a worthy
> and noble end for man's word, which is spoken to be heard. To write as we
> write in Madrid is to jot down a note, it is to write in a diary, it is to carry
> on a desperate and sad dialogue solely for oneself. To write in Madrid is to
> weep, it is to search for a voice without finding it, as in an overwhelming
> and violent nightmare.]

The formulation once again reveals a lucid grasp of key features of
the discourse of northern European cultural imperialism. Long before the

postcolonial critique of Eurocentrism, Larra apprehends the logic according to which modern Europe is positioned as the unquestioned home of the universal ("civilization," "humanity"), while its exterior—here, peripheral Spain—is taken to be merely a realm of depressing particulars. Precisely because it engages a structure of thought that would continue to inform Spanish culture throughout the modern era, Larra's image of writing as mournful weeping in "Horas de invierno" subsequently became one of the quintessential expressions of the quandary of the modern Spanish writer. Taken in the broader context of the essay, however, the pathos of Spanish cultural abjection is tempered by the philosophy of history from which it has emerged. One cannot overlook the fact that Larra's lament in "Horas de invierno" remains thoroughly within a Hobbesian logic of perpetual war: Historical protagonism, national vitality, cultural life, artistic creativity, and literary genius have been positioned figuratively as the precipitates of military and economic power. As was the case with Tediato and Don Alvaro, the pain of the romantic subject—in this case, Larra's Spanish writing subject—elicits an ideologically charged kind of readily sympathy. The cultural politics of Larra's famous "escribir en Madrid es llorar" [to write in Madrid is to weep] encode not only grief over a symbolically dead Spanish culture, but also imperial nostalgia and, perhaps more disturbingly, the image of life as domination.

While thoroughly undermining the narrative of enlightenment progress by suggesting that the modern liberal world is nothing but a newer form of oppression, Larra's implacable law of history thus also marks the ideological limits of his thinking. The notion that history might in some future be something other than a process driven by conquest, domination, exploitation, and death is rendered almost unthinkable. It is as if, defrauded by the widening chasm between the realities of the modern liberal world on the one hand and its emancipatory rhetoric on the other, Larra relinquishes historical aspiration altogether. Just as the passing of the Count of Campo Alange in the "Exequias" figured the restriction of a more expansive understanding of subjective possibility, the lifelessness of Spanish culture in "Horas de invierno" signals a snuffing out of historical possibility within the collective, transnational domain of European politics. In a landscape strewn with modernity's victims, the extinction of hope, the hope that the life of some, whether individuals, classes, or nations, might one day cease to be predicated on the exploitation of others, is the essay's ultimate, and perhaps most fateful death.

No Souls' Day

Within the Catholic liturgical calendar, All Souls' Day, also known as the Day of the Dead, is a day of remembrance and prayer for the deceased. "The theological basis for the feast"—usually celebrated on 2 November—"is the doctrine that the souls which, on departing from the body, are not perfectly cleansed from venial sins, or have not fully atoned for past transgressions, are debarred from the Beatific Vision, and that the faithful on earth can help them by prayers, almsdeeds and especially by the sacrifice of the Mass" ("All Souls' "). By offering prayers for the dead in the hope of aiding their passage from purgatory to heaven, the living are reminded that they participate in a spiritual economy whose purpose is to help realize the Christian narrative of the triumph of eternal life over death. The third article we shall consider, "El Día de Difuntos de 1836. Fígaro en el cementerio" [All Souls' Day 1836. Fígaro in the Cemetery], takes this religious festivity and its theological framework as its point of departure, but, in a characteristic reversal, the essay delivers something quite contrary to the promise of eternal life implied by its title.

Indeed, the basic conceit of this piece famously turns the principle of the Christian afterlife on its head by figuring what might aptly be termed the *foredeath* of the living; that is, by constructing a narrative in which Madrid, its inhabitants and its institutions, are uncannily more dead than alive. In this sense "El Día de Difuntos" offers a more sustained meditation on the motif of "living death" that surfaced at key moments of the "Exequias" and of "Horas de invierno." At the same time, the essay elucidates the tension between Catholic theology and the basic death narrative that informs Larra's late essays generally. To the extent that the plot which underpins Larra's representations of modern suffering can be described as a tale of death's triumph over life, or the story of a process by which possibility itself is painfully extinguished from a world that nevertheless continues to live, it becomes clear in "El Día de Difuntos" that such a tale is the very antithesis of the Catholic narrative of the attainment of life everlasting. Analysis of this fundamental reversal and of Larra's ensuing itinerary through the streets of a metaphorically dead Madrid will consequently allow us to pursue further the question of death's meaning and its relationship to the modern in his late essays.[19]

As the essay opens, the reader finds Larra's literary alter ego, Fígaro, brooding in his home. Awakening on the morning of All Souls' Day, he is perplexed, not by the mystery of death as one might expect, but rather by the simple fact that so many people are alive: "no me asombra precisamente que haya tantas gentes que vivan; sucédeme, sí, que no lo comprendo" [it does not exactly amaze me that so many people live; what *is* happening to me is that I do not understand it] (580). It is an intriguing confession of estrangement. The ordinary baffles; the familiar world of the living, the very fact that so many people live, is perceived as something odd, as something almost incomprehensible. Although the reasons for this state of affairs are not yet articulated, the implication is clear. Given the way of things, a world less alive would be far more understandable, and as Fígaro dwells on this thought, a melancholy mood overcomes him. "No tardó en cubrir mi frente una nube de melancolía; pero de aquellas melancolías de que sólo un liberal español en estas circunstancias puede formar una idea aproximada" [It was not long before a cloud of melancholy covered my face; but one of those melancholies about which only a Spanish liberal in these circumstance can form an approximate idea] (580).

The analogies that follow as Fígaro describes this sentiment emphasize the characteristic grounding of melancholy in the experiences of loss and deferral: To feel melancholy—he writes—is to be like a man who loses faith in friendship, like an inheritor whose rich relative dies without a will, like a congressional representative who wins an election that is later annulled, and so forth (581).[20] In sociohistorical terms, unrealized hope becomes for Larra an image of the unfulfilled promise of liberal modernity in Spain: The Carlist war rages on, liberal governments are themselves becoming increasingly authoritarian, and behind the celebrated image of a free press, censorship continues (581). One might conclude from this initial series of observations that Fígaro's melancholy stems from the frustratingly slow pace of modernization in Spain, from the fact that the many wonders of the modern, secular world had not yet fully manifested themselves in Spain. And yet, as the previous articles we have considered suggest, Larra's critique is rarely as simple a plaint.

As Fígaro seems to come out of his melancholic torpor, for example, the complex, double-edged quality of his critique begins to come into view. A ringing of bells jars him out of his brooding: "Un sonido lúgubre y monóntono [. . .] vino a sacudir mi entorpecida existancia.—'¡Día de Difuntos!'—exclamé." [a lugubrious, monotonous sound { . . . } came to

shake up my benumbed existence—"All Souls' Day!"—I exclaimed] (581).
For just a moment, the call to the stable, familiar territory of religious tradition promises to assuage Fígaro's disquiet, but if the tolling of the bells
momentarily dispels his melancholy thoughts, its fleeting promise quickly
gives way to an image of the desacralizing ravages of the modern:

> el bronce herido que anunciaba con lamentable clamor la ausencia eterna
> de los que han sido, parecía vibrar más lúgubre que en ningún año, como si
> presagiase su propia muerte. Ellas también, las campanas, han alcanzado su
> última hora, y sus tristes acentos son el estertor del moribundo; ellas también
> van a morir a manos de la libertad, que todo lo vivifica, y ellas serán las únicas
> en España, ¡santo Dios!, que morirán colgadas. ¡Y hay justicia divina! (581)

> [the wounded bronze that with a lamentable clamor was announcing the
> eternal absence of those who have been, seemed to ring more lugubriously
> than any other year, as if it presaged its own death. They too, the bells, have
> reached their final hour, and their sad sounds are the death rattle of the mori
> bund; they too are going to die at the hands of liberty, which brings life to
> everything, and they will be the only ones, holy God!, who will die hanged.
> And there is divine justice!]

Twentieth-century editors of the passage have noted that its most immediate historical reference is the sale of convent bells that was part of
the project of liberal disentailment of church property under Mendizábal,
and later Calatrava. At the same time, it is not difficult to see in the pun
on hanging an allusion to widespread frustrations over the liberal government's inability to bring a "criminal" Carlist insurrection to justice. Less
commented, however, is the more general line of reasoning that informs
this passage, a pattern of thought that we considered in the "Exequias."
To put it simply, modern liberty, one of liberalism's sacrosanct values, is
once again figured as an agent of death. In becoming merchandise, church
bells are symbolically executed. Entry into the world of exchange value is
a march to the gallows, and for readers familiar with the disentailments,
the tacit equation established between liberty, selling, and death would
not have been difficult to apprehend. The fact that such bells ostensibly
bring Fígaro *out* of his melancholic brooding on liberal hopelessness is
one of the essay's bleaker ironies, and it serves to subtly underscore the

ineluctable quality of Larra's despair. Fígaro awakens from one nightmarish chain of thought, but only to find himself within another.

It is at this point that the basic reversal which will govern the rest of the essay takes place. Breaking away from his ruminations, Fígaro steps out into the street and momentarily scrutinizes the masses as they head toward the cemetery for the day's celebration, and the view before him prompts a macabre insight:

> Dirigíanse las gentes por las calles en gran número y larga procesión, serpen-teando de unas en otras como largas culebras de infinitos colores: ¡al cemen-terio! ¡al cementerio! ¡Y para eso salían de las puertas de Madrid!
>
> Vamos claros, dije yo para mí, ¿dónde está el cementerio? ¿Fuera o dentro? Un vértigo espantoso se apodereo de mí, y comencé a ver claro. El cementerio está dentro de Madrid. Madrid es el cementerio. Pero vasto cementerio donde cada casa es el nicho de una familia, cada calle el sepulcro de un acontecimiento, cada corazón la urna cineraria de una esperanza o de un deseo.
>
> Entonces, y en tanto que los que creen vivir acudían a la mansión que presumen de muertos, yo comencé a pasear con toda la devoción y recogi-miento de que soy capaz las calles del gran osario. (582)

> [People were heading through the streets in great numbers and in a long procession, winding from one street to another like long snakes of infinite colors: To the cemetery! To the cemetery! And for that they were coming out of the doors of Madrid!
>
> We're in a fine one, I said to myself, Where is the cemetery? Outside or in? I was overpowered by a frightening dizzy spell, and I began to see clearly. The cemetery is inside of Madrid. Madrid is the cemetery. But a vast cem-etery where each house is a family niche, each street the tomb of an event, each heart the cinerary urn of a hope or of a desire.
>
> At that point, and while those who think they are alive were going to the mansion they presume to be of the dead, I began to stroll the streets of the great ossuary with all the devotion and absorption of which I am capable.]

The sudden understanding that the city is dead paradoxically marks a be-ginning of sorts, for the epiphany quite literally sets the stage for the char-acteristic wanderings of Fígaro the *costumbrista*, Fígaro the flaneur. The initial surprise that so many people were alive has ceded to the intuition that they may in fact be less alive than they seem, and, not unlike Tediato before him, Fígaro steps out to peruse the city-as-graveyard.

In evoking Fígaro as a *costumbrista* or flaneur of the dead, however, we once again confront the challenges to critical inquiry posed by Spain's peripheral status within the grand narrative of Western modernity, for a significant conceptual gap continues to separate these two very different names for nineteenth-century urban meandering. On one hand is a well-known, authoritative critical and theoretical tradition that has taken the flaneur as the very paradigm of the modern. For Baudelaire, readers may recall, the flaneur would famously become one of the privileged sites for the perception of that particular play of the eternal within the ephemeral, which he defines as *modernité*. "For the perfect idler, for the passionate observer"—he notes in "The Painter of Modern Life"—"it becomes an immense source of enjoyment to establish his dwelling in the throng, in the ebb and flow, the bustle, the fleeting and the infinite" (*Selected*, 399). In the twentieth-century, Walter Benjamin's classic work on Baudelaire—bolstered by the recent publication of *The Arcades Project*—along with an immense twentieth-century critical bibliography, would serve to reinforce Baudelaire's status as the ineluctable "figure who gives voice to the shock and intoxication of modernity" (Gollich, 134). Chris Jenks has recently summarized the flaneur's rhetorical function as a placeholder for that space from which the experience of the modern comes to be understood:

> The flaneur, though grounded in everyday life, is an analytic form, a narrative device, an attitude towards knowledge and its social context. It is an image of movement through the social space of modernity. [. . .] The flaneur is a multilayered palimpsest that enables us to move from real products of modernity [. . .] through the practical organization of space and its negotiation by inhabitants of a city, to a critical appreciation of the state of modernity. (148)

But behind even this rudimentary genealogy of *flanerie*-as-modernity—from Baudelaire's Paris, to Benjamin's Baudelaire, to Jenks's discursive formation—it is not difficult to apprehend once more the "imperial privilege" that subtends such universalizing claims: It is *Paris* that becomes representative of urban modernity in general, it is *Baudelaire* who becomes the transnational representative of the modern writer, it is

the French word, *flaneur,* that names Jenks's abstracted discursive position.[21] The point is not to dismiss this indispensable body of work on the
modern but to note again the ways in which some of the more powerful
literary and cultural theory concerning modernity has unwittingly replicated rather than contested the cultural imperialism encoded into the
metageography of modern Europe. One need only juxtapose the flaneur
with its analogue within Spanish literary historiography, the *costumbrista,*
in order to note the very different series of associations that the latter
term prompts.[22] Despite compelling recent work that has underscored
the radical novelty of *costumbrista* discourse in Spain—see Escobar ("Costumbrismo")—even today the analytic framework applied to the phenomenon is rarely that of the "image of movement through the social space
of modernity" (Jenks, 148). Indeed, it is only a slight exaggeration to
claim that next to the flaneur's intoxicating experience of the modern,
the *costumbrista* has tended to be construed as a more-or-less picturesque
sketch artist, a quaint observer of social customs, or a nostalgic gatherer of
disappearing traditions. The vestiges of the ideological structure by which
flanerie speaks to modernity, while *costumbrismo* can only speak to Spanish
tradition, are still with us.[23]

As we return to the image of Fígaro stepping out into the city of the
dead, the question thus seems to be whether he should be read—within
the framework sketched above—as a flaneur or as a *costumbrista.* Is the
necropolis that opens up before Fígaro a modern one, or is the dead city
a sign of modernity's absence? If the bells that prompt Fígaro's voyage are
symbolically executed *by* the modern, what is the status of Madrid more
generally? In order to address these questions, it will be useful to review
briefly the various gravesites that Fígaro encounters, for a catalogue of the
funereal monuments he contemplates offers useful insights into the nature
and causes of Madrid's collective death.[24] The first edifice Fígaro sees is the
Royal Palace:

> ¿Qué monumento es éste?—exclamé al comenzar mi paseo por el vasto
> cementerio. [. . .] "¡Palacio!" [. . .] En el frontispicio decía: "Aquí yace el
> trono; nació en el reinado de Isabel la Católica y murió en La Granja de un
> aire colado" (583).

> [What monument is this?—I exclaimed as I began my stroll through the vast
> cemetery { . . . } "The Palace!" { . . . } On the frontispiece it said: "Here lies

the throne; it was born in the reign of Isabel the Catholic, and it died in La
Granja from an air that blew in."]

Referencing the August 1836 military insurrection that had forced the
Regent María Cristina to adopt the liberal Constitution of 1812, the symbolic death of the throne in this passage is ushered in by liberal militarism.
In a similar vein, the next building Fígaro views, the National Armory, is
dead because of other, decidedly modern phenomena: "Y este mausoleo
a la izquierda? 'La armería.' Leamos: 'Aquí llace el valor castellano, con
todos su pertrechos' " [And this mausoleum on the left? "The armory."
Let us read: "Here lies Castilian valor, with all of its provisions"] (583).
A wry comment on the logistical difficulties that were plaguing the army
in its confrontation with Carlism, the passage also echoes the disappearance of the heroic that we considered in the "Exequias." Following the
armory, Fígaro's gaze falls upon the governmental ministries: "Los min-
isterios: 'Aquí llace media España: murió de la otra media' " [The ministries: "Here lies half of Spain: it died from the other half"] (583). In this
instance, death names the characteristic process by which, upon assuming
power, the two basic factions within Spanish liberalism—the conservative
moderados and the more progressive *exaltados*—tended to systematically
undo the work of predecessors. Among the initial tombs Fígaro sees is also
the Inquisition, the emblem of Catholic reaction and intolerance, which
liberalism had finally abolished: "Más allá: ¡Santo Dios!, 'Aquí yace la In-
quisición, hija de la fe y del fanatismo: murió de vejez' " [Further along:
Holy God! "Here lies the Inquisition, daughter of faith and fanaticism: it
died of old age"] (583).

If one were to judge by this sequence of images alone, it would not be
unreasonable to conclude that what is dead in Madrid is the past of the
Ancien Régime: the unfettered sovereignty of the crown, an older world
of heroic valor, the Inquisition. Death would name those impulses within
modern Spanish liberalism that sought to systematically dismantle and
reform the practices and institutions of absolutist tradition. In fact, death
would be an image for the liberal destruction of the nonmodern; and
yet, even in this initial series of images, it becomes apparent that death's
shadow falls across much more than Spain's reactionary past. As we have
just seen, the internal divisions within liberalism itself are also represented
as a kind of death. More striking is the fact that as the essay continues

it becomes evident that the city-as-cemetery is home to numerous liberal cadavers as well. Fígaro will encounter the sepulchers of the Liberal Triennium (1820–1823) and the moderate Estatuto Real (1834–1836); he will find the tombs of the stock market, freedom of the press, and the Spanish House of Commons; and even more significantly, commerce, industry, and business will also be imagined to slumber away under death's spell (583–84).

When it comes to the question of modernity, "El Día de Difuntos" paints a decidedly mixed landscape. To discuss this essay solely as a representation of Spanish historical stagnation is to miss the enigmatic fact that death names both the insufficiencies within Spain's liberal modernity and the modern extinction of Spain's past. Madrid cannot easily be reduced to the image of "nonmodern" Spain, for at times the city is dead *because of* the modern. The very heterogeneity of Madrid's living dead (i.e., a cemetery of moderns and nonmoderns) speaks to a rather complex understanding of the social space of 1830s urban life in the Spanish capital. Larra's cityscape represents a space which neither the figure of the flaneur and the hefty theorization of the modern he represents, nor the figure of the *costumbrista*, dressed in the garb of traditionalist nostalgia, are able to capture fully. Fígaro in "El Día de Difuntos" is neither, or to put it another way, he is both, for the cemetery before him is an irremediably hybrid entity. Its modernity does not intoxicate, and its past customs do not enchant; instead, the essay suggests, both lead to a kind of death in life.

For the critical tradition that has approached nineteenth-century Spanish culture as always already insufficiently modern, these features of Larra's Madrid can, no doubt, be explained away by appealing to the all-too-familiar story of Spain's incomplete or uneven modernization. The city as cemetery would in this scheme become the image of Spain's painfully slow path to the modern. If, however, the macronarrative of modernity is itself a suspect entity in need of revision, then Larra's representation of the Madrid of the mid-1830s can also be read for a very different series of insights. This is not to claim that nineteenth-century Madrid was as "modern" as London or Paris, nor is it to make new assertions about the pace of modernization in Spain. It is merely to suggest that the obsessive focus on Spanish difference, along with the image of nineteenth-century Spain as presumptively backward, have tended to occlude a more substantive reckoning with the status of the modern itself. Rather than figuring a defective *Spanish* modernity, for example, one might legitimately ask whether Larra's hybrid (modern/nonmodern) urban landscape is not in fact a compellingly lucid representation of the inherent logic of modernization *per se*. "El Día de Difuntos" might even be marshaled as an exemplary case of a text that—like "Horas de invierno"—tacitly dismantles the celebratory myth of modernity by depicting an intrinsically inchoate, ominously deadening process.

The tendency to evoke "uneven modernity" as a distinctly Spanish phenomenon has often unwittingly engaged in the common fantasy that such a thing as an "even modernity" ever existed. It has perpetuated the myth that in modern Europe (Britain, France, and Germany), or anywhere else for that matter, there ever existed a "sufficient," "complete" modernity. One need only bring into view the impoverished urban peripheries of most European capitals today, or the "underdeveloped" quality of many American inner cities, or the areas of rural immiseration on both continents—Galicia or Extremadura, but also Appalachia—in order to appreciate that modernity, in and of itself, has been anything but a homogenous affair. (And it is worth noting that here we are still within the framework of a putatively prosperous First World.) Even the more philosophically rigorous defenders of enlightened modernity such as Habermas concede that it remains an "unfinished project," and recent debates tend to focus on the question of whether the project can be fully realized or whether it is constitutively doomed.[25] The notion of a cohesive, "even" entity called modernity is, on the face of it, a contradiction, and it is for this reason that, after reviewing the countries that have traditionally been taken as paradigms of the modern, Fredric Jameson has recently concluded that

> what is most significant in all these cases is that the modernity of the states in question is *a modernity for other peoples*, an optical illusion nourished by envy and hope, by inferiority feelings and the need for emulation. Alongside all the other paradoxes built into this strange concept, this one is the most fatal: that modernity is always a concept of otherness. (my emphasis; *Singular*, 211)

The point, once again, is thus not to deny the different patterns of social, political, and economic change within Europe, but rather to note the illusory quality of the myths that have traditionally accounted for such differences and to ask whether peripherally modern cultures might not be privileged rather than deficient sites for inquiry into the modern. Larra's Madrid, like peripheral Europe more generally, speaks to the question of modernity in a way that Baudelerian *flanerie* and its subsequent theorization have tended—perhaps too easily—to overlook. The essay is, among other things, an occasion to reexamine the ways in which the modern has been and continues to be imagined. While it may register the historically incomplete nature of modernization in Spain, "El Día de Difuntos" also openly begs the question of the possibility of modernity's completion more generally. As such it provides a useful example of how reading the modern *from* Spain—rather than reading a deficient Spain from "European modernity"—may yet yield useful insights on both.

Insofar as Larra's hybrid graveyard suggests that reaction and modernity both kill, Madrid in "El Día de Difuntos" is not unlike the corpse-strewn fields that we considered in "Horas de invierno." The city of the dead carries within it traces of Larra's Hobbesian *bellum omnium contra omnes*, the image of life as domination, and the disquieting suggestion that modernity is but the newest agent of this historical "truth."[26] It is thus no coincidence that the poignant suggestion of the extinction of hope, which hovered over the previous articles, becomes concretized in the closing image of "El Día de Difuntos." The essay ends with Fígaro's discovery of one final, heart-numbing tomb. As night falls, the melancholy cloud that afflicted Fígaro at the beginning of the essay threatens to return. But when Fígaro turns his gaze inward, hoping to find some solace in the inner life of the heart, he is shocked to discover that the macabre, funereal world he has contemplated throughout the essay extends to his own innermost recesses as well:

> Una nube sombría lo envolvió todo. Era la noche. El frío de la noche helaba mis venas. Quise salir violentamente del horrible cementerio. Quise refugiarme en mi propio corazón, lleno no ha mucho de vida, de ilusiones, de deseos.
>
> ¡Santo cielo! También otro cementerio. Mi corazón no es más que otro sepulcro. ¿Qué dice? Leamos. ¿Quién ha muerto en él? ¡Espantoso letrero! "¡Aquí yace la esperanza!!!"
>
> ¡Silencio, silencio!!! (585–86)

> [A dark cloud covered everything. It was the night. The chill of the night was freezing my veins. I violently tried to leave the horrible cemetery. I tried to

shelter myself in my own heart, which was filled not long ago with life, with hopes, with desires.

Holy Heaven! Also another cemetery. My heart is nothing more than another tomb. What does it say? Let's read. Who has died in it? A frightening sign! "Here lies hope!!!"

Silence, silence!!!]

Like the masses that were the initial object of his gaze, Fígaro discovers that, devoid of hope, he too is more dead than alive. Following this final insight, nothing remains to be said, and by way of a powerful rhetorical maneuver, silence becomes the essay's final figure of hopelessness. The article's ending in effect performs the silence it announces, extending the death of hope to language itself by appearing to renounce words.

Given this climactic ending in silent hopelessness, it is evident that for Larra hope designates much more than mere expectation or the sense of a future. To the extent that it is analogized with desire and with life itself, its disappearance is charged with significance. Larra positions himself within a longstanding tradition when he represents hopelessness as a kind of death, for the concepts of hope and life had long been associated with one another. For much of its history, the word for the negation of hope, despair, was in fact synonymous with death, and more specifically with suicide. Within a religious framework, suicide was considered a sin precisely because it was understood as a form of despair, implying a loss of faith in an ultimate, metaphysical, divine source of hope.

Larra's images of living death dialogue with this tradition, to be sure, but they also seem to announce the general contours of the problem of despair as subsequently taken up by existential philosophy. Readers of Kierkegaard will recall, for example, his famous conception of despair as "the sickness unto death." "Despair," he writes, "is veritably a self-consuming, but an impotent self-consuming that cannot do what it wants to do" (18). Commenting on this passage, Patrick Shade has more recently described the kind of death-in-life stasis that Keirkegaard has in mind:

We are trapped in a present and restricted [. . .] to such an extent that the self is intolerable. This self cannot become anything better, and yet it is inescapable. [. . .] Consequently, one despairs over being incapable of consuming the self, of being rid of it with all its limitations. Despair, then, is the inability to escape or die, the curse of being condemned to an intolerable present that stretches out indefinitely. (163)

Modern psychological approaches to despair similarly stress stasis and diminished liveliness as key features of the condition. As we saw in connection with *Noches lúgubres*, Freud initially conceived of melancholy as a kind of psychic stagnation tinged with the qualities of the lost or dead beloved; more recently, depression, the contemporary face of despair, has increasingly been described not only in terms of sadness but also as a generalized loss of vitality and a deadening of affect altogether.[27]

Independent of the specific framework, what each of these formulations shares with Larra's representation of hopelessness is an implied understanding that there are substantive gradations of intensity and quality within the experience commonly called "living." If the trope of living death that surfaces in Larra's late writing is an expression of suffering, disillusion, and disappointment, it also registers a muting of life experience itself, a muffling out of vitality. More specifically, it speaks to a painful curtailing of the particular facet of the self that is future-oriented, the self that anticipates, decides, and acts. The death of hope names a crippling of the human agency traditionally taken to be the ground of moral philosophy; it speaks to a squelching of the animating principle that theology has commonly called the "soul." To the extent that "El Día de Difuntos" suggests that such a death is the product not only of reactionary Spain or of the deferred promises of liberalism, but also of liberal modernity itself, it is a historically prescient image of those forces within the modern whose effect is to deaden or otherwise flatten the experience of living. Within the hybrid cityscape of Larra's Madrid there are intimations of that decidedly modern form of alienation, which the Lukàcs of *History and Class Consciousness* would describe as a "ghostly objectivity," an objectivity that "stamps its imprint upon the whole consciousness of man," rendering subjective qualities like hope, for example, "things which he can 'own' or 'dispose of'" like the various objects of the external world" (100). The word for this process is of course *reification*, and Lukàcs famously locates its source in the commodity form itself, that peculiarly beguiling entity in which a social relation between human beings takes on "the fantastic form of a relation between things" (Marx, *Das Kapital*, 52–53). Indeed, one of the fundamental insights of Lukàcs's 1923 work is that consciousness—in more contemporary terms, subjectivity—is itself progressively reified as the logic of the commodity form increasingly permeates the social order.

This is not to claim that the reifying machinery of modernity was the cultural dominant in 1830s Spain; it is simply to observe that, contrary to what has been suggested by the image of backward Spain, reification is clearly among those forces at work in Fígaro's Madrid. This is so, not only because as we have seen in previous chapters, reification belongs to a vaster historical time scale, with important roots in early modern Spain, but also because 1830s Spanish culture was undergoing an unprecedented liberal economic "shock treatment" of sorts, as the legal codification of private property began to supplant the structures of ownership of the Ancien Régime. While commodity production was far from becoming a dominant in the Lukàcsian sense, liberal disentailment and economic reform more generally had rather clearly begun to reconfigure the place of markets, commerce, and exchange within the Spanish polity.

To the extent that death is a word that attempts to come to terms with the moment in which bodies are no longer conceived as subjects able to act in the hic et nunc of the material world, the concept has always named the fear of becoming an object, merely matter after all, a thing. In this regard it is no coincidence that over the 1800s—and in Larra's work particularly—the idea of death would slowly come to be invested with anxieties over the objectifying effects of liberal modernity. To reify, it is worth recalling, literally means "to make into a thing." The modern is not the only agent of death in Larra's late essays, to be sure, but within the bleak world he evokes there is a recognition of the deadening, reifying effects of the emergent world of liberal modernity in Spain. In Madrid's living dead—a city of zombies—and in the poignant death of Fígaro's hope, there is more than merely the representation of "nonmodern" Spain. Such images also speak to the painful reifying effects of modernity itself, and they encode a decidedly contemporary despair over the emergence of an increasingly "soulless" world.

Christmas Eve between the Liturgy and the Market[28]

Among the most widely anthologized of Larra's works, the final essay we shall consider, "La Noche Buena de 1836" [Christmas Eve 1836], ranks as one of the most highly canonical and critically celebrated essays in his production. The immediate reasons for its privileged status are not difficult to discern. As the work of critics as methodologically disparate as Ricardo Gullón, Susan Kirkpatrick, and John Rosenberg has demonstrated, few of Larra's essays so efficiently convey the hallmark topoi of romanticism—introspection, anguished self-consciousness, alienation, suicidal exhibitionism—while fusing these subjective elements with the collective concerns—social, political, and historical life—that sustain the satirical impulse throughout his work. "La Noche Buena de 1836" seems to promise the best of both worlds for cultural historians: It is a densely poetic and highly subjective discourse that simultaneously renders Fígaro's consciousness an image of the contradictions we have encountered in preceding essays, the contradictions of the emergent modern culture wrought by Spain's uneven and intermittent, modern, liberal revolution.[29]

The narrative scaffolding of the essay is relatively simple. Brooding in his home on Christmas Eve, Larra's alter ego, Fígaro, gives his servant some extra money for the evening before he himself steps out to wander the streets of Madrid. As Fígaro contemplates a series of urban scenes, he experiences what has become a habitual alienation from his surroundings, and he eventually returns to his home. There he encounters his servant, who has used his holiday pay to inebriate himself. A verbal confrontation ensues, and after suffering a series of excoriating recriminations from his servant, Fígaro retires to his bedroom for the evening. As the essay ends, he contemplates a box at his bedside that is inscribed with the word "mañana" [morning/tomorrow]. In the last lines of the article he wonders what that tomorrow will bring, and he sarcastically plays with the double meaning of "Noche Buena": "En tanto, la *Noche buena* era pasada y el mundo todo, a mis barbas, cuando hablaba de ella la seguía llamando *Noche buena*" [Meanwhile, Christmas Eve had passed and, to my face, the whole world, when it spoke of it, kept calling it the Good Night].[30]

In contrast to the relative narrative simplicity of "La Noche Buena de 1836," however, recent interpretations of the essay have diverged rather widely: MacCurdy has read Fígaro and his servant as Jungian "opposed tendencies of the psyche" (143); Del Vecchio has described the encounter as an emblematic representation of the romantic imagination's fateful struggle with the vitiated medium of language (140); Teichmann has construed the narrating subject as a magician who symbolically produces a ritualistic act of expiation (120–26); Kirkpatrick has identified the divided self as a paradigm of romantic subjectivity (*Las Románticas*, 98–109); and, more recently, Rosenberg has argued that Larra is "a clear example of the ego's entrapment within itself; he represents the dangers of a solitude that collapses on itself" (388).

While such critical pluralism undoubtedly reflects the richly nuanced range of meanings that the essay has been capable of putting into play, it also suggests that a reconsideration of the sociohistorical forces that suffuse Fígaro's subjectivity in "La Noche Buena de 1836" may be especially fruitful, for as we have seen in the previous three articles, it is precisely the turbulent romantic encounter between the self and social reality that often imbues Larra's late essays with their rhetorical force. The following pages will be an attempt to reevaluate the encounter between self and social world in "La Noche Buena." More specifically, my objective is to historicize more fully the writing subject constituted in the essay by delineating heretofore unexplored contours of the modern selves that are represented—and there are several—by reexamining the social forces for which those selves are figures and by analyzing the ideological function of the very gesture by which Fígaro and Spanish social life are seemingly fused. If "El Día de Difuntos" progressed from the dead cityscape of Madrid to a pained recognition of modern hopelessness within the self, "La Noche Buena" in turn offers the most protracted examination of the liberal subject's paradoxical position as both victim and perpetrator of modernity's violences.

It will be useful to begin our analysis with a phenomenon as seemingly distant from the social realities of modern liberalism as is the question of literary form. Among the initially striking and scarcely commented upon rhetorical features of Larra's essay is its repeated, dramatic juxtaposition of two distinctive narrative tempi. Fígaro's account of Christmas Eve 1836 consistently oscillates between what appear to be temporally unmarked, meditative passages on one hand, and discretely punctuated moments of the essay's rudimentary narrative on the other.[31] From the seemingly atemporal, discursive present of the narrator's opening musings on superstition in the first paragraph, for example—"El número 24 me es fatal: si tuviera que probarlo" [The number 24 is fatal to me; if I had to prove it]—Fígaro and the reader pass to the historically specified beginning of the action per se in the second paragraph—"El último día 23 del año 1836 acababa de expirar" [The last day 23 of the year 1836 had just finished expiring] (604). And this initial juxtaposition establishes a pattern that will be repeated throughout the essay. The discursive time of Fígaro's reflections is systematically disrupted by intrusions of a more immediate, historical hic et nunc, such as the sequence in which his commentaries on office life are interrupted by his servant's call:

¡Dichoso el que tiene oficina! [. . .] Al menos no está obligado a pensar, puede fumar, puede leer la *Gaceta*.

    —¡Las cuatro! ¡La comida!—me dijo una voz de entonación servil y sumisa. [. . .] Esta palabra me sacó de mi estupor. (605)

[Happy is he who has an office! { . . . } At least he is not obliged to think, he can smoke, he can read the *Gaceta*.

    —Four o'clock! Time to eat!—a voice said to me with a servile and submissive intonation. { . . . } Those words brought me out of my stupor.]

Conversely, just as narrative sequences begin to build, they quickly dissolve into the time of meditative discourse, as when *Fígaro* dawns his cape, pulls on his hat, and finally steps out of the house in which he has been brooding, only to engage in new musings on the arbitrary nature of calendrical time:

Tercié la capa, calé el sombrero y en la calle.

    ¿Qué es un aniversario? Acaso un error de fecha. Si no se hubiera compartido el año en trescientos sesenta y cinco días, ¿qué sería de nuestro aniversario? (606)

[I draped on my cape, pulled down my hat, and off through the street.

    What is an anniversary? Perchance a mistaken date. If the year had not been divided into three hundred sixty-five days, what would be of our anniversary?]

While such oscillation might readily be understood as inherent to the loosely narrative structure of the *costumbrista* genre itself, the extent to which Larra's essay exploits the convention's figurative potential is striking inasmuch as the abrupt shifts between these two extremes in narrative tempo mirror a more fundamental dichotomy that is thematized by the title of the piece itself—that is, the opposition between the ahistorical, cyclical time of Christian ritual—"La Noche Buena"—and the secularized, quantifiable time of linear history—"de 1836." In a manner reminiscent of the oscillation between prose and verse in *Don Alvaro*, the essay's staccato tempo consequently functions as a figure of the two distinctive, and ostensibly irreconcilable, temporal modes that govern the essay from the outset; and, not surprisingly, the selves that are constituted in the essay will be inflected through these contrasting forms of temporality. More specifically, two of those selves will alternatively be construed either as the protagonist of a liturgical ritual or quite literally as a commodity destined for consumption in the secular time and space of the market.

The messianic dimension of Fígaro's self-representation in "La Noche Buena de 1836" has not gone unnoticed, and the initial semiosis of the opening lines of the essay, in which Fígaro identifies himself as having been born "en día 24," immediately positions him as a Christ figure by tacit association with Christmas Eve.[32] To the extent that the Christian divinity efficiently figures the traditional, contradictory poles of exalted romantic subjectivity—the inspired deity on the one hand and the misunderstood outcast on the other, the supernatural seer and the sacrificial victim—such an identification is by no means an exceptionally novel rhetorical move. What is intriguing, however, is the extent of the symbolic itinerary this initial figurative gesture inaugurates, for in what is a typological inversion that would certainly not go unnoticed by readers schooled in biblical exegesis, the Nativity in "La Noche Buena de 1836" doubles for the Passion. Fígaro in fact explicitly states the central tenet of Catholic dogma that links the Christ's birth and death: "Hace mil ochocientos treinta y seis años nació el Redentor del mundo, nació el que no reconoce principio; y el que no reconoce fin, nació para morir. Sublime misterio" [One thousand eight hundred thirty-six years ago the world's Redeemer was born; he was born to die. A sublime mystery] (606). To the extent then that he has consciously self-encoded as a Christ figure, Fígaro's wanderings through the streets of Madrid on Christmas Eve will in fact double for that centerpiece of the Catholic liturgy, the Passion and Crucifixion.

Indeed, Larra's celebrated polysemic play, so often deployed in the service of acerbic political commentary, here becomes the vehicle by which Fígaro's night of anguish is repeatedly figured as Christian martyrdom, from the initial coupling of "24" and "fatal" (604), to the ascetic rhetoric with which he describes his anticipation of the day— "desde el 23 me prevengo para el siguiente día de sufrimiento y resignación" [from the 23rd on, I prepare myself for the following day of suffering and resignation] (604)—to the evocation of the time of imperial Rome by way of the Saturnalia, the pagan palimpsest to Christmas that models the subsequent encounter between Fígaro and his servant—"me acordé de que en sus famosas saturnales los romanos trocaban los papeles y los esclavos podían decir la verdad a sus amos" [I remembered that in their famous Saturnalias the Romans switched roles and could speak the truth to their masters] (606).[33]

It is not difficult within this context to posit the biblical analogues onto which Fígaro's sojourn through Madrid might be grafted. In the introspection and brooding sense of impending doom of his study are the traces of Gethsemane. The description of the road that takes him to the theater by way of the marketplace remits to the *via dolorosa* with an ironic, almost Counter-Reformation severity: "Para ir desde mi casa al teatro es preciso pasar por la plaza, tan indispensablemente como es preciso pasar por el dolor para ir desde la cuna al sepulcro" [To go from my house to the theater one must traverse the plaza, as unavoidably as one must traverse pain to go from crib to tomb] (606). And the reality that wounds and bruises Fígaro's sensibility as he wanders the streets after exiting the theater doubles for the torments preceding the Crucifixion:

> Dos horas, tres horas, y yo rondo de calle en calle a merced de mi pensamiento. La luz que ilumina los banquetes viene a herir mis ojos por las rendijas de los balcones; el ruido de los panderos y de la bacanal que estremece los pisos y las vidrieras se abre paso hasta mis sentidos y entra en ellos como cuña a mano, rompiendo y desbaratando. (607)

> [Two hours, three hours, and I wander from street to street at the mercy of my thought. The light that illuminates the banquets streams through the balcony rails, wounding my eyes; the sound of the tambourines and of the bacchanal that shakes floors and windows makes its way to my senses and enters them like a wedge in hand, breaking and ruining.]

Moreover, it is precisely as the faithful are called to Midnight Mass, the liturgical reenactment of the Passion, that Fígaro returns to what will be his figurative crucifixion, the self-annihilating encounter with his servant.

But perhaps the most compelling allusion to Fígaro-as-Christ is the densely figurative passage that in a sense sets the wheels in motion for the final exchange between master and servant; it is the scene in which Fígaro sends his servant out with a few coins to celebrate the evening:

> Miré a mi criado y dije para mí: "Esta noche me dirás la verdad." Saqué de mi gaveta unas monedas; tenían el busto de los monarcas de España: cualquiera diría que son retratos; sin embargo eran artículos de periódico. Las miré con orgullo:—Come y bebe de mis artículos—añadí con desprecio. (606)

[I looked at my servant and said to myself: "Tonight you will tell me the truth." I took some coins out of my desk drawer; they had the bust of Spain's monarchs on them; anybody would say they are portraits; and yet they were newspaper articles. I looked at them with pride:—Eat and drink of my articles—I added with scorn.]

This parodic restaging of the Last Supper, with its echoes of "This night one of you will betray me," its reminiscence of the coins that bought Judas, and its play on the very words of consecration that the priest utters over the communal host, would certainly not be lost on readers with even a rudimentary religious education; and the liturgical underpinnings of the passage, specifically the latent image of the host, will extend to the encounter itself, which will be framed not only as a crucifixion but also as a kind of grotesque communion.

The figural complexity of the passage, however, is by no means exhausted by this frame of reference, for in what is one of the most astounding rhetorical maneuvers of the essay, it is from within the evocation of this very core of the Catholic liturgy that the reified, self-as-commodity augured by the aforementioned time of secular history literally rears its head as the busts of temporal kings inscribed on coins. Moreover, the chain of metonymic associations initiated by the transformation of coins into articles leads not only to the pending, unexpressed metonymy—articles as Fígaro—but also fuses this new triad—coins as articles as Fígaro—with the preceding sequence—Fígaro as Christ as communal host—by way of the tacit metaphor, coin as host. The result is a most dialectically charged image of Fígaro as both the suffering incarnation of a transcendent logos and as an inert unit of material exchange. The image captures with extraordinary economy one of the central dramas that unfolds in the process of Spain's nineteenth-century secularization. It is a drama we have considered in the previous articles: the encounter between the desacralizing machinery of an incipient modern market culture, on the one hand, and a profoundly entrenched Catholic culture of the sacred on the other. In this sense, the image of the host-as-coin is of a piece with earlier images, such as the church music that no longer consoles in the "Exequias" or the strangled bells of "El Día de Difuntos."

The ostensibly incommensurable spheres to which coin and host belong, however, are in fact bridged by the shared semantic fields of "consumption" and "representation" in which both images operate: that is, the communal consumption of the host and its function as a sign of divinity, on the one hand, and the market consumption enabled by the coin as a sign of exchange value on the other. It is consequently no small coincidence that the two primary public spaces occupied by Fígaro in the essay—the market and the theater—which are in a sense emblems of the secular, are dialectically linked to the liturgy and its communal centerpiece. For the images of consumption that preside over the market scene are the degraded, secularized counterparts to the meaning-endowed, transcendent spiritual consumption of communion:

> ¿Hay misterio que celebrar? "Pues comamos," dice el hombre. [. . .] Montones de comestibles acumulados, risa y algazara, compra y venta, sobras por todas partes y alegría. [. . .] Todos aquellos víveres han sido aquí traídos de distintas provincias para colación cristiana de una capital. En una cena de ayuno se come una ciudad a las demás. (606–7)

> [Is the a mystery to celebrate? "Let's eat then," says man. { . . . } Piles of accumulated foodstuff, laughter and clamor, buying and selling, leftovers everywhere and happiness. { . . . } All those provisions have been brought from different provinces for the Christian meal of a capital. In a fasting meal one city eats the rest.]

Similarly, the theater remits to Catholic liturgy both by way of its historical origins and by way of the privileged role each phenomenon accords the act of representation.[34] Again the link is dialectical. The two plays Fígaro views are disapprovingly summarized as "una representación en que los hombres son mujeres y las mujeres hombres" [a play in which men are women and women men] and "un novio que no ve el logro de su esperanza; ese novio es el pueblo español" [a suitor who does not see the realization of his hope; that suitor is the Spanish people] (607). Stable meanings, significantly represented here by gendered vehicles, are either subverted or eternally deferred.[35] And this crisis in representation is the negative, secularized analogue to that *fusion* of representation and meaning that is codified in Catholic dogma by the tenet of transubstantiation, which construes the liturgy not merely as a representational act but as a ritual that actually brings about the incarnation of transcendent meaning in the host. To reiterate then, both the market and the theater might be said to dialectically invert or secularize the respective values of consumption and representation as they are represented in the liturgy.

And just as the call to Midnight Mass that is juxtaposed with Fígaro's return home is no mere backdrop to the narrative action but actually points figuratively to a self that is plotted in terms of the liturgy, so the market and theater are more than the mere secularized analogues of liturgical ritual. They too perform a deictic function, pointing as they do to the alienated and commodified subjectivity that is figured by the articles and coins. Indeed, it might be claimed that it is through the mechanisms of theater and market that the self is in fact commodified. For readers familiar with his writings, the theatricality of Larra's subjectivity would be anything but novel; his public persona is not only inextricably linked to his role as the preeminent theater critic of his time, but the very distinction between public and private and the very notion of a discursive "persona" are thematized by the many *dramatis personae* behind the pseudonyms that span Larra's production—theatrical roles that range from Duende Satírico del Día, to Bachiller Juan Pérez Munguía, to Andrés Niporesas, to M. J. de Larra, to Fígaro.[36]

In the metonymic chain Fígaro-as-articles-as-coins, then, is the embedded history of a Larra who has come to fully acknowledge and exploit both the shifting identities that are inherent to the writing process and the market value of these various writerly selves. And as Ermitas Penas Varela demonstrated in his classic documentation of the publishing contracts that explicitly stipulate the pseudonym under which Larra was to write, publishers were by no means oblivious to this value either. Beyond this personal history, however, are also the traces of that more general history of the material conditions of literary production. It is the history of that gradual but profound eighteenth- and early nineteenth-century transition in which, with the emergence of a burgeoning public sphere, aristocratic patronage cedes to market forces as the primary engine of literary production.[37] In the context of this ever-intensifying commodification of writing, the logic of the commodity form takes over, such that by the time of Larra's writings, a radical schism has opened up between—to use the terms of Marx's classic critique—the use value of writing and writing subjects, on the one hand, and their exchange value on the other. What was intimated in "El Día de Difuntos"—the sense that interior life itself is subject to the reifying, deadening effects of the modern—is concretized in the image, as is the reenchanted, divine flip side of this dialectical coin.

It is in the wake of these simultaneously deified and reified selves that "La Noche Buena de 1836" finally turns to Fígaro's third self, the self toward whom he has been traveling throughout the circular itinerary of the essay, the self that is his servant. The process by which the servant is at once constituted as an independent agent and subsumed into Fígaro echoes the dialectal play between the liturgical Fígaro and the commodified Fígaro, but this time the drama is played out within the field of literary creativity, such that the servant is marked as both Fígaro's autonomous antagonist and as his creation, the displaced voice of his conscience. Hence, while there is a readily identifiable humanizing and individuating process at work in Fígaro's progressively less-disparaging representations of the servant—he is first described as nothing more than "un mueble cómodo" [a comfortable piece of furniture], then as "un ejemplar de la gran edición hecha por la Providencia de la humanidad" [a copy of the grand edition of humanity created by Providence] (608), and finally as a speaking, reasoning subject—"mi criado encontró entonces y de repente, voz y palabras, y habló y raciocinó" [my servant then found, suddenly, a voice and words, and he spoke and reasoned] (609)—the moment in which he is accorded this fully fledged expressive subjectivity is also the moment in which Fígaro links the servant with his own narrative voice: "los fabulistas hacen hablar a los animales, ¿por qué no he de hacer yo hablar a mi criado? [. . .] En fin yo cuento un hecho" [the fabulists make animals speak, why should I not make my servant speak? { . . . } All said, I am recounting a deed] (609). And this dialectic tension between identity and difference—that is, between the servant as self and the servant as accusing other—in turn remits to the two frames in which the encounter has been figuratively positioned—the frames of communion and crucifixion.

Significantly, Fígaro's return from the public spaces of Madrid to the domestic sphere in which his servant awaits is governed by a passage that explicitly continues the metonymic chain initiated in the Last Supper parody:

> ¿Qué es esto? ¿Va a expirar el 24 y no me ha ocurrido en él más contratiempo que mi mal humor de todos los días? Pero mi criado me espera en mi casa, como espera la cuba al catador, llena de vino; mis artículos hechos moneda, mi moneda hecha mosto se ha apoderado del imbécil como imaginé, y el asturiano ya no es hombre; es todo verdad. (608)

> [What is this? The 24th is going to expire and I have had no mishaps other than my daily bad mood? But my servant awaits me at home, like the cask

awaits the taster, full of wine; my articles-become-coin, my coin-become-must has overpowered the imbecile as I imagined, and the Asturian is no longer a man; he is all truth.]

The new chain of figuration—coins as wine as truth—brings the servant into the previously outlined symbolic logic of communion and consumption. On the one hand, he again figuratively communes with Fígaro. He has partaken of the body—coins as hosts—and the blood—coins as wine—of his master in order to experience the truth of him. On the other hand, in a secular sense he has "ingested" Fígaro to the point of inebriation, and—recalling the *in vino veritas* topos—the wine is about to talk: "has de oir al vino una vez que habla" [You will listen to the wine once it begins to speak] (610). Moreover, to the extent that the servant will himself be identified with Fígaro's voice, it is the image of self-consumption that looms large as servant launches into drunken diatribe against master.

As the confrontation begins, the shift from the first-person narrative and monologue that have predominated throughout the essay to dialogue formally conveys the oppositional or self-oppositional nature of the exchange. The seemingly heterogeneous burst of accusations that follow are thus loosely structured by the dialogical pronominal opposition (*tú–yo*) that is repeated throughout the encounter. The servant almost seems to take pleasure in hammering away at Fígaro with these pronouns, from the opening "tú vienes triste de costumbre; yo estoy más alegre que suelo" [you arrive sad, as usual; I am happier than I accustom] (609), to "tú buscas la felicidad [. . .] yo nada busco" [you look for happiness { . . . } I seek nothing] (610), to the concluding "yo estoy ebrio de vino, es verdad; ¡pero tú lo estás de deseos y de impotencia!" [I am drunk on wine, it is true; but you are drunk on desires and on impotence!] (611). At the same time, this closing allusion to questions of desire and power names the two processes that accord the dialogue as a whole with its easily overlooked thematic coherence. Power and desire are in a sense the conceptual anchors around which the various charges coalesce.

As part of a bourgeois power structure that defines the very terms within which the criminal justice system operates, for example, Fígaro is free to commit crimes with legal impunity and thus must face the excruciating pain of his own recriminating conscience:

No pareces criminal; la justicia no te prende al menos; verdad es que la justicia no prende sino a los pequeños criminales, a los que roban con ganzúas o a los que matan con puñal; pero a los que arrebatan el sosiego de una familia seduciendo a la mujer casada o a la hija honesta, a los que roban con naipes en la mano, a los que matan una existencia con una palabra dicha al oído, con una carta cerrada, a esos ni los llama la sociedad criminales, ni la justicia los prende. [. . .] Tú acaso eres de esos criminales, y tienes un acusador dentro de ti. (609)

[You do not look like a criminal; at least the police do not detain you; the truth is that justice only pursues the small criminals, the ones that rob with a lock pick or kill with a knife; but those who snatch away the tranquility of a family by seducing the married woman or the honest daughter, those who rob with playing cards in their hand, those who kill a being with a word whispered in the ear, with a sealed letter, those society does not call criminals, and the police do not arrest them. { . . . } You in all likelihood are one of those criminals, and you have an accuser inside of you.]

Similarly, as an actor within the bourgeois sphere of public discourse, Fígaro is doubly engaged in a never-ending, frightfully paralyzing power struggle, both to maintain the readerly approbation on which his status and critical authority depend and to subdue the potential political rivals who constantly threaten his position:

Tú eres literato y escritor, y ¡qué tormentos no te hace pasar tu amor propio, ajado diariamente por la indeferencia de unos, por la envidia de otros, por el rencor de muchos! [. . .] Hombre de partido, haces la guerra a otro partido; o cada vencimiento es una humillación, o compras la victoria demasiado cara para gozar de ella. [. . .] Adulas a tus lectores para ser de ellos adulado, y eres también despedazado por el temor, y no sabes si mañana irás a coger tus laureles a las Baleares o a un calabozo. (610)

[You are a man of letters and a writer, and yet what torments your pride makes you suffer, disparaged daily by the indifference of some, by the envy of others, and by the scorn of many! A party man, you wage war against the other party; each defeat is a humiliation, or you buy victory at too high a price to enjoy it. { . . . } You adulate your readers in order to be adulated by them, and yet you are also torn apart by fear, and you do not know if tomorrow you will gather your laurels on the Balearic Islands or in a prison cell.]

More blunt even is the servant's ideological unmasking of Fígaro's liberalism as merely a bourgeois grab for power. "Te llamas liberal y despreocupado, y el día que te apoderes del látigo azotarás como te han azotado" [You call yourself an unworried liberal, and the day you get hold of the whip you will beat the way you have been beaten] (610).

Desire, the correlate to such power, is not surprisingly related to the new economic conditions in which the bourgeois class is beginning to flourish. It is, for example, the desire generated by an expanding commodity culture forced to guarantee ever-increasing appetites for its products that informs the servant's following accusation: "yo en fin no tengo necesidades; tú, a pesar de tus riquezas, acaso tendrás que someterte mañana a un usurero para un capricho innecesario, o para un banquete de vanidad en que cada bocado es un tósigo" [I have no needs; you, despite your riches, might have to subject yourself to a moneylender for an unnecessary whim, or for a banquet of vanity in which each mouthful is poison] (610–11). Transposed to his readerly habits, this frustrated desire similarly structures Fígaro's search for truth: "Tú lees día y noche buscando la verdad en los libros hoja por hoja, y sufres de no encontrarla ni escrita" [You read day and night looking for the truth in books, page by page, and you suffer from not finding it, even in writing] (611). And it is the desire for an all-too-illusory amorous plenitude that sets the stage for Fígaro's inevitably tragic liaisons:

> Tú echas mano de tu corazón, y vas y lo arrojas a los pies de la primera que pasa, y no quieres que lo pise y lo lastime, y le entregas ese depósito sin conocerla. Confías tu tesoro a cualquiera por su linda cara, y crees porque quieres; y si mañana tu tesoro desaparece, llamas ladrón al depositario, debiendo llamarte imprudente y necio. (611)

> [You take a hold of your heart, and you go and hurl it at the feet of the first woman that passes, and you do not want her to step on it or wound it, and you make that deposit without knowing her. You entrust your treasure to anybody for her pretty face, and you believe because you want to; and if tomorrow your treasure disappears you call the receiver a thief when you should call yourself imprudent and stupid.]

Finally, language itself can only frustrate the sublimated desires Fígaro futilely attempts to satiate with words, as the servant observes in a pivotal passage that I will return to shortly: "inventas palabras [. . .] y cuando descubres que son palabras, blasfemas y maldices" [you invent words { . . . } and when you discover that they are words, you blaspheme and curse] (611).

To the extent that the servant is, among other things, the voice of Fígaro's own conscience, this series of accusations is one of the most powerful representations within nineteenth-century Spanish letters of the modern liberal subject's self-critique. In the exchange between Fígaro and his servant, Larra stages precisely the kind of dynamic self-reflexivity that philosophy has traditionally taken to be the touchstone of modern subjectivity; and yet it is not merely self-reflexivity that characterizes the enterprise, for Larra's tale is at the same an exercise in self-indictment. "La Noche Buena" represents an ethically and politically critical kind of self-awareness, and in doing so it suggests that within the romantic critique of the modern in Spain there was by 1836 a tacit acknowledgment that liberal modernity and the problem of the modern liberal self were two sides of the same coin. In this essay Larra implicitly notes that the limits of liberalism's emancipatory potentials are at work not only within the external arena of social and political life, but also within the subjective domain of the self and in its quotidian relation to others.

One of the more intriguing turns in "La Noche Buena de 1836" in fact stems precisely from Larra's attempt to give voice to a historically silenced, co-opted other. In psychic terms, the servant is something akin to the skeptical voice within the modern self, the self that recognizes its structural complicity in the unfreedom of others. It is a voice that knows that the modern self participates, wittingly or not, in modes of power in which its own freedom is linked to another's oppression. Indeed, what the servant unmasks within Fígaro is the very thing that leads to historical hopelessness in "Horas de invierno," the intuition that liberal freedom may merely be the name for a new regime of domination. The servant's "azotarás como te han azotado" [you will beat as you have been beaten] is of a piece with the Hobbesian "to devour or be devoured," which, in his desperation, Larra had taken to be history's engine. The difference between the two moments, however, is that "La Noche Buena de 1836" relocates the phenomenon by suggesting that the law of domination is at work within the self, governing not only the fate of nations but also individual, subjective modes of comportment. We thus confront again in

Larra the sense that modern liberal freedom is not free enough, the sense that, in the end, the modern liberal self betrays the emancipatory ideals it so famously espouses.

If "La Noche Buena" is read in an autobiographical register, it is not difficult to identify the reasons behind such self-recriminations. Well-known for his liberal positions, by mid-1836 Larra found himself on the conservative side of the increasingly pronounced rift between moderate and progressive liberals. In the public eye, his support for the moderate government of Istúriz, which collapsed after the famed military coup at La Granja in August 1836, had left Larra on the side of those who favored reform and social stability over more radical, populist, revolutionary models of social transformation. By an unpredictable turn of events Larra, one of the paradigmatic voices of liberalism in Madrid, suddenly found himself cast in the role of moderate crony. Cayetano Cortés succinctly summarized Larra's position within the tumultuous and complex political landscape of the late 1830s as follows:

> Unos se pusieron de parte de la corona en aquella ocasión y se hicieron con-servadores. [. . .] Otros por el contrario se pusieron de parte del pueblo u obraron en nombre suyo. [. . .] Fígaro se decidió por el bando conservador; no ciertamente porque sus ideas liberales no fuesen suficientemente avanza-das. [. . .] Fígaro no veía la necesidad de exponer el país a nuevos trastornos, ni las instituciones a nuevas conmociones. [. . .] Por consiguiente cuando estalló el movimiento de agosto se encontró sorprendido y sin comprender unos sucesos, [. . .] lanzado en el partido de la resistencia, no por simpatía alguna hacia él, sino por la fuerza misma de las cosas.

> [Some decided to back the crown on that occasion and they became con-servatives. { . . . } In contrast others decided to back the people, working in their name. { . . . } Fígaro opted for the conservative faction, but not because his liberal ideas were not advanced enough. { . . . } Fígaro did not see the need to expose the country to new convulsions nor the new institutions to new commotions. { . . . } Consequently, when the August movement erupted he was surprised and did not understand events. { . . . } He was thrown in with the party of resistance, not out of any sympathy for it, but due to the force of circumstances.]

It is against this backdrop that "La Noche Buena" finds its most immediate sociopolitical resonance. Indeed, for habitual readers of Larra, the servant's accusatory demystification of Fígaro's interests in "La Noche Buena de 1836 " would most certainly have been read as a kind of public acknowledgment on Larra's part of the bind in which he had been caught.

A merely autobiographical or national-political reading of this moment in "La Noche Buena de 1836" runs the risk, however, of overlooking the fact that Larra's life, and Spanish politics more generally, do not fully account for the sort of betrayal Larra represents in his self-recriminations. The tendency to read Larra within the framework of "the problem of Spain"—a framework widely disseminated by the turn-of-the-century Spanish writers of the "Generation of 1898"—seems to have made it difficult see that, while undoubtedly embedded in his biographical, sociopolitical, and historical moment, Larra's work also speaks more broadly to the problem of the ways in which modernity's promise has so often been betrayed. The curtailing of the emancipatory potentials within liberalism was not simply a Spanish phenomenon; it was and is a constitutive element of modern revolution as such. Indeed it is precisely this process—the reactive recontainment of emancipatory impulses—that the Marx of *The Eighteenth Brumaire of Luis Bonaparte* highlights, for example, in his study of the quintessentially "modern" French political culture at the mid-century. In this work Marx notes rather matter of factly that bourgeois revolutions are by their very nature "short lived," inasmuch as demands for social order inevitably follow moments of upheaval. "A long crapulent depression"—he observes—"lays hold of society before it learns soberly to assimilate the results of its storm-and-stress period" (19).

It is similarly worth recalling that, on a grander historical stage, the spectacle of the French Revolution and its aftermath had already made clear to most observers the extent to which revolutionary energies could usher in periods of reactionary, repressive restraint; and by the mid-century, the bloody crushing of the working-class uprisings that swept across Europe in 1848 left little doubt as to the class interests that subtended bourgeois liberalism's rallying cries of *family, church, tradition,* and *society.* The point of reconsidering Larra against this broader historical canvass is, again, to note the degree to which his work speaks to the question of modernity itself as much as it does to the question of Spanish culture. The servant's accusation—"azotarás como te han azotado" [you will beat as you have been beaten]—addresses more than Larra's political falterings, and it is more than a lucid recrimination of the hypocritical shortcomings of moderate liberalism in Spain. The servant's words are also an indictment of the more fundamental betrayal of freedom that by 1836 was already understood to inhere—in Spain and elsewhere—within the bourgeois order of modernity.

Such are the charges that lead to the closing image of a sleepless Fígaro, deliriously eyeing a mysterious yellow box inscribed with the word "mañana" and asking himself what that tomorrow will bring. That box would become famous just over two months after the essay's publication when, in addition to the firearm with which he killed himself, a revolver box of the same color was found at the scene of Larra's suicide. It was at this point that the nexus between Larra's late essays and his suicide began to form, for it was a two-way bridge that went up between boxes (the box in the essay and the revolver box in Larra's home) at that moment of discovery. If Larra's death reframed "La Noche Buena de 1836" as a kind of literary suicide, Fígaro's rhetoric of martyrdom in the essay was instantly extended to the accounts of Larra's death and, subsequently, to much of the criticism dedicated to his work. In large measure, the reception of this essay as a veiled suicide letter inaugurated the interpretive tradition that, to this day, is forced to grapple with the social significance of Larra's death. This is so because the fusion of boxes established a framework in which Larra's self-annihilation was irrevocably suffused with the metaphysical, political, and historical suffering as transmitted by the figure of death in essays such as the "Exequias," "Horas de invierno," and "El Día de Difuntos." "La Noche Buena de 1836" is in this sense a key—perhaps the key—to understanding the shifting status of death and its meanings that we considered at the beginning of this chapter.

And yet one is obliged to return to the problem that hovered over the work of other authors we have considered—the disquieting nature of Tediato's pain and compassion, or *Don Alvaro's* curious blindness to slavery—in order to ask whether Larra's pained critique of the modern, even in its most self-reflective moment, does not also carry within it a similar kind of ideological mystification. The question that must be asked is the question of the ideological significance and function of the representation of Fígaro's self-annihilation in "La Noche Buena." It will be useful in this regard to retrace our steps in order to consider once again the selves that the essay has constituted, for it is through those selves that the text's ideological dimensions may be more readily apprehended. Indeed, from a distance, Fígaro's subjectivity seems to have been the stage for a historical allegory. The liturgical time and space of Fígaro-as-Christ represents the stable, hieratic metaphysics associated with the Ancien Régime; the secularized time and space of Fígaro-as-commodity is a figure of the emergent bourgeois market-world; and the mostly silent Fígaro-as-servant—who cannot yet make an appearance in this new public sphere but who, given the opportunity, lashes out at his master—clearly doubles for a laboring class that has begun to understand the relations of power behind the nineteenth-century bourgeois cult of freedom. Moreover, the discursive dialectical play we have seen between Fígaro's various selves and between the spaces they occupy appears to figure the social dialectic between the forces that those selves and spaces represent. It is as if "La Noche Buena de 1836" has in a sense textualized the very gears of the Ancien Régime grinding against the new secularizing forces of the market, as if it has captured the desacralization inherent to this process in the communal host that is also a coin, as if it has attempted to represent the emerging opposition between the bourgeoisie and its laboring others at the level of pronouns. But to what end has this history has been deployed? What has been the purpose of this Saturnalian slave revolt?

Historical narrative is, of course, always more than the disinterested representation it may try to be. As Frederic Jameson has observed, "the production of aesthetic or narrative form is an ideological act in its own right with the function of inventing imaginary or formal solutions to unresolvable social contradictions" (*Political*, 79). And it is precisely this dimension of "La Noche Buena de 1836," its status as an ideological act, that has been veiled by Larra's suicide and the rhetoric of modern suffering with which it has been fused. The agenda behind the essay's historical allegory is ultimately anything but complicitous with the figurative revolution it enacts. Indeed, the carnivalesque inversion of the roles of master and servant imaginatively resolves the ever-intensifying social problem of class friction by giving Fígaro's servant a figurative voice and power that labor did not in fact have in 1836. It is, in the Jamesonian sense, a kind of collective wish fulfillment, a symptomatic palliative for the latent, unresolvable contradictions lurking in Spain's early nineteenth-century political unconscious.

One need only scrutinize the representation of the servant, however, to begin to outline the class interests served by this highly touted social critique. While the vehemently accusatory rhetoric directed at his master quite successfully draws attention away from the way the servant himself is characterized, the image of him that emerges from the encounter is nothing short of a bourgeois dream about the working class:

> Yo nada busco, y el desengaño no me espera a la vuelta de la esperanza. [. . .] ¿A mí quién me calumnia? ¿Quién me conoce? Tú me pagas un salario bastante a cubrir mis necesidades. (610)

> [I look for nothing, and disillusion does not await me on the other side of hope. { . . . } Who slanders me? Who knows me? You pay me a sufficient salary to cover my needs.]

> Concluyo, yo en fin no tengo necesidades; [. . .] Cuando yo necesito de mujeres echo mano de mi salario y las encuentro, fieles por más de un cuarto de hora. (611)

> [In conclusion, I have no needs; { . . . } When I need women I make use of my salary and I find them, faithful for over a quarter of an hour.]

> El pobre asturuiano come, bebe, duerme, y nadie le engaña, y, si no es feliz, no es desgraciado, no es al menos hombre de mundo, ni ambicioso ni elegante, ni literato ni enamorado. (611)

> [The poor Asturian eats, drinks, sleeps and nobody deceives him; and if he is not happy, he is not wretched, at least he is not a man of the world, nor is he ambitious, nor elegant, nor a man of letters, nor in love.]

In short, he is an untroubled, simple, almost mindless man whose desires extend no further than easily satisfied bodily needs and who is fortunate to be free from the terrible injuries to which the exercise of power and unbridled desire have subjected his master.

Moreover, the servant's accusations have been positioned not as the expression of legitimate class interests but rather as the terrible instruments of a symbolic crucifixion such that readerly sympathies fall with the master. It is one of the essay's rhetorical coups that modern bourgeois power and hegemony have been rewritten as suffering. To murder with impunity, to participate in a libidinal machinery the precondition of which is material comfort, to have a voice in the public sphere—in "La Noche Buena de 1836" these class privileges ironically become part of an extended proof of the servant's initial assertion to his master that, of the two, it is Fígaro who most deserves pity: "Lástima—dijo una voz, repitiendo mi piadosa exclamación—. ¿Y por qué me has de tener lástima, escritor? Yo a tí, ya lo entiendo" [Pity—a voice said, repeating my compassionate exclamation. And why should you pity me, writer? My pitying you, that I understand] (609). The extent to which mainstream critical receptions since 1836 have tacitly accepted and reproduced this sentiment speaks most eloquently both to the rhetorical force of such discourse and to the persistence with which the modern bourgeois subject continues to function, to this day, as an invisible, naturalized standard of reference. Perspicacious as Fígaro's self-critique is, in the end it is he and not the servant who is figured as a victim of the modern order.

The essay also symbolically resolves the fundamental tension between those two contradictory impulses of the bourgeois revolution, freedom and domination, by staging—to use a term John Rosenberg proposes in a different context—an "ethical nightmare." That is, it displaces the question of power relations into the language of ethics, such that while Larra's bourgeois readers might grapple with the their consciences, they would not need to fully confront their own rise to class hegemony in political terms. To the contrary, "La Noche Buena" would serve as a convenient badge of conscience, an emblem of their morality if ever there was a question; and, as Teichmann has argued, Fígaro's pseudo-Christian "sacrifice" would symbolically redeem the very culture ostensibly under critique. In this sense the allusion to the carnivalesque inversions of the Saturnalia could not be more appropriate, for the carnival's function in the essay is, ultimately, to legitimize the status quo it momentarily subverts.

In this light it is well worth reconsidering the much commented linguistic skepticism that afflicts Fígaro, for it too is more than it seems: "inventas palabras y haces de ellas sentimientos, ciencias, artes, objetos de existencia. ¡Política, gloria, saber, poder, riqueza, amistad, amor! Y cuando descubres que son palabras, blasfemas y maldices" [you invent words and make of them feelings, sciences, arts, objects of existence. Politics, glory, knowledge, power, wealth, friendship, love! And when you discover that they are words, you blaspheme and curse] (611). This disenchantment paradigm that structures the passage initially seems to replicate within language itself the tension between transcendence and material contingency that has characterized Fígaro's deified and reified selves. The quasi-religious transcendence that informs Fígaro's desire for words to be more than mere words, for example, is apparent in his decidedly *sacrilegious* reaction upon confronting their contingent, mundane existence. As a metacommentary about "La Noche Buena de 1836" itself, this view of words might also be read as a kind of aporia or short-circuiting in which language turns on itself, much as the servant has turned on Fígaro. This crisis of referentiality, however, is not devoid of political implications. If on the one hand it enacts a powerful unmasking of the foundational ideals of the liberal cultural revolution—for which Larra should continue to be credited—on the other it also undermines the very categories with which the prevailing order might be challenged. As Terry Eagelton has observed with regard to more recent, but similar, postmodern gestures:

> The anti-foundationalist road is perilous [. . .] only to a degree, for in boldly kicking out the foundations from under one's own life forms, one inevitably drags them out from beneath one's opponents too. They can now no more finally ground their challenge to you than you can metaphysically copperplate your defense against them. [. . .] The move serves to swaddle the dominant system from any searching critique at the same time as it serves to enhance its liberal credentials. (*Illusions*, 40–41)

Larra's disillusioning experience with words is, in this regard, a luxury made possible precisely because the political question of whose words ultimately count has already been answered.

The socially symbolic dimensions of the essay, however, extend beyond its uses of historical allegory or its demystification of language. They are also apparent in the epistemological preconditions that have allowed Fígaro's selves to fuse with each other, with their object-world, and with social realities in the first place. I am referring to that well-known romantic shift to an idealist, subject-based epistemology, the famous Kantian "Copernican turn," whereby the empiricist separation between subject and object is blurred, opening the door to the world of subjectivity at work in "La Noche Buena de 1836."[38] A celebrated passage in which the windows of Fígaro's study become an emblem of the porous threshold between mind and reality thematizes the figurative process that is at work throughout the essay:

Ora volvía los ojos a los cristales de mi balcón. [. . .]. Los vapores conden-
sados se deslizaban a manera de lágrimas a lo largo del diáfano cristal; así se
empaña la vida, pensaba; así el frío exterior del mundo condensa las penas en
el interior del hombre. (605)

[From time to time I turned my eyes on the windows of my balcony. { . . . }
Condensed vapors ran like tears across the length of the crystal; that's how
life becomes clouded, I thought; that's how the cold exterior of the world
condenses pains within man's interior.]

Behind the rhetoric of suffering is the deeply utopian, romantic dream
of a fragile unity between the perceiving self and the external world, and
in this sense "La Noche Buena" and the other winter essays of 1836 are
far less distant from romantic lyric poetry than might be expected of the
genre. At the same time, the reality that this utopian impulse necessarily
carries with it as its conceptual antithesis is not difficult to identify, for
to negate the key terms of Larra's conceit by positing a radical *separation* between subject and object is to open a very different window onto
that increasingly inert, atomized, quantifiable, and alienated reality of the
emerging world of liberal modernity. In this context it is not difficult to
appreciate, as we have seen elsewhere, that romantic idealism itself is a
kind of symbolic compensation, the counterpart to the increasingly desa-
cralized, objective reality of modernity.

Arguably, it is ultimately this utopian dimension of the "La Noche
Buena de 1836," and not its more explicit forms of civic self-flagellation,
that invests the essay with its most lasting value. For the profoundly anti-
empirical epistemology that characterizes this piece, and Larra's late essays
generally, models a romantic subject whose very fusion with his social
world is grounded in a desire to resist, at the level of language itself, an
alienating reality that is coming into being; it represents a desire to think
and write beyond what is. It is a phenomenon we encountered repeatedly: The Count of Campo Alange is more than the friend Larra lost;
"Horas de invierno" is more than the translation of an anthology; Madrid
is more than an agglomeration of buildings; Fígaro's coins are more than
money; and throughout, death is always more than simply death. In the
end it may be the imaginative power and vitality of the act of figuration
itself rather than its particular contents that imbue Larra's work with a

paradoxically contemporary significance. For while "La Noche Buena de 1836" clearly registers the romantic subject's deep complicity with the reality against which he dreams, the act of dreaming itself—the wavering will to think that things might be different—continues to speak to our present and its numbing "the way things are" with a most poignant and thoroughly modern urgency.

Afterword

An anguished gentleman dialogues in a cemetery with the gravedigger he has hired to unearth the body of his beloved; a Peruvian noble is driven to suicide at the edge of a cliff on a stormy night; in Madrid, a journalist's essays chillingly ruminate on images of death shortly before he takes his life. In the works we have considered in the preceding chapters, a pained response to the modern has repeatedly manifested itself with a strangely moving insistence. It is a kind of anguish that bespeaks the restrictions of the modern, a mournful sort of longing that implies that one of the prices of modernity may in fact be a stifling rather than an enabling of subjective possibility. And yet, just over a decade after Larra's death, Charles Baudelaire, the poet of European modernity par excellence, would give emblematic expression to the symbolic geography of the modern that, as we considered at the outset of this book, presumed a European south devoid of suffering, of romanticism, and, by extension, of modern art altogether. In the well-known essay, "Qu'est-ce que le Romantisme?" [What is Romanticism?], Baudelaire lucidly expresses the literary commonplace concerning the differing artistic "spirits" that purportedly animated northern and southern European cultural production:

> Qui dit romantisme dit art moderne,—c'est à dire intimité, spiritualité, couleur, aspiration vers l'infini, exprimées par tous les moyens que contiennent les arts. [. . .] Le romantisme est fils du Nord [. . .] les rêves et les féeries sont enfants de la brume. En revanche le Midi est naturaliste, car la nature y est si belle et si claire, que l'homme, n'ayant rien a désirer, ne trouve rien de plus beau à inventer que ce qu'il voit. [. . .] (*Oeuvres*, 421)

> [He who says romanticism says modern art; that is, intimacy, spirituality, color, aspiration for the infinite, expressed by all of the means the arts con-

tain. { . . . } Romanticism is a child of the North { . . . } dreams and fancies
are children of the mist. In contrast the South is naturalistic, for nature there
is so beautiful and so clear, that man has nothing to desire, he finds nothing
more beautiful to invent than what he sees.]

The passage carries out a climate-inflected distribution of aesthetic qualities that in effect spatializes the classic schism of philosophical dualism. To
the north, spirit, mind, and depth; to the south, matter, surface, the body.
In this account northern Europe comes to represent subjective agency
itself—interiority, imagination, aspiration, and the like—while the south
figures a nondesiring, nonmodern locus of creative indolence. It is not difficult to hear in these lines the echoes of Hegel's modern Europe, and one
of the objectives of this book has been to make visible the links between
this representational legacy and the shifting power structures of modern
European cultural politics.

To contrast the preceding chapters—that is, the figures of Tediato,
Alvaro, and Fígaro—with such a legacy is to face the fissure that most attempts to think historically about the writing of Spain's romantic era have
had to confront in one way or another. It is to experience the conceptual
gap between, on the one hand, a textual archive that evinces complex
engagements with the modern in Spain, and, on the other hand, a master
narrative of European modernity from which Spanish culture was systematically purged. This fissure was historical, to be sure, and it can be traced
to the northern displacement of imperial power that accompanied the
transition from early modern to modern Europe. But the effects of this
historical process continue to inform our contemporary landscape in numerous ways; they persist within European literary studies today. All too
often, "modern European literature" continues to designate the national
literatures of only three countries—the three countries that appeared in
my opening evocation of the international news. And while this pattern
of thought has been dismantled intellectually, it lives rather robustly in
institutional practices that range from the structuring of departments of
"literature," to questions of literary curricula, to the world of academic
publishing. Similarly, the metageography of modern Europe is often still
subtly at work within the analytic assumptions of contemporary cultural
theory and criticism; it persists as a mode of reading. In each of the preceding chapters, for example, we have encountered moments in which the
historical presumption of Spanish backwardness was at odds with a more

substantive historical reckoning with the texts in question. This is not to say that Spain did not differ from its neighbors to the north in significant ways; it is simply to suggest that the amplification of national difference within a narrative of Hispanic nonmodernity or "failure" needs to be recognized as the mythic thinking it is, rather than as the given for which it has so often been taken.

In practice this means acknowledging that, as a word-thought, modernity is at its core a relational term; its meanings are unavoidably relative insofar as they always imply some other state of affairs. If the concept is meant to name a definitive break with the past in order to underscore the novelty of the now, its claim to singularity soon dissolves into a deeper understanding of historical time. Modernity paradoxically proliferates into its familiar adjectival forms: early modernity, mercantile modernity, liberal modernity, industrial modernity, the contemporary (post) modernities of the present. Similarly, if for nineteenth-century modern Europe, Spain was imagined as one of the most proximate sites of poetic nonmodernity, for the writers we have considered in the preceding pages, the modern was rather clearly perceived as a powerful, disturbing force at work *within* Spanish culture.

Even in those places where the traditional tale tells us that modernity was fully established—the symbolic centers of the modern—the concept is far more relational and porous a notion than one might suspect. As Homi Bhabha has recently observed:

> What one expects to find at the very center of life or literature—as the summation of a Great Tradition, the core values of a culture—may, in large part, be the dream of the deprived, or the illusion of the powerless. The canonical center may, indeed, be most interesting in its elusiveness, as an enigma of authority. ("Afterword," 195)

Precisely because of the questionable ways in which that authority has been wielded, Bhabha goes on to remind twenty-first-century readers of the need "to refuse to accede to arrogant claims to cultural supremacy based on some normative sense of cultural hierarchy or racial and historical supremacy" (196). Another of the aims of this book has been to resist such assertions of cultural supremacy by developing new readings of the culture of "peripherally modern," romantic Spain. They are readings that have attempted to register the historical impact of northern European cultural imperialism on Spanish culture—and on the discipline of Spanish studies—without replicating its "you are not modern" at the level of critical analysis. In practice this has entailed an attempt to read modernity *from Spain*, rather than reading a deficiently modern Spain from the imperial difference of modern Europe. It has meant acknowledging, for example, that the pained sense of the modern that has repeatedly surfaced in the preceding works is often not a distinctively Spanish anguish but rather a feature of modernity itself.

Cadalso, Saavedra, and Larra were deeply concerned with the collective life of the Spanish nation, and their intellectual biographies make clear that each of them was a proponent of what today would be called "modernization." At the same time, however, in the writings we have examined each author also gathers together the elements of a cautionary tale concerning the modern. It is a tale that continues to resonate in the present, despite the historical distance that separates them from it: As contemporary twenty-first-century cultures are increasingly dominated by the cult of economic self-interest, for example, Tediato's melancholy may still speak to the more nocent effects of instrumental reason. In an emergent global culture fraught with nationalist xenophobia, Alvaro's tragic impossibility may yet resound in disturbingly familiar ways. And as the logic of perpetual war openly makes its claim on international politics today, Fígaro's disquieting insight that one of modernity's more common masks is the face of death may seem strangely prescient. This is so not only because the modernity of the romantic era shares fundamental features with the present, but also because, as the preceding chapters suggest, romantic pain in the face of the modern is not merely nostalgia for the past. In Spain, it is certainly not reducible to nationalist historicism. There is something in the romantic's wounded recoiling from the way things are that is more than mere evasion.

The numerous terms that have historically named this suffering—spleen, mal du siècle, *Weltschmerz, fastidio universal*—tend to pathologize the subject who experiences it; but this suffering also carries within it a tacit indictment of the socioeconomic order that produces it. As we have seen in each of the preceding chapters, romantic pain accuses. For recent theorists such as Löwy and Sayre, the name of the socioeconomic order that is the object of romantic critique is simply modern capitalism, which they conceive as follows:

As a socioeconomic system, capitalism has various aspects: industrialization, the rapid and correlated development of science and technology [. . .] the hegemony of the market, the private ownership of means of production, the enlarged reproduction of capital, "free" labor, and an intensified division of labor. Around it have emerged integrally related aspects of modern civilization: rationalization, bureaucratization, the predominance of [. . .] urbanization, secularization, reification, and so on. As a mode of relations and production, capitalism is the principle that generates and unifies the overall phenomenon, rich in ramifications, that we know as "modernity." (19)

In this view, romantic discourse is best grasped as a response "to a certain number of features of modernity that it finds unbearable" (29), and among the more salient of those features are several of the phenomena we have encountered in the preceding pages: the disenchantment of the world, its quantification, its mechanization, the dominance of rationalist abstraction, and the dissolution of social bonds (29–43). There can be little doubt that Spain's progressive entry into capitalist modernity took place at a different historical pace than it did in northern Europe, but to disregard or otherwise mute the importance of the transformation that *was* taking place in the eighteenth and nineteenth centuries is to remain enthralled to the myth of modern Europe. Another of the objectives of this book has been to show that the writing of Spain's late eighteenth and early nineteenth centuries clearly engaged these facets of the modern, despite the nation's different, non-northern path to the modern.

If Tediato's melancholy can be related to the self-interested values of eighteenth-century mercantilism, if the rift between the poetic and the prosaic in *Don Alvaro* might have a basis in nineteenth-century political economy, and if there are suggestive links between Fígaro's macabre rhetoric and the implementation of liberal economic reform, this is because, as we have seen at various moments in this book, the history of modernity cannot easily be located in one time or one place. The features that Löwy and Sayre describe did not suddenly arrive on the scene. They were not simply the result of punctual transformative events, but accrued intermittently over vast time spans. Before they crystallized into a coherent framework, these features coexisted in an irregular patchwork, with differing degrees of development; and this more complex understanding of modernity and its histories has repeatedly been on display in Spanish cultural production of the romantic era.[1] Precisely because of its symbolically peripheral status, the writing of romantic Spain teaches that the modern cannot be reduced to a standard series of revolutionary narratives—whether political, economic, or scientific. It gestures to other timescales that are equally important; it reminds readers that modernity and empire have historically been two sides of the same coin; and it demonstrates that the concept of the modern is awash in questions of power more generally: the power to define it, narrate it, and locate it historically.

At the same time, the texts we have examined bear witness to a distinctively macabre tradition within the writing of Spain's romantic era. As David Gies has noted, Spanish romantic discourse seems to have an especially strong gothic tenor ("Larra"). The gothic could easily be read as yet another instance of a belated Spanish cultural movement, to be sure, but if one discards this sequential, teleological view of literary history, it might just as easily be envisaged as an especially effective mode of symbolic engagement with the turmoil of the modern. Even in the present, "Gothic figures have continued to shadow the progress of modernity with counter narratives displaying the underside of enlightenment and humanist values" (Botting, 2). "Perhaps the Gothic is an entirely serious attempt"—David Punter has recently observed—"to get to grips with the difficulties of social organization, or in the organization of the psyche" (xix).

In the texts we have considered, wrestling with the modern via the darkness of gothic discourse enables a particularly potent form of critique. It is a mode of representation that is suffused with utopian negativity, that is, a negativity that suggests the need for alternatives. In their quasi-obsessive engagement with modernity's underside, these texts often suggest the possibility of another, better state of affairs that nevertheless remains unstated. Commenting on similar gestures within twentieth-century cultural criticism, Simon Jarvis has recently characterized utopian negativity as follows:

> It cannot provide a blueprint for what the good life would be like, but only examine what our "damaged" life is like. It hopes to interpret this damaged life with sufficient attention and imagination to allow intimations of a possible, undamaged life to show through. (9)

Such utopian intimations manifest themselves in the texts we have considered as the questions that each project leaves behind it: In what state of affairs would Tediato's suffering be less implacable? In what kind of world would Alvaro truly be free? What would authentic life look like in contrast to Fígaro's fateful encounters with death-in-life? To ask such questions is to entertain the possibility that things could be otherwise, and it is to acknowledge that something is deeply amiss within the given. In short, *Noches lúgubres, Don Alvaro o la fuerza del sino*, and Larra's late essays each respond to the modern by communicating a symbolic "not like this," and far from nostalgia, such rhetorical gestures create the ground from which to imagine an as-yet-unarticulated, better future. Ultimately, it is this dissatisfied, negative utopian impulse that accounts for the continued purchase of these texts on the imagination of the present; for as artworks that symbolically communicate dissent, their utopian kernel—the implicit "it might be otherwise" that they carry within—represents a standard of measure from which any status quo comes into question.[2]

If the romantic subject's pained response to the modern carries within it unexpressed utopian intimations, however, it also tells a cautionary tale of a very different sort. Time and again, we have witnessed the way in which the self—the very center of the rhetoric of romanticism—can become a stumbling block or limit, a force that curtails the scope of the emancipatory ideals it asserts. In historical terms it is clear, for example, that despite proclamations to the contrary, the subject of culture throughout much of nineteenth-century Europe was usually limited to a bourgeois man of property, and such ideological limitations were often structurally embedded within the cultural production of the moment. It is a limitation that reminds contemporary readers of the restrictive nature of the freedoms initially imagined by liberalism, and it begs the question of just how successful subsequent liberal democratic regimes have been in extending the idea of freedom beyond its historically parsimonious home.

The texts we have considered, however, also display a limit that is less historically contingent, a limit that is intimately linked to the experience of pain, and it too may still speak to our present. A common, disquieting feature of the anguish represented in the texts we have considered is the ease and frequency with which such pain eclipses the suffering of others. Tediato's compassion paradoxically effaces the qualitatively different nature of Lorenzo's suffering; Alvaro's nightmarish trajectory takes place against an unquestioned backdrop of slavery; and Fígaro, although keenly aware of the contradictions of his class position, is ultimately incapable of recognizing in his servant anything more than an agent of his own suffering. The modern selves we have considered often fail to see the pain of subordinate others around them, and even when they do, their gaze tends to transmute alterity into identity: The other becomes a figure of the self's pain.

One of the final paradoxes of romantic anguish is thus how often such pain is coupled with unacknowledged privilege, how often the self in sorrow is blind to its own participation in structures that inflict pain on others. There is surely something to be learned from the fact that, even as they decry the alienating effects of the modern, the suffering spirits we have considered are each shadowed by laboring bodies whose toil is either unrepresented or, more commonly, poeticized as a figure of their masters' tribulations. To the extent that romantic writing remained within the bourgeois order it sought to indict, it is no surprise that labor should consistently appear as its blind spot. More broadly, however, this pattern of representation and omission also echoes the gesture that characterized modern Europe itself when, confronted by the alienating effects of its own purportedly autonomous civilization, it began to imagine its exterior—in this case Spain—as a space of poetic reprieve. The analogy is possible because in both cases the experience of pain is represented across an asymmetrical field of power; put more simply, the structural, political superiority of the self/modern Europe marks the limit of its ability to recognize the subordinate.

Whether interpersonal, between classes, or across national boundaries, the paradox of privileged pain makes visible the contradictions of coming to terms with suffering from differing—and usually unacknowledged—positions of power. Nationally, the culture of romantic Spain installed itself within the emergent forces of a modern liberal social order whose reifying power it often sought to critique; internationally, however, it was viewed as part of a declining Spanish Empire whose culture was increasingly subordinated to the more contemporary imperialisms of northern Europe. In large measure it is such shifting power structures that make the romantic era in Spain such a fascinating and particularly instructive site of inquiry, for Spanish historical experience foregrounds the fundamental question of the relationship between power and culture in ways that the field of "modern European literature" has, until very recently, tended to overlook.

At the same time, so long as the question of modern social justice remains unresolved within our own world, works such as those we have examined will continue to engage the now of our reading in revealing ways. The opening years of this century have made clear, for example, that the paradox of privileged pain could scarcely be more of a present-day concern. One need only turn to the twenty-four-hour news, to the talking heads beaming with info-youth, to see that the suffering of some is systematically privileged over the routine pain of others. Indeed, as new forms of imperial power respond to First World pain and vulnerability by promising relentless war in the name of modern civilization, the possibilities of utopian dissent that the preceding Spanish texts have intimated, and the lessons that they have taught about the historical hubris of modernity, may come to be seen as an especially modern, perhaps even contemporary, form of literary engagement.

Notes

Introduction

1. For recent discussion of the "globalization" of literary studies, see for example Moretti, the *PMLA* special topic, *Globalizing Literary Studies* (Gunn), or more recently, Shih.
2. For a historical overview of this mode of thought and of its impact on the writing of Spanish history well into the twentieth century, see Alvarez Junco (Introduction, 1–10).
3. The most sustained analysis of romantic subjectivity and its relationship to Spanish liberal ideology remains Kirkpatrick (*Románticas*, 37–48).
4. For a classic essay on the distinction between art—in this case, narrative art—and information, see Benjamin's "The Storyteller" (*Illuminations*, 83–109). The engagement with the limits of empiricism that will unfold in the pages that follow is, in this regard, not unlike the claims that Frankfurt School thinkers—themselves inheritors of romantic thought—would famously come to make about modernism in the twentieth century.
5. The Foucault I have invoked here tends to be overshadowed by the one for whom, as James Kinkaid has recently noted, "the concept of power remains oddly secure, mystic and immune, protected and idealized, because it is metaphysical through and through" (1328).
6. The most notable, recent exception is Hillgarth's *The Mirror of Spain*. The work examines European images of Spain during the early modern era. Although it does not explicitly relate such representations to the theorization of Western modernity, it offers a thorough inventory of northern European images of Spain.
7. For a recent evaluation of the question of canon in modern Spanish literature, see Ríos-Font. It is worth noting that my interest in taking up the work of Cadalso, Saavedra, and Larra is not to reassert their canonical status within Spanish letters but rather to highlight the distance between the Spanish literary canon and the international "modern European" canon.

Chapter 1

1. All translations from Spanish texts, unless otherwise indicated, are my own.

2. Paz situates his search within a Symbolist genealogy of modern poetry: "Mi caso no es único ni excepcional: todos los poetas de nuestra época, desde el período simbolista, fascinados por esa figura a un tiempo magnética y elusiva, han corrido tras ella. El primero fue Baudelaire. El primero también que logró tocarla y así descubrir que no es sino tiempo que se deshace entre las manos" [My case is neither unique nor exceptional: from the Symbolist period, all modern poets have chased after that magnetic and elusive figure that fascinates them. Baudelaire was the first. He was also the first to touch her and discover that she is nothing but time that crumbles in one's hands] (18).

3. "Hegel used the concept of modernity first of all in historical contexts, as an epochal concept: The 'new age' is the 'modern age.' This corresponded to contemporary usage in English and French: 'modern times' or *temps moderns* denoted around 1800 the three centuries just preceding. The discovery of the 'new world,' the Renaissance, and the Reformation—these three monumental events around the year 1500 constituted the epochal threshold between modern times and the middle ages" (Habermas, *Philosophical*, 5). For Habermas, Hegel is "the first philosopher to develop a clear concept of modernity" (4). In what follows, I shall be using Hegel in order to map the locations of "European modernity" and "universal history." For a brief synopsis of the persistence of this paradigm in the twentieth century, see Lewis and Wigen (106–9).

4. Weber himself would make clear that for him *rationalization* extends beyond mathematics and empirical reasoning. "There can equally be rationalizations of the economy, technology, scientific work, education, war, the administration of justice, and other forms of administration. Furthermore, each one of these spheres can be 'rationalized' from extremely varied perspectives and aims" (*Protestant* 365–66).

5. Jameson notes recently in his *A Singular Modernity* that "the double standard of the two moments or versions of modernity—the scientific one of the seventeenth century, and the industrial one of the late eighteenth and nineteenth centuries—is a doxa so widely held as to be largely commonsensical and unchallenged" (63). He later describes a pattern of thought that perfectly describes the rift we have considered in Hegel: "It is as though the intensification of our attention turned upon itself, and began to distinguish the detail of what was somehow less modern in modernity from what was more so, thereby generating a pre-modern moment within modernity as such" (74). For Jameson, it is not until Foucault's *The Order of Things* that

the continuity between these two modernities is shattered and productively problematized. "The merit of Foucault [. . .] is then evidently to assign these moments to radically different historical systems, and to turn that very succession or progression into a historiographic and even a philosophical problem" (63).

6. Within the long, complex history of the idea of progress, several phases have traditionally been postulated. Its early formulation in the Greco-Roman world is evident (Edelstein), as is its presence within Renaissance thought (Wagar). For most historians of the idea, however, the (Counter) Reformation marks an important reinvigoration of the concept, and the eighteenth and nineteenth centuries bear witness to its definitive triumph. Robert Nesbit's classic history of the idea of progress offers the following synthesis: "During the period 1750–1900 the idea of progress reached its zenith. [. . .] From being one of the important ideas in the West it became the dominant idea [. . .]. It was possible to show—as did Turgot, Condorcet, Saint-Simon, Compte, Hegel, Marx, and Spencer, among others—that all history could be seen as a slow, gradual, but continuous and necessary ascent to some given end [. . .]. What we also find [. . .] is the beginning and development of the secularization of the idea of progress—detaching it from its long-held relationship with God, making it a historical process activated and maintained by purely natural causes" (174–75). Bury, Ginsberg, and Van Doren chart similar progressions.

7. Following Löwith's *Meaning in History*, the narrative of progress has traditionally been understood as a secularization of Christian eschatology; Blumenberg, however, challenges such a formulation by arguing that it is in fact modernity's autonomy from Christian theology that underpins its claims to legitimacy. For his part, Cascardi warns more recently against the reduction of modernity to a self-reflexive rational subject, whether Cartesian, Weberian, or Habermasian; in its place he posits a multidiscursive modern subject (*Subject*, 1–71).

8. While scientific or technological progress continues to be championed in some sectors, it is primarily the idea of the moral progress of humanity that has been resoundingly refuted. Reviewing the century, Hobsbawm poses the problem in the following terms: "Why [. . .] did so many reflective minds look back upon it without satisfaction, and certainly without confidence in the future? [. . .] Because it was without doubt the most murderous century of which we have record, both by scale, frequency and length of the warfare that filled it [. . .] [and] by the unparalleled scale of the human catastrophes it produced, from the greatest famines in history to systematic genocide" (13).

9. Greenblatt has recently argued that "we need more a sharp awareness of accidental judgements than a theory of the organic; more an account of purposes mistook than a narrative of gradual emergence; more a chronicle of carnal, bloody, and unnatural acts than a story of inevitable progress from traceable origins" (62). The historiography Greenblatt envisions, however, seems remarkably uninterested in the extent to which history has been and can be shaped by purposive human action over time. One need not adopt a metaphysics of progress in order to note goal-oriented historical phenomena. The contemporary globalization of capitalism, for example, hardly seems a function of "accidental judgements" or "purposes mistook." For a left critique of the antiteleological vogue, see Eagleton (*Illusions,* 45–68).

10. Perhaps the most succinct, recent formulation of this view of modernity is Cascardi's: "My claim is that the traditions represented by thinkers like Descartes, Hume, and Kant on the one hand, and by Nietzsche, Heidegger, and Derrida on the other, must be seen as one tradition and not two, and that the genealogy of the modern age may be seen to conform to the antinomic configuration which *together* these lines represent" (*Subject,* 35).

11. Mignolo offers a useful synthesis of the commonalities behind the various postcolonial vocabularies engaged with what might be termed the creolization of thought, or to use his term, border thinking: "All of them are changing the perspective, the term rather than the content, of the conversation. All of them critically reflect on the imaginary of the modern world system from the perspective of the coloniality of power and from particular, local histories of modernity/coloniality. [. . .] Or they reflect on the "double translation" allowing for an intersection between incommensurable (from the perspective of modernity) forms of knowledge [. . .]. What all these key words have in common is their disruption of dichotomies through being themselves a dichotomy. This, in other words, is the key configuration of border thinking: *thinking from dichotomous concepts rather than ordering the world in dichotomies.* Border thinking, in other words, is logically, a dichotomous locus of enunciation and, historically, is located at the borders (interiors and exteriors) of the modern/colonial world system" (*Local,* 85).

12. The centrality of the question of modernity in the construction of Spain's cultural identity is readily on display in the bourgeoning bibliography on the subject that has emerged in recent years. See for example: Fox, Fusi, Onainda, Alvarez Junco (*Mater*), Pérez Magallón, and Labanyi (*Constructing*).

13. For analysis of the relationship between hegemony and modernity, see Taylor (38–43).

14. This is the paradigmatic formulation of modern European imperialism. One of the important shifts in the passage from early modern to modern imperialism is the secularization of the pretext with which Europe symbolically

authorized its activities. In the fifteenth and sixteenth centuries the putative objective was to Christianize infidels; from the eighteenth to the mid-twentieth century, the goal would be to civilize the primitive. As Mignolo observes, "The very self-description by European intellectuals of the notion of 'civilization,' which will then become the foundation of the colonial 'civilizing mission,' is basically a construction of the European Enlightenment" ("Globalization," 32). For an extensive analysis of the idea of civilization, see Elias's two-volume study, *The Civilizing Process*. For discussion of the relationship between "diffusionist" notions of modernity and Eurocentrism, see Blaut (*Colonizer's*).

15. Dussel draws primarily from Wallerstein's groundbreaking work in world-systems analysis in order to inscribe the limits of modernity within a planetary interpretive horizon (3).

16. "It is necessary to carry out an abstraction (favoring *quantum* to the detriment of *qualitas*) that leaves out many valid variables (cultural, anthropological, ethical, political, and religious variables [. . .]) that will not allow adequate, "factual" or technologically possible management of the world-system. This *simplification* of complexity encompasses the totality of the life-world (*Lebenswelt*), of the relationship with nature [. . .] of subjectivity itself (a new self-understanding of subjectivity), and of community (a new intersubjective and political relation)" (Dussel, 13).

17. "From 1492 to 1500 approximately 50,000 square kilometers are colonized. [. . .] In 1515 these numbers will reach 300,000 square kilometers, with about 3 million dominated Amerindians; by 1550 Spain has colonized more than 2 million square kilometers (an area greater than the whole of the Europe of the center) and more than 25 million indigenous peoples (a low figure), many of whom are integrated into a system of work that produces value (in Marx's strict sense) for the Europe of the center (in the encomienda, mita, haciendas, etc.). We would have to add, from 1520 onward, the plantation slaves of African provenance (about 14 million until the final stage of slavery in the nineteenth century, including those in Brazil, Cuba, and the United States)" (Dussel, 11–12). Whether or not one accepts the proposition that the conquest of America was *the* determinant of Europe's competitive advantage, his work makes a compelling case for the importance of the event.

18. For Dussel the Hegelian notion "of an absolute Truth that determines or realizes itself through itself without owing anything to anyone" is the very essence of the "Eurocentric paradigm." The countervailing position from which Wallerstein, Dussel, Quijano, and Mignolo write holds that modernity and coloniality are mutually constitutive, two sides of the same coin.

19. To my knowledge, the history of northern Europe's racial codification of

Spaniards is a largely unexplored subject. Despite the well-known *pureza de sangre* agenda within Spain, it seems clear that in the early modern period, northern Europeans often perceived Spaniards in terms of racial as well as national alterity. Bataillon recalls that for Erasmus Spain was "one of those strange countries where Christianity enters into contact with semites who rebel against the faith, and it mixes with them." He concludes that for Erasmus the Iberian Peninsula "reveals itself as profoundly semiticized" (78). In the Low Countries, William of Orange makes clear that for him Spaniards are racially other. "I will no more wonder at that which all the world believeth: to wit, that the greatest part of Spaniards, and especially those that count themselves as noblemen, are of the blood of the Moors and Jews" (cited by Kamen, 310). More importantly, the northern European face of modernity was itself conceived in terms of racial superiority. Blaut recalls that Weber's thinking was influenced by prevalent racial assumptions of his day: "Weber saw race as one primordial, or presociological, factor explaining the greatness of the Europeans" (*Eight,* 21).

20. For a classic analysis of the relationship between narrative and empire, see Said (*Culture*). "The power to narrate, or to block other narrations from forming and emerging"—he writes—"is very important to culture and imperialism, and constitutes one of the main connections between them" (xiii). The representations we will consider in what follows in effect testify to northern Europe's power to narrate Spain.

21. By "common denominator" I do not mean to diminish the historical specificity of each of the images and the contexts that generated them. My interest in what follows is simply to foreground the structural homologies that such representations share when it comes to the question of Spain's relationship to the modern or the idea of the "West."

22. The fact that the representation of the Inquisition came out of fierce conflict has made it difficult for researchers to distinguish between history and myth. In a chapter entitled "The Invention of the Inquisition," Peters offers the following overview: "The Inquisition was an image assembled from a body of legends and myths which, between the sixteenth and the twentieth centuries, established the perceived character of inquisitorial tribunals and influenced all ensuing efforts to recover their historical reality" (122).

23. Peters recalls that "every European state based its legitimacy on religious grounds, and virtually every European state persecuted religious minorities" (122). The following example is instructive: "The Netherlands already possessed an Inquisition of its own which Phillip II of Spain confessed was 'more merciless than the one here.' At the very time that magistrates in Antwerp were objecting to the possibility of a Spanish tribunal, they themselves were

executing heretics. The Antwerp courts between 1557 and 1562 executed 103 heretics, more than died in the whole of Spain in that period" (Kamen, 310). Needless to say, the point is not to engage in a defense of the Spanish Inquisition, or for that matter, the Spanish empire, but rather to note the ideologically charged tenor of initial northern European critiques.

24. The term was fist introduced by Julián Juderías in 1912. Since then the Black Legend has constituted a bourgeoning subspecialty within Hispanism, with an extensive bibliography. For an overview, see for example, Gibson or Maltby (3–11). For a more recent discussion, see Sánchez. My intention here is not to revisit the Black Legend in depth, but rather to position it rhetorically within the discourse of modernity I have been attempting to outline.

25. Kamen attributes the text to Antonio Pérez, a Spaniard residing in England during the 1590s (310).

26. "A los *philosophes* les bastaba con escribir la palabra 'España' para evocar sin nececesidad de mayores explicaciones, lo erróneo, lo autodestructivo del oscurantismo monárquico-clerical, de la falta de libertad, de la cerrazón ante la ciencia moderna y el librepensamiento" [For the *philosophes* it was enough to write the word "Spain" to evoke, without need of further explanation, the erroneous, the self-destructive facets of monarchic and clerical obscurantism, of the lack of freedom, of the rejection of modern science and free-thinking] (Alvarez Junco, *Mater,* 106).

27. The basic contradiction between the two paradigms (fanatical barbarism vs. laziness) seems not to have been perceived as a problem by most of the *philosophes*: "There is not a single page in Montesquieu's work which shows the least appreciation of the astonishing physical feat carried out by the conquistadors; nor does his work contain the smallest semblance of a discussion of the difficulties encountered by Spain in trying to reconcile its need for rational management, arising from its status as a pioneer modern state in the world, with the ideals of an ecumenical world order almost unavoidably fostered in the political context of Europe at the dawn of the modern age" (Iglesias, 148).

28. Although this was the dominant pattern of the tour, there were of course numerous travelers to Spain throughout the eighteenth century. See, for example, Sarrailh (290–338).

29. Preston has argued against the notion of a revolution in historical consciousness, and Lowenthal reminds readers that modern historical thought "was no historical revolution [. . .] but a plant of slow growth nurtured by secularism, increasing scrutiny of evidence, and awareness of anachronism" (232). The nationalist historicism of the early nineteenth century is in this regard perhaps more accurately grasped as a particularly compelling bourgeoning of

historical thinking within the vaster history that Lowenthal charts. Foucault too would locate the beginning his "age of history" at the end of the eighteenth century (*Order,* 217).

30. Torrecilla has noted the phenomenon: "un problema temporal o interno adquiere una dimensión, por así decirlo, 'espacial' " [A temporal or internal problem acquires, so to speak, a "spatial" dimension] (Torrecilla, *Tiempo,* 12).

31. Ford is representative of the numerous tour books on Spain that proliferated over the course of the century. Fernandez-Herr has studied the role of travel writing in the production of the image of "romantic Spin" that Ford inherits. See also García Mercadal, López Cepedo, and Casado. For analyses of the cultural politics of tourism and the asymmetrical power relations they imply, see Crick, Culler, Lanfant, MacCannell, Urry, and Pratt. Torrecilla (*Tiempo* and *Imitación*) has studied the impact of modern European colonialism on nineteenth-century Spanish cultural production. More recently, and in a similar vein, Monleón reads *La Gaviota* against Merimée's *Carmen* in order to chart Cecilia Böhl de Faber's response to the stereotypes of *espagnolisme.*

32. For a recent analysis of British romantic figurations of Spain—in Byron, Coleridge, Landon, Southey, Grimstone, and others—see Saglia (Poetic).

33. Flitter offers the following definition of romantic historicism: "the 'historical sense' adumbrated in Germany by Johann Gottfried Herder (1744–1803), who opposed the belief in universal laws or ideals which had formed an essential part of the philosophy in the Classical tradition, and instead sought to promote an individualizing attitude the placed greater value upon the local and temporal conditions of human existence" (5). As the summary reflects, when Herder is invoked as the putative father of romantic historicism, the complexity of his philosophy of history is unavoidably simplified. This reduction, however, tends to reproduce the simplification of his ideas that accompanied their initial dissemination. The same can be said for the Schlegel brothers. For more protracted discussion of Herder's philosophy of history, see Gillies, Clark, Barnard, and Berlin (*Three*). As we shall see shortly, the relative importance of German historicism within Spanish romanticism has been the subject of much debate.

34. As we shall see in chapter 2, this is not the only account of the genesis of Spanish romanticism.

35. Juretschke has observed that Böhl's readings in German literature included, among others, Herder, Goethe, Bürger, Lessing, and Schiller. It is primarily the Schlegelian paradigm, however, that informs Böhl's exchanges in the *querella* ("Presencia," 304).

36. A recent exception has been Torrecilla, who discusses nineteenth-century

Spanish culture in terms of its colonial subordination to northern Europe (*Imitación* and *Tiempo*).

37. Recent scholarship on German romanticism has suggested that it is perhaps best grasped as a relatively early and important moment within the history of the West's critique of rationality. See for example, Cavell, and Nancy and Lacoue-Labarthe. Acknowledging the critical potential of the aesthetic has also been one of the more cogent ways of grasping the various continuities that have traditionally been perceived between romanticism and modernism. One of the insights of Adorno and Horkheimer that much contemporary thinking seems to have forgotten or abandoned is that these movements are themselves part of the structure of Western modernity, rather than a departure from it. The case in favor of aesthetics as the indispensable agent of modernity's self-criticism has been made recently by Cascardi's reframing of Kant (*Consequences*).

38. It is worth noting that both romantic historicism and the narrative of the modern—here represented by Hegel—remain thoroughly metaphysical in conception. Where one narrative posits the historical unfolding of reason, however, the other asserts the expression of a transhistorical ethnic national spirit.

39. It is primarily the ideas of August Wilhelm, rather than Friedrich Schlegel, that shape the discussion of romantic historicism in Spain. In what follows, unless otherwise noted, "Schlegelian" will refer to the historiography advanced by August Wilhelm.

40. Alvarez Junco has recently summarized the deep appeal of historicist thought in the following terms: "En esa visión nacional del mundo, España salía beneficiada en relación con la imagen negativa elaborada por la *Leyenda Negra* de los siglos XVI y XVII y por los ilustrados del XVIII. Podía aceptarse, como creía Montesquieu, que España era una nación decadente, pero ¿no era hermosa la decadencia para un romántico? Era también cierto que España no sabía adaptarse a la modernidad, pero eso demostraba su superioridad espiritual" [In that national view of the world, Spain came out benefiting in comparison to the negative image crafted by the *Black Legend* in the fifteenth and sixteenth centuries and by the enlightenment thinkers of the eighteenth. One could accept, as Montesquieu believed, that Spain was a decadent nation, but wasn't decadence beautiful for a romantic? It was also true that Spain didn't know how to adapt itself to modernity, but that demonstrated its spiritual superiority over the rest of Europe] (*Mater,* 389). See also Saglia's cogent treatment of the subject along similar lines ("True").

41. Following Lanfant, Monleón has recently suggested that Spanish national identity entailed an internalization of the northern gaze. "A pesar de las reac-

ciones o resistencias internas, los símbolos propios de la identidad española se fueron forjando desde afuera, al gusto de la visión extranjera" [Despite internal reactions and resistances, the symbols that belong to Spanish identity were forged from the outside, according to the taste of the foreign gaze] (6). If that is the case, Schlegelian romanticism was one of the primary vectors for the interpellation of such an identity. What is equally clear, however, is that nationalist historicism took on a life of its own within Spanish letters. See, for example, Torrecilla (*España*).

42. This view has often been identified with the thinking of Menéndez Pelayo. While each moment gives the historicist paradigm a different inflection, what is common to all of them is the presumption of an immutable national Spanish essence. See Maravall (*Mentalidad*) for discussion of the eighteenth-century Spanish historical consciousness that sets the stage for romantic historical thought. For an overview of Spanish historiography from the 1700s through the 1900s, see Sánchez Marcos. For treatment of nineteenth-century Spanish historiography, see Cirujano and Moreno Alonso. A useful overview of *noventayochista* interest in foundational nationalist ideas is Shaw (*Generation*). For more protracted analysis of the subject see Fox. In a similar vein, Silver argues that romantic historicism was largely responsible for the "invention of modern Spain" (*Ruin*, 3–46), and Alvarez Junco notes that romantic historicism was, among other things, a catalyst for the consolidation of an essentially Catholic national identity in Spain during the nineteenth century (*Mater*, 383–91). See also Nuñez Florencio (21–44). On the role of the ideology of Reconquista within Francoist historiography, see Richards (7–25). For the implications of nationalist historiography in the twentieth century, particularly as it pertains to the novel, see Herzberger.

43. This shift may itself be taken as reflecting the transition at mid-century from the "European Age" to other transnational and regional configurations. For a straightforward overview the subject see Halecki, particularly chapter 3, "The Chronological Limits: The End of European History" (45–61), where the author envisages the second half of the twentieth century as the "Atlantic Age."

44. The scholars cited here are meant to function as a representative sample of work that has taken up such questions. It is not intended to exhaust the field of scholarship—too extensive to enumerate—that has focused on such issues.

45. Significantly, the Spanish authors that do seem to have made it into the European literary canon belong either to imperial, early modern Spain (i.e., Cervantes, and with less frequency, Lope de Vega and Calderón de la Barca) or to the twentieth century (i.e., García Lorca).

46. The latter half of the twentieth century appears to have witnessed rather clearly a displacement of the center of enunciation of "culture" away from "modern Europe." In its place, an ostensibly global conception of literary production that is loosely managed by those forms of power and empire currently represented by the United States has emerged. See Hart and Negri for recent analysis of this new configuration. For an insightful essay on the effects of this displacement, see Baucom, who returns to the question of place and its relationship to thought. At the same time, one cannot help but notice the degree to which postcolonial studies—and now "global cultural studies"—are disproportionately produced, disseminated, and consumed within an Anglo-American "international" academic field dominated by the United States. Were an American Hegel continuing his lessons on the philosophy of history, we would undoubtedly find that "Geist" crossed the Atlantic at the mid-twentieth century. Indeed, Hegel famously intimated America's future in his *Philosophy of History*: "America is therefore the land of the future, where, in the ages that lie before us, the burden of World's History shall reveal itself" (cited by Jameson, *Singular*, 202). For present purposes, it will be the earlier construct, "modern Europe," that has the most bearing on the problem of thinking about romanticism in Spain.

47. To be sure, the successful propagation of Schlegelian historicism was as much a function of the conservative political uses to which the discourse could be put within Spain as it was a reflection of modern European cultural power. One framework does not annul the other; the point here is to underscore that, for all of its emphasis on national tradition, romantic historicism was clearly a transnational phenomenon that reflected the power relations between hegemonic and nonhegemonic Europe.

48. Once more, my intention is not to give an exhaustive account, but rather to recall key moments of the historicist paradigm and its transformation in twentieth-century literary historiography. The itinerary we will be following is one side of an ongoing debate concerning the historical meanings of romantic discourse in Spain. I will be taking up the basic countervailing positions in the next section of this chapter.

49. Juretschke has returned to the problem of the origins of Spanish romanticism more recently in an extensive work that could stand as a book in its own right (*Epoca*, 5–209). He closes his detailed review of the question by concluding with the argument that his earlier work had sketched: that A. W. Schlegel's Course on Dramatic Literature was the principle catalyst for Spanish thinking about the past and that this process was modified by the influence of other French and German thinkers over the course of the century. He acknowledges, however, the presence of multiple, alternative lines of romantic thought and writing.

50. The sequence Flitter charts is, in amplified form, a restatement of the trajectory that Juretschke sketches. Several section titles from Juretschke's essay—"Böhl de Faber. El introductor del Schlegelianismo," "La formación del romanticismo histórico español," "La penetración del romanticismo liberal," and "La reacción contra el romanticismo liberal"—find their correlates in chapter titles from Flitter: "Böhl von Faber and the establishment of a traditionalist Romanticism," "The consolidation of Romantic ideas: 1820–1833," "The exiles, liberal Romanticism and developments in criticism," "Condemnation and clarification in the literary debate." As we shall see later in this chapter, Flitter's opposition of "historicist" and "liberal" romanticism sets up something of a false choice.

51. By the mid-1830s liberalism in Spain had split into what would become two basic factions, *progresistas* and *moderados*. The *moderados*, generally upper-class liberals who were as frightened by democratic violence as they were supportive of royal prerogatives, represented the conservative tendency within liberalism. The *progresistas*, their opposition, were the heirs of the Constitution of 1812, and they represented a lower echelon within the middle class; the *progresistas* often capitalized on the discontent of the masses—particularly in cities—in order to achieve their political ends.

52. One of the classic formulations of this thought-pattern is Berlin (*Roots*, 46–67), who locates the "true fathers" of romanticism precisely where Weber had located the heart of modernity: in the ethno-religious subjectivities of Protestantism. De Man's deconstructive reading of European romanticism, while dismantling a series of fundamental assumptions, leaves this basic geography untouched, as does Silver. It is worth emphasizing that the point here is not to revisit whether or not there was a "high romanticism" in Spain, but to argue that "high romanticism" itself, with its authority as *the* standard of measure from which Spanish romantic writing is judged, needs to be reexamined.

53. I use the term metageography to designate "the set of spatial structures through which people order their knowledge of the world: the often unconscious frameworks that organize studies of history, sociology, anthropology, economics, political science, or even natural history" (Lewis and Wigen, ix). Needless to say, literature figures just as easily on the list.

54. Blanco Aguinaga has made similar arguments, noting that the "so-called Hispanic world is a privileged site for understanding not only the economic and political relationships between center and periphery but their cultural relationships as well. [. . .] Both Spain and Spanish America became the first neocolonial societies. The originality of the case is precisely what makes it a privileged model of study" (4). For a collection of essays that explore this

peripheral status in relationship to modernism, see Geist. More recently, see Santiáñez.

55. For more extensive treatment of myth as a semiological system, see Barthes's final chapter, "Myth Today," (109–36). For discussion of the relationship between Barthes's conception of myth and its relationship to ideology, see Brown 24–38.

56. One of the more powerful, brief refutations of the mystification of the West can be found in Lewis and Wigen's *The Myth of Continents*: "The formula 'modernization = westernization' assumes a priority of origin over process, or geography over history. It holds, in essence, that modernization represents the cultural essence of Western Europe, because Western Europe is (supposedly) where it all began. The present work posits a different metageography of modernity. For one thing, we would like to challenge the claim that individualism, democracy, secularism and the like reveal anything essential or transhistorical about Western culture. [. . .] In fact all the familiar 'isms' of modernization were resisted by important elements of the establishment in Western Europe. Moreover, all were driven by processes that were in important ways global from the start, and all have proven both incomplete and contingent, even in the West. [. . .] A recognition of contingency in history discredits our simple glosses of both Westernization and modernity, as well as sundering the presumed identity between the two" (101).

57. For discussion of the various convergences and tensions between the postmodern and the postcolonial, see for example, Appiah or Bhabha (*Location*, 245–84).

58. See Hutcheon for discussion of the strategic reasons for which traditionally marginalized groups often turn to otherwise questionable models of history when faced with the imperative to tell *their* story.

59. One should not forget that, undaunted by its secondary status within European power politics, and undeterred by the emancipation of its South American colonies, Spain would continue to think of itself and act as an imperial power throughout the nineteenth century. Sebastian Balfour has noted that "the retention of fragments of the Empire, in particular its richest colony, Cuba, sustained the illusion that Spain was still an imperial power of some rank" (2). It would take the loss of its last transatlantic colonies to the United States in 1898—known within Spain as "el desastre"—for the country to begin to "awaken" from its imperial daydream.

60. More recently, scholars have traced the genealogy of the modern in Spain to the early stirrings of scientific rationality in the period between 1675 and 1725, the time of the *novatores*. In his *Construyendo la modernidad: la cultura española en el tiempo de los novatores (1675–1725)*, Pérez Magallón, for

example, documents the gestation of the discourses of modernity (scientific rationality, experimentalism, skepticism, the critique of authority, etc.) and of national identity among the men of letters who lived and wrote in the transition from Habsburg to Bourbon Spain. Significantly, the author closes by contrasting this panorama with the discourse of modernity in Hegel. "La visión hegeliana de la historia y de la cultura resulta absolutamente inadecuada para captar el proceso específico por el cual se configura tal discurso" [The Hegelian vision of history and culture turns out to be absolutely inadequate for grasping the specific process by which such a discourse is configured]. To accept the Hegelian framework, he adds, "implica asumir las imposiciones 'colonizadoras' de las potencias dominantes" [implies accepting the "colonizing" impositions of the dominant powers] (338).

61. Flitter's discussion of Schlegelian historicism as if it were opposed to what he calls "liberal romanticism" is one example. The sense of opposing conceptions of the movement in Spain is already evident, however, in two categories that Tarr juxtaposes in the title of his 1939 study, *Romantic Spain and Spanish Romanticism.* Part of the confusion stems from the conflation of the historical sense of the term *liberal* with its present-day use to designate the Left or progressive politics more generally.

62. Navas Ruiz deals with the issue as follows: "Se ha dicho que existe un romanticismo conservador, concretamente aquel que enfatizó las bellezas del cristianismo, el esplendor del pasado, la utilidad de la monarquía [. . .]. Ahora bien, ¿este romanticismo conservador no era liberal? En algunos casos, como el de Böhl de Faber, no: estaba al servicio de una reacción absolutista. Per en general, sí." [It has been said that there is a conservative romanticism, concretely the one that emphasized the beauties of Christianity, the splendor of the past, the utility of monarchy { . . . }. Now then, wasn't this conservative romanticism liberal? In some cases, such as Böhl von Faber's, it was not: it was at the service of an absolutist reaction. But in general it was.] (*Romanticismo* 48). Kirkpatrick also observes that "with the exception of the soon-to-be-defeated Carlist faction, the principal political tendencies, both conservative and progressive, assumed some inalienable human rights and the necessity of some degree of political and economic expression of self-interest" (*Románticas* 43).

63. As a vast bibliography on European nationalism makes clear, the "factitiously unitary" sense of national culture that Silver decries was by no means a distinctively Spanish creation. See for example, Schulze or Llobera. In this sense, I do not mean to minimize the importance of nationalist historicism in Spanish romantic culture, but rather to recontextualize it within the broader framework of European nationalism. Virtually every European state

cultivated a robust romantic nationalism; at the same time, each national literary tradition bears witness to a romanticism that is not easily reduced to this paradigm.

64. "One of the tasks of the liberal revolution was the creation of private property. As it affected the land this protracted liberal revolution had three main points: the abolition of entail, the disentailment of all land held in mortmain and the abolition of the seigneuries. This was achieved by 1840 and for virtually a century the reign of private property was questioned only by those who wanted more" (Shubert, *Social,* 57).

65. For a suggestive overview of the notion of plural temporalities and their applicability to the problems of literary history in Spain see Santiáñez (51–85).

66. For a lucid synthesis of how a distorted idea of "Europe" is structurally embedded within North American departments of history, for example, see Shubert ("Spanish"). For a series of essays on the ways in which the poetic mystification of Spain was integral to the foundation of Hispanism in the United States, see Kagan (*Spain*).

Chapter 2

1. The basic contours of the debate are not difficult to delineate. Those who have acknowledged or argued for Cadalso's romanticism in some measure include Menéndez Pelayo (296), Azorín (*Clásicos,* 184), Gómez de la Serna, Lunardi, Helman (Introducción, 32–48), Martínez Torrón, Basalisco, and—perhaps the most protracted—Sebold (*Cadalso* and *Fronteras*). Among those who reject, question, or substantially modify claims of a romanticism in *Noches lúgubres*—often in the name of a nonromantic or preromantic, enlightened eighteenth-century sentimentalism—are Maravall ("Estimación" 269–90), Arce (17–35), Bermúdez-Cañete, Rudat ("Lo prerromántico" and "Artificio"), Froldi ("Literatura"), Caso González (*Conceptos,* 16–19), Aguilar Piñal (*Historia,* 202–11), Glendinning (*Vida* and "Sobre"), and Quinziano. This list is by no means exhaustive. Most scholars working on Cadalso's text have in one way or another had to confront its contested historiographic status. For a useful summary of the basic tenor of the debate, see Martínez Mata (lxi–lxvi).

2. For a summary of eighteenth-century conceptions of the sublime and their relation to *Noches lúgubres,* see Glendinning (Introducción, 32–34). For a more detailed linguistic analysis, see Vázquez de Castro.

3. Over the course of the eighteenth century in Spain, as in much of Europe, classical medical authority—primarily Aristotle, Hippocrates, and Galen—

was slowly modified and replaced by chemical and mechanistic medical theory as scholasticism gave way to the empirical sciences. By the 1770s many of the century's major polemics had been settled. A pragmatically eclectic approach to medicinal theory had become commonplace, and while some vestiges of humoral theory continued to be defended, numerous new hypotheses regarding the physiology of affective states circulated as well. For a detailed discussion of the history of medicine during the period, see Granjel. For analysis of the relationship between language and the body in eighteenth-century Spanish debates, see Haidt (*Embodying,* 13–48).

4. Glendinning has found in these lines traces of Rousseau's *Emile*: "tous sont nés nus et pauvres, tous sujets aux misères de la vie . . . tous sont condamnés à la mort" [all are born naked and poor, all are subject to the miseries of life . . . all are condemned to die] (Prólogo, lxvii). Others who have studied the intertextual references to Rousseau include Spell, Raimondi, and Sebold (*Colonel,* 166–70). As Martinez Mata has recently observed, however, the sentiment expressed here is common enough in the period to preclude an exlusively Rousseauian source (Notas, 386).

5. For a recent analysis of Tediato in vaguely Lacanian terms, see LaRubia-Prado, who reads the protagonist as a case of arrested psychological development. The author suggests that Tediato is to be read as caught in Lacan's Imaginary stage, somehow never having managed to enter the Symbolic stage. While suggestive, such a reading poses a perplexing problem inasmuch as Lacan's Symbolic stage is the realm of language, a realm Tediato seems to have managed to inhabit.

6. Helman, for example, recounts the following episode, which led to the work's prohibition in Córdoba in 1817: "Una viuda se había quejado, a un vecino, de un hijo suyo que maltrataba a sus hermanos y amenazaba quitarse la vida; este joven leía en un libro que, por fin, había podido quitarle, y le ruega al vecino que lo lea y lo queme si puede serle perjudicial al hijo. El vecino, después de haberlo léido, lo denunció, por 'contener muchas expresiones escandalosas, peligrosas e inductivas al suicidio' " [A widow had complained to a neighbor about a son of hers who was abusing his brothers and threatening to take his own life; this young man was reading from a book that, at last, she had managed to take away from him, and she begs the neighbor to read it and burn it if it could be harmful to the boy. The neighbor, after reading it, reported it for 'containing many scandalous, dangerous expressions that could induce suicide'] (Introducción, 54). *Noches lúgubres* was subsequently prohibited by the Inquisition on 13 November 1819.

7. For samples of such endings, see Glendinning (Apéndices, 99–109)

8. In Graf's view, the failed attempt to unearth the beloved "borders on Pe-

trarchan and Freudian bathos" and the "lengthy discourses on love, family, friends and society" are "simply sublimated effects of Tediato's psychosexual drama" (212). I will be arguing for a less dismissive account of Tediato's "lengthy discourses," which as it happens comprise most of the text. It is precisely the bearing of Tediato's loss on his views of love, friends, and society that signal Cadalso's profound rewriting of late-Petrarchan melancholy. Rather than reading the text as a bathetic exaggeration of Petrarchism, I posit a series of important transformations of the tradition.

9. Significantly, when literary historians have looked for "precursors" to the antisocial dimensions of the romantic figuration of amorous sentiment, they have turned not to the Rennaissance lyric tradition, but rather to the more chaotic passions of the *novela sentimental.* See, for example, Río's discussion (220–21). At the same time, it is worth noting that the exploration of the social dimensions of Tediato's suicidal suffering in *Noches lúgubres* intimates the kind of thinking that Emile Durkheim would systematize in the twentieth century.

10. "Indiano" was the designation for the emigrant who returned from the Americas after having made his fortune. An important figure in the colonial culture of metropolitan Spain, the indiano had become a common character on the eighteenth-century Spanish stage. See for example, Ripodas.

11. The presence of ascetic discourse in *Noches lúgubres* has been analyzed at length by Glendinning (Introducción). Many have noted, however, that Cadalso seems to have decoupled asceticism from its religious framework. There is no invocation of a Christian afterlife that accords meaning to suffering. The problem of suffering seems to be approached in entirely secular terms.

12. The 1819 Inquisitorial records make clear that the Enlightenment theorization of the family—perceived as a threat to more traditional, theocratic conceptions of family and state—was readily understood by nineteenth-century readers. The inquisitors refer to Cadalso's "doctrina impía [. . .] muy consonante y análoga con la de Rousseau y Hobbes que establecen el origen del estado y union recíproca *viri et femines* del propio modo de las bestias" [impious doctrine { . . . } very much consonant and analogous with that of Rousseau and Hobbes, who establish the origin of the state and the reciprocal union *viri et femines* in the same manner as that of the beasts] (Cited by Martínez Mata, Footnotes, 236–37).

13. The most lucid discussion of the difference between baroque *desengaño* and the rationalist *desengañar* of the *novatores* and *ilustrados*, is Pérez Magallón (23–32).

14. In Fray Luis de Granada: "¿Qué es un cuerpo humano, sino un muladar

cubierto de nieve, que por defuera parece blanco y dentro está lleno de in-
mundicias? [What is a human body but a dunghill covered in snow that on
the outside looks white and on the inside is full of filth?] (cited by Martínez
Mata, Footnotes, 238).

15. See for example, Cano, Aguilar Piñal ("Moratín"), Arce (331–41), Gies
    ("*Ars*"), Camarero ("Didacticismo"), and Sanchez-Blanco Parody. For a more
    extended analysis of male friendship in *Cartas marruecas*, see Haidt (*Embody-
    ing*, 151–71).

16. "La influencia de Adam Smith sobre los ilustrados españoles, muchos de los
    cuales hicieron de *The Wealth of Nations* una especie de libro de cabecera—
    Jovellanos, en el año 1796, confiesa haberla leído ya tres veces [. . .]—fue
    inmenso en lo que se refiere a [. . .] los temas estrictamente económicos, la
    libertad económica, el comercio, la tierra, la necesaria desamortización de los
    bienes inmuebles" [The influence of Adam Smith on enlightened Spaniards,
    many of whom turned *The Wealth of Nations* into a kind of bedside book—in
    1796 Jovellanos confesses to having already read it three times { . . . }—was
    immense when it came to { . . . } strictly economic subjects, economic free-
    dom, commerce, the land, the necessary disentailement of landed property]
    (Aranguren, 13–14).

17. See Cadalso's *Memoria de los acontecimientos más particulares de mi vida*
    (*Escritos*. 3–32).

18. Readers of Walter Benjamin's writings on melancholy—both in his
    Trauerspeil study and in his well-known engagements with Baudelaire—will
    perhaps recognize the resonance of his thinking in the preceding examina-
    tion of melancholy subjectivity. Not unlike the Benjaminian project of read-
    ing Baudelairean *Spleen*, a deeper, preexisting conception of melancholy has
    functioned here as the historical foil against which the distinctive quality of
    Tediato's more contemporary form of subjectivity comes into view. Benjamin
    observes that "because Baudelaire knew that his affliction, *Spleen*, the *te-
    diatum vitae*, was an age-old one, he was in a position to bring into relief
    the imprint of his own experience with the utmost precision" (Benjamin,
    Charles, "Central Park", 2.2). The same case can be made for Cadalso's repre-
    sentation of melancholy. It is worth noting, however, that key concepts such
    as "symbol" and "allegory"—notions that are central to the Benjaminian con-
    ception of melancholy and to the discourses of "European romanticism" and
    its theorizations more generally—have been absent in the preceding analysis.
    Indeed, my discussions of melancholy without recourse to these analytic
    categories throughout the book represent an attempt to rethink melancholy
    in relation to decidedly Spanish cultural and political history.

19. For a discussion of the distinction between nomothetic and ideographic

explanation, terms common to anthropological analysis, see Harris (*Cultural*, 78–79).

20. It is worth noting that my argument here is not about the political efficacy (or lack thereof) of Spanish discourses of compassion within the colonial enterprise. Rather, it is about the existence of such debates in early modern Spain and their occlusion by post-Enlightenment, "modern European" discourses concerning Amerindians. In the next chapter we shall discuss the "Rousseau effect" and its relationship to the metageography of modern Europe more extensively.

21. In the work's first printing, the reference to class distinctions as "useless" was excised.

22. "We are talking about characteristic elements of impulse, restraint, and tone; specifically affective elements of consciousness and relationships: not feeling against thought but thought as felt and feeling as thought: practical consciousness of a present kind, in a living and interrelating continuity. We are then defining these elements as a 'structure': as a set, with specific internal relations, at once interlocking and in tension" (Williams, *Marxism*, 132).

Chapter 3

1. Before dying, Ferdinand had promulgated a decree known as the Pragmatic Sanction, which allowed his daughter to succeed him. The decree, in effect, preempted the eighteenth-century Salic Law of succession, by which the crown would have passed to Ferdinand's brother Carlos. The First Carlist War (1833–1839) broke out shortly after Ferdinand's death. For a history of the Carlist movement in Spain, see Oyarzun or Holt.

2. Saavedra returns to Spain on 9 January 1834. Several months later, upon the death of his older brother, the firstborn, he inherits the title of Duke of Rivas.

3. The play opened at the Príncipe Theater on 22 March 1835. In what would subsequently become one of the most-cited pronouncements concerning Spain's romantic theater, Alcalá Galiano made the following observation in the pages of *Revista Española* two days later: "Quien niegue o dude que estamos en revolución, que vaya al teatro del Príncipe y vea representar el drama que ahora me toca dar cuenta a mis lectores" [If anyone denies or doubts that we are in a revolution, let him go to the Príncipe Theater and let him see the drama of which I will now give an account to my readers.] (Cited by Caldera, "Estudio," ix).

4. Lama (Prólogo, 9–32) offers a useful overview of the play's initial reception. For analysis of the significance of the play's debut within the field of Madrid's

1830s theater production see Andioc ("Sobre"); for a discussion of the *Don Alvaro* within the broader context of nineteenth-century theater in Spain, see Gies (*Theater*, 108–11)

5. For discussion of the Inca Garcilaso as a source for *Don Alvaro*, see Alonso Seaone.

6. For an analysis of the basic changes that accompanied the transformation from play to libretto, see Busquets. For a briefer treatment of the subject, see Sedwick.

7. It is worth recalling that even as Baudelaire famously articulated the concept of modernity in "The Painter of Modern Life," he pointed to this dialectic of permanence and impermanence. Baudelaire's painter "is looking for that indefinable something we may be allowed to call 'modernity,' for want of a better term to express the idea in question. The aim for him is to extract from fashion the poetry that resides in its historical envelope, to distil the eternal from the transitory" (*Selected*, 402).

8. These are relative observations; even in Ghislanzoni's libretto, for example, Don Alvaro's mestizo lineage is mentioned. What diminishes, however, is the relative weight or importance of the colonial context as a whole in comparison to *Don Alvaro o la fuerza del sino* or to the Inca Garcilaso's biography.

9. One need only turn to figures such as Don Juan, for example, to note that the most widely circulating modern incarnations of the seducer have for the most part emerged from non-Spanish cultures (Mozart/DaPonte, Byron, Kierkegaard, Bernard Shaw). As discussed in the first chapter, the phenomenon can be read as a symptom of Spain's status as an object rather than a subject of representation within the international arena during much of the modern era.

10. See Lama (Prólogo, 32–44) for a synthesis of the numerous structural analyses dedicated to the work. Drawing on Shaw ("Acerca") and Rey Hazas, he makes a compelling case for reading the first of the work's five acts as a self-contained one-act play or overture; the remaining acts then align themselves according to a circular spatial itinerary—II (Hornachuelos), III–IV (Veletri), V (Hornachuelos)—that symbolizes the protagonist's inability to elude destiny. Independent of the particular meanings one ascribes to the structure, it seems rather clear that there is a well-defined, albeit romantic, *dispositio* at work throughout the play's five acts.

11. The tendency to read romantic drama in Spain primarily as reaffirmation of the baroque theater is itself a symptom of the metageography that posited Spain as a naturally nonmodern "romantic" country. For an incisive refutation of the neobaroque thesis, see Sebold (*Trayectoria*, 43–73).

12. There had, of course, been a long tradition of texts written in verse and prose.

Kittay and Godzich note, for example, that "the technique of versiprosa texts (also called *prosametrum*), which alternate passages of prose and verse had been known in medieval Latin since the time of Boethius" (46). The point here, however, is to underscore Saavedra's novelty vis-à-vis contemporary dramaturgical conventions. Lama notes that "la escritura en prosa cumplía con una marca característica del teatro francés del momento, cuyas piezas eran compuestas en verso o en prosa, pero no en una mezcla de ambas, como al cabo sucedería en *Don Alvaro*" [writing in prose followed a characteristic feature of the French theater of the moment, whose works were composed in verse or in prose, not in a mix of both, as would ultimately happen in *Don Alvaro*] (Prólogo, 10).

13. Prose is used for the social sketches or *cuadros de costumbre* with which all but the fourth act begin; it appears in transitional scenes that function as preludes to especially important moments; it is used in informational scenes, when characters narrate events that have taken place off stage; and the shift from verse to prose often marks climactic moments and their respective dénouments (Lama, Prólogo, 63). For detailed treatment of Saavedra's choice of verse forms, see Busquets and Casalduero.

14. Levinas has articulated the oft-overlooked paradox by which artistic novelty—from romanticism through modernism—grounds itself in the claim to be more authentic, and ultimately more realistic, than what has preceded it. "Though it be disparaged as an aesthetic canon, realism nevertheless retains all its prestige. In fact it is refuted only in the name of higher realism. Surrealism is a superlative" (117). For discussion of the intentionally uneven quality of romantic discourse and its relationship to modernity in the work of José Espronceda, see Talens. At the same time it is worth recalling that in his classic study of the avant-garde, Poggioli observes that "the cult of novelty [. . .], which is the basis for avant garde art's [. . .] unpopularity, was an exquisitely romantic phenomenon even before it became typically avant-garde" (50).

15. For a brief synopsis of Alvaro's deadly desire over the course of the work, see Lama (Prólogo, 58–61).

16. For analysis of the relationship between Saavedra's *costumbrismo* and the visual arts, see Lama ("Escribir").

17. As numerous editors have observed, theatergoers would have recognized the plot of a highly popular baroque play, Luis Belmonte Bermúdez's *El diablo predicador, y mayor contrario amigo*, which had been performed repeatedly during the early 1830s. See Lama (Prólogo, 18–20) for a review of the scholarship dedicated to the subject.

18. Kirkpatrick has argued that mystery is in fact constitutive of Alvaro's sub-

jectivity: "The question mark that hovers over don Alvaro is the sign of an uncertain identity—not only the social identity of name, origins, and rank that traditionally resolved the enigma of the dramatic protagonist but also of self-identity, the subjective possession of one's own being that Romantics sought in the quest for selfhood" (*Las Romanticas*, 110). Pattison also notes that, as was common throughout romantic rhetoric, the "light" of reason is often figured as a form of pain (223–24).

19. *Don Avaro* is set during the reign of Charles III (1759–1788), who by the 1830s was already recognized as a secularizing, enlightened reformer. Rather than the more typical Middle Ages of romantic historical drama, it is a relatively recent past that would readily have been identified with modernization in Spain. For commentary on the play's historical location, see Quinn and Mansour. For a discussion of modernization under Carlos III, see Herr (*Eighteenth*).

20. The suggestion that Don Alvaro's death signals a collective death of hope is conveyed by the pose of the Anti-Christ that he adopts immediately prior to his suicide: "Yo soy un enviado del infierno, soy el demonio exterminador. [. . .] ¡Infierno, abre tu boca y trágame! ¡Húndase el cielo, preezca la raza humana; exterminio, destrucción!" [I am an envoy of hell, I am the exterminating demon. { . . . } Hell, open your mouth and swallow me! May Heaven fall, may the human race perish; extermination, destruction!] (189). For more extensive analysis of Alvaro as an ironic Christ figure, see Gray and Sebold ("Nuevos").

21. For most historians, the Napoleonic invasions, the 1812 Cortes de Cadiz, Fernandine repression, and liberal revolution—that is, the traditional historical home of Spanish romanticism—created the conditions for the possibility of Spanish American independence. See for example, Kinsbruner (9–24).

22. "The loss of the continental American Empire was a devastating blow for Spain's economy. Denied revenue from trade with mainland Spanish America, the treasury plunged into chronic deficit. The end of the special relationship with huge areas of America, which had provided Spain with a reserved market for her finished goods and a cheap source of raw materials, deprived the economy of its comparative advantage over others" (Balfour, 2). For a recent study that does link *Don Alvaro* to colonial *mestizaje*, see Galdo.

23. Alda Blanco has recently come to similar conclusions concerning the historiography of nineteenth-century Spanish literature more generally: "el pasado imperial se ha reprimido de una manera sumamente efectiva" [the imperial past has been repressed in an highly effective way] ("El fin" 16).

24. For an analysis of the links between imperialism, nationalism, and Pan-Hispanism later in the century, see Loureiro.

25. Sebold has been among the most explicit in evoking the Rousseauian paradigm. Summing up Alvaro's relationship to the protagonist of Jovellanos's 1773 lacrimose drama, *El delincuente honrado*, he notes: "los dos son buenos salvajes, o salvajes nobles, a lo Rousseau, por haberse visto obligados a vivir al margen de la sociedad conservadora guiándose por su natural instinto de bondad [both are good savages or noble savages, a la Rousseau, for having been obliged to live on the margin of conservative society, guiding themselves by their natural instinct for goodness] ("Jovellanos," 416).

26. For the most recent, extensive analysis of the relationship between European colonialism and representations of the savage, see Ellingson's *The Myth of the Noble Savage*, particularly 9–95. The author historicizes the noble savage as a discursive construct with its own history, and one of the key features of his thesis supports what I mean to suggest here: that it is the *story of Rousseau as progenitor of the myth of the noble savage* that becomes dominant over the course of the nineteenth and twentieth centuries. "Rousseau's invention of the Noble Savage myth"—he notes—"is itself a myth" (4).

27. The following example is one among many: In a series of collected essays on political theory published in 1997 under the title of *The Legacy of Rousseau*, a well-known specialist asserts that "Rousseau was unusual in siding with the 'savages' against the colonial conquests that followed Columbus's discovery of the Americas" (Masters, 128). No Spanish writers are ever mentioned, and among the fourteen specialists contributing to the volume, not one references Bartolomé de Las Casas or the debates in early modern Spain concerning the legitimacy of the conquest. It is an example of what, following Chakrabarty, I have elsewhere called asymmetrical ignorance: to discuss the noble savage without Rousseau seems immediately suspect; to discuss Rousseau without any reference to the writing of Iberoamerican colonialism generally passes with little if any comment.

28. For a more extended analysis of the way in which the idea of History was intimately bound to European imperialism, see Wolf's *Europe and the People without History*.

29. The sociohistorical realities that underpinned such representational asymmetries during the romantic era in Spain have been elucidated by Kirkpatrick: "Woman's existence was confined to the private domestic world, within which she shared man's existence. Since she had no place in the public arena, she was attributed no political rights or economic interests of her own; only through a man—father or husband—did she have legal status. Even in her only space of existence, the private circle, she was not seen as an autonomous individual but as man's adjunct, the source of his domestic happiness" (*Las Romanticas*, 49).

30. For discussion of Spain's nineteenth-century constitutional history, see Farias, García Fernández, or Clavero.

31. Notable abolitionist representatives at Cadiz included Miguel Guiridi y Alcócer and Agustin Agüelles. See for example, Saco (vol. 3, 83–85).

32. For a more detailed history of slavery in Spain, particularly as it applied to Cuba, see Corwin. For analysis of the legal dismantling of slavery in the 1870s and 1880s, see Navarro Azcue.

Chapter 4

1. For more extended interpretation of this poem and its implications for the romantic conceptions of authorship and poetry see Ramírez (159), Sebold ("Larra y la Misión"), and Valis ("Romanticism," 330; *Culture*, 123–24).

2. The following are represntative commentaries, recently gathered by Escobar ("Larra: esperanza"): "Cada uno de esos artículos que el público lee con carcajadas eran otros tantos gemidos de desesperación que lanzaba a una sociedad corrompida y estúpida que no sabía comprenderle" [Each of thos articles that the public reads with guffaws were so many cries of desperation that he hurled at a corrupt and stupid society that was unable to understand him] (Roca de Togores). "Larra se mató porque no pudo encontrar la España que buscaba, y cuando hubo perdido toda esperanza de encontrarla" [Larra killed himself because he could not find the Spain he was searching for] (Antonio Machado); "le mató la sociedad de su tiempo" [the society of his time killed him] (Eduardo Haro Tecglen, commenting on Buero Vallejo's *La detonación*).

3. Larra had famously been involved in extramarital relations with Dolores Armijo, for whom he had abandoned his pregnant wife. Hours before his suicide, Dolores met with Larra in his home and apparently broke relations with him definitively. For testimony from Larra's brother Eugenio concerning the event, see Burgos (259). For early commentary on the implcations of Burgos's work, see Cotarelo.

4. Paul Ricouer repeatedly draws attention to the nexus between narrativity and Heidegger's being-towards-death. In his three-volume classic, *Time and Narrative*, he notes: "The most serious question this work may be able to pose is to what degree a philosophical reflection on narrativity and time may aid us in thinking about eternity and death" (vol. 1, 87).

5. Before Durkheim, Marx and Engels had arrived at similar conclusions regarding the individual in their *Economic and Philosophical Manuscripts of 1844*: "Man, much as he may therefore be a particular individual (and it is precisely his particularity which makes him an individual, and a real in-

dividual social being), is just as much the totality—the ideal totality—the subjective existence of imagined and experienced society for itself; just as he exists also in the real world both as awareness and real enjoyment of social existence, and as a totality of human manifestation of life" (105).

6. Recent observations by Löwe and Sayre have underscored this facet of romantic writing more generally: "Even as the romantics rebel against modernity, they cannot fail to be profoundly shaped by their time. Thus by reacting emotionally, by reflecting, by writing against modernity, they are reacting, reflecting, and writing in modern terms" (21). Before them, Escobar had already observed of Larra that "Esto es, precisamente, lo que encierra la contradicción del romanticismo progresista; el querer compaginar la afirmación optimista de la modernidad, según los principios de la Ilustración, con la rebelión angustiosa contra esa misma modernidad" [This is precisely what is enclosed in the contradiction of politically progressive romanticism: the desire to reconcile the optimistic affirmation of modernity, according to the principles of the Enlightenment, with the anguished rebellion against that very modernity] ("Larra y la revolución" 50).

7. The poem from which Larra draws these verses is Cienfuego's "A un amigo en la muerte de un hermano."

8. Weber himself was more attuned to the play of dis/re-enchantment than many of his commentators, who have emphasized only the first moment of the dialectic. The following passage, from "Science as Vocation," makes his own position clear. Speaking of the present, he notes: "It is just like the old world, which was not yet disenchanted with its gods and demons, but in another sense. Just as Hellenic man sacrificed on this occasion to Aphrodite and on another to Apollo, and above all as everybody sacrificed to the gods of his city—things are still the same today, but disenchanted and divested of the mythical" (23).

9. Land reform is arguably the most researched phenomenon within Spanish historical scholarship dedicated to the nineteenth century, and in recent years emphasis has fallen on its particular local and regional effects. For classic reviews of the phenomenon within a national framework, see, among others, Tomás y Valiente, Simón Segura, Bernal, and Rueda Hernanz.

10. Over the course of the 1840s, as *moderado* liberalism became hegemonic, a less strained relationship between church and state was established. For many, Spain's Concordat of 1851 with Rome represents the consolidation of this new pact. Nevertheless, historians of the church in Spain have traced a "dechristianizing process" at work throughout the nineteenth century. See, for example, Callahan (53–54, 106–7, 181–82) and Shubert (*Social History*, 160–63).

11. For reflections on the question of class in Larra's work, see, for example, Perry or Schurlknight ("Larra").

12. As Nöel Valis persuasively argues in *The Culture of Cursilería*, it is precisely the negotiation of such shifting class identities, along with the collective negotiation of Spain's symbolic subordination to modern Europe, that shapes the sociohistorical matrix in which *lo cursi*—an unsuccessful attempt at elegance—will become an important nineteenth-century Spanish cultural trope.

13. Drawing on the work of Georg Simmel, Löwy and Sayre make similar observations: "It follows that the Romantics' 'individualism' is fundamentally different from that of modern liberalism. The difference has been analyzed with a good deal of subtlety by Georg Simmel: he calls individualism of the Romantic type 'subjective individualism' to distinguish it from eighteenth-century 'numeric individualism' and from French and English liberalism" (25).

14. In Letter X of his *On the Aesthetic Education of Man*, Schiller characterizes human personality as "nothing but the pure virtuality of a possible infinite manifestation [. . .] it is nothing more than a form, an empty power" (43). For his part, Hegel describes the "beautiful soul" as follows: "It lives in dread of besmirching the splendour of its inner being by action and an existence; and in order to preserve the purity of its heart, it flees from contact with the actual world" (400). For a more protracted treatment of the tensions between such conceptions of the self and the actualities of liberal legalism, see Rosenblum (34–56).

15. The terms of subscription, on the back cover of the first volume, offer intiguing insight into what had become a common practice in the publishing industry: "Esta obra se publica por suscripcion, en cuadernos de cinco ó seis pliegos de impresion: cada cuatro cuadernos componen un tomo—el precio por suscripción es 2 reales cada entrega, llevada el domingo por la mañana á casa de los Señores Suscriptores" [This work is published through subscription in booklets of five or six print sheets: every four notebooks compose one tome—the subscription price is two reales for each installment, which is delivered to the home of subscribers on Sunday morning.]

16. The daring, and at times jarring, movements of Larra's thought have been noted as one of his stylistic hallmarks. In addition to exploiting the freedom of conceptual association that had come to characterize the essay form— since Montaigne, at least—many of the stylistic features of Larra's writing have been also been linked to the tradition of Menippean satire. Summarizing Larra's relationship to this tradition, Romero Tobar observes that "Larra

es el primer periodista español que entrevera la tradición de la sátira moderna y la antigua sátira menipea para hacer de la mezcla una ágil respuesta a las incitaciones de cada día" [Larra is the first Spanish journalist who intermingles the tradition of modern satire with the ancient Menippean satire in order to create out of the mix an agile response to the incitements of each day] ("Estudio" xii).

17. It is worth recalling Nietzsche's observations in "The Use and Abuse of History." "We do need history"—he observes—"but quite differently from the jaded idlers in the garden of knowledge. [. . .] We need it for life and action, not as a convenient way to avoid life and action. We would serve history only so far as it serves life" (3).

18. The *Curso* saw multiple editions throughout the 1830s, 1840s, and 1850s. The work synthesized and disseminated well-known works of the day for a Spanish reading public. In addition to the presence of Smith's thought throughout, Flórez Estrada's sources included the following: McCulloch's *Principles of Political Economy* (1825), Mill's *Elements of Political Economy* (1821–1826), Say's *Traite d'economie politique* (1827), Ricardo's *On the Principles of Political Economy and Taxation* (1821), Storch's *Cours d'economie politique* (1823), Sismondi's *Etudes sur l'economie politique* (1837), and, in Spain, the works of Jovellanos and Canga Argüelles (Almenar, LXIII). For a discussion of the life and works of Flórez Estrada and his impact on Spanish liberal economic reform, see Martínez Cachero and Lancha.

19. For an analysis of the shift from the figure of the city to the necropolis in Larra, see Baker; for a discussion of Larra's dialogue with the highly popular gothic discourse of his day, see Gies ("Larra") and Haidt ("Gothic").

20. The allusion is biographical as well as symbolic. Larra had in fact been elected—by customarily fixed means—but the results were revoked by the 12 August uprising known as the "Motín de la Granja."

21. Harvey nicely sums up this pattern of thinking in the title of his most recent study: *Paris, Capital of Modernity.* Casting a slightly wider net, Habermas notes that "in the European languages of the modern age the adjective 'modern' only came to be used in a substantive form in the middle of the nineteenth century [. . .] in the realm of the fine arts. This explains why *Moderne* and *Modernität, modernité* and *modernity* have until our own day a core aesthetic meaning fashioned by the self-understanding of avant-garde art" (8). The three languages Habermas happens to reproduce (French, German, and English), as well as the European languages that go unrepresented, are symptomatic of the "modern European" metageography we explored in chapter 1.

22. The juxtaposition of the two terms also highlights what I have elsewhere called the "asymmetrical ignorance" produced by modern European cultural imperialism. Ignorance of the figure of the *flaneur* would establish grounds for questioning the intellectual credentials of "any self-respecting nineteenth-century scholar." In contrast, to ignore the *costumbrista* is to disregard a more or less important figure within Iberoamerican culture.

23. A veritable subspecialty within nineteenth-century Hipanic studies, *costumbrismo* has engendered a vast bibliography. For a classic overview of the "cuadro de costumbres" and its relationship to the nineenteenth-century novel see Montesinos. For a discussion of the genre's roots in the eighteenth century, see Marun and Froldi ("Anticipaciones"). See also Kirkpatrick ("Ideology") and Fontanella. Navas Ruiz (*Romanticismo*) provides a useful summary of the basic tendencies within Spanish *costumbrismo*: to record sociohistorical changes in Spanish society (often through the lens of conservative nostalgia for a disappearing past), to correct foreign misrepresentations of Spanish customs, and—as is particularly true of Larra—to mount an ethico-political critique of the Spanish status quo (145). Escobar ("Costumbrismo") has made one of the strongest cases for reframing critical discussions of *costumbrismo* within the theorization of modernity.

24. The gothic echoes of *Noches lúgubres* are not difficult to discern here. See Sebold ("Cadalso y Larra") for an analysis of the bio-temperamental similarities between the two authors.

25. Habermas is genarally credited with the formulation of modernity as an "unfinished project." McCarthy offers the following useful summary: "Habermas agrees with the radical critics of enlightenment. [. . .] Like them he views reason as inescapably situated, as concretized in history, society, body and language. Unlike them, however, he holds that the defects of Enlightenment can only be made good by further enlightenment" (xvii). For examples of various contemporary responses to Habermas, see Passerin d'Entrèves.

26. Strikingly, Jameson has recently come to conclusions not at all unlike Larra's late thinking about the modern: "The West"—he writes—"has long [. . .] found itself unable to think the category of the 'great collective project' in terms of social revolution and transformation. But we have a convenient substitute, in any case far less demanding on the imagination: for us, and as far back in 'modernity' as we can determine, the great collective project—the 'moral equivalent of war'—is simply war itself. It is finally as a war machine that the efficiency of a state is judged; and no doubt modern warfare offers a very advanced form of collective organization indeed. But a fundamental structural and ideological limit on our Utopian imagination is surely demonstrated by the lack of alternatives" (*Singular*, 211–12).

27. The U.S. National Institute of Mental Health currently lists the following among the array of symptoms associated with depression: "a persistent sad, anxious or 'empty' mood; feelings of hopelessness, pessimism; [. . .] loss of interest or pleasure in hobbies or activities; decreased energy" ("Depression"). The point of course, is not to diagnose Fígaro with a depressive disorder but rather to underscore the consonance between this diminished vitality and the death of hope in Larra. At the same time, it is worth noting that the death of hope is not solely a subjective affair; it is represented as the effect of objectively existing social conditions.

28. Portions of this analysis were first published in *Revista de Estudios Hispánicos* 33 (1999): 41–63.

29. For analyses of Larra's work in the context of the "properly bourgeois revolution" that begins with the Enlightenment (Jameson, *Political*, 96), see Escobar ("Larra y la revolución") and Kirkpatrick (*Las Romanticas*, 3–9).

30. Given this wordplay, I will follow Pérez Vidal in citing the title of the essay as "La Noche Buena" rather than the more frequent "Nochebuena."

31. See Gennette's chapters on "Duration" and "Speed" for a discussion of tempo in narratological terms (*Narrative Discourse*, 86–112; *Narrative Discourse Revisited*, 33–37.)

32. In his study of Larra's ritualistic settings, for example, Teichmann makes the connection explicit: "Larra se considera un mártir a la manera de Cristo [. . .] es éste un papel que desempeña en su grado máximo en 'La Nochebuena de 1836' " [Larra considers himself a martyr in the manner of Christ { . . . } this is a role that he plays to the greatest degree in 'Christmas Eve 1836'] (124). Many of Larra's annotators have also noted a scarcely veiled autobiographical reference here; Larra was born on 24 March.

33. For the most exhaustive analysis of Larra's play on contemporary and often highly ephemeral political rhetoric, see Ullman. See also Centeno, who reads the encounter as a modernization of Horace (Satire 7, book II).

34. For a discussion of the historical links between theatricality and Catholicism, see, for example, Young, Donovan, or Hardison. For an overview of medieval drama, see Harris (*Medieval*).

35. Pérez Vidal notes that the obseervation is a reference to the play, *Las colegialas son colegiales*, which was preformed on 24 December 1836 in the Teatro de la Cruz (607).

36. See Romero Tobar ("Larra") for an analysis of the Larra's various literary pseudonyms.

37. For a classic analysis of the changes that accompany the bourgeoning of a public sphere see Habermas (*Structural*).

38. The evocation of Kant in this context, a familiar critical reference in discus-

sions of romantic subjectivity, is, of course, more emblematic than factual. The Copernican revolution mentioned in the famous second preface to the *Critique* is in fact quite limited within Kant's epistemology—it is circumscribed to what in Kantian nomenclature are known as *a priori synthetic truths*. At the same time, the foundational role of Kant for what would become a more full-blown German idealism cannot be disregarded, nor can his appropriation by the English romantics, particularly Coleridge, as the philisophical authority behind a new, creative "imagination." For a reading of the Kantian legacy and its relationship to solipcism in "La Noche Buena de 1836," see Rosenberg.

Afterword

1.   Santiáñez proposes a similar notion of modernity in his attempt to reframe Spanish modernism within multiple, overlapping historical frameworks. See, in particular, chapters 1 and 2 (13–85).

2.   Perhaps the best-known formulation of this facet of the aesthetic is Adorno's. At the end of his essay, "Commitment," he observes: "Art, which even in its opposition to society remains a part of it, must close its eyes and ears against it: it cannot escape the shadow of irrationality. [. . .] Even in the most sublimated work of art there is a hidden 'it should be otherwise' " (*Adorno*, 202).

Works Cited

Abellán, José. *Historia crítica del pensamiento español. Liberalismo y romanticismo 1808–1874.* Madrid: Espasa Calpe, 1979.

Abrams, M. H. (Meyer Howard). *The Mirror and the Lamp: Romantic Theory and the Critical Tradition.* New York: Oxford University Press, 1953.

———. *Natural Supernaturalism: Tradition and Revolution in Romantic Literature.* New York: Norton, 1971.

Adams, Nicholson. *The Heritage of Spain.* New York: Henry Holt, 1943.

Adorno, Theodor. *The Adorno Reader.* Oxford: Blackwell, 2000.

Agamben, Giogio. *Language and Death: The Place of Negativity.* Minneapolis: University of Minnesota Press, 1991.

Aguilar Piñal, Francisco. *Historia literaria de España en el siglo XVIII.* Madrid: Consejo Superior de Investigaciones Científicas, 1996.

———. *Introducción al siglo XVIII.* Madrid-Gijón: Júcar, 1991.

———. "Moratín y Cadalso." *Revista de Literatura* 42 (1980): 135–50.

Aldaraca, Bridget. *El ángel del hogar: Galdós and the Ideology of Domesticity in Spain.* Chapel Hill: North Carolina Studies in Romance Languages and Literatures, 1991.

"All Souls' Day." *Catholic Encycolpedia Online.* 1997. www.newadvent.org (accessed December 2005).

Alonso Seaone, María José. "Sobre Don Alvaro y su verdadero origen. (Presencia de la obra del Inca Garcilaso de la Vega en el drama del Duque de Rivas)." In *Homenaje al Profesor Antonio Gallego Morell.* 3 vols. Granada: Universidad de Granada, 1989. Vol. 1: 189–204.

Althusser, Louis. "Ideology and Ideological State Apparatuses (Notes Toward an Investigation)." In *Mapping Ideology*, ed. Slavoj Zizek, 100–40. London: Verso, 1994.

Almenar, Salvador. "Estudio Preliminar." In *Curso de economía política*, by Alvaro Flórez Estrada, vol. 1: XXXV–CXIII. Madrid: Instituto de Estudios Fiscales, 1981.

Alvarez Junco, José. Introduction to *Spanish History since 1808,* ed. José Alvarez Junco and Adrian Shubert. New York: Arnold, 2000.

———. *Mater dolorosa: la idea de España en el siglo XIX.* Madrid: Taurus, 2001.

Andioc, René. *Teatro y sociedad en el Madrid del siglo XVIII.* Madrid: Fundación Juan March, 1976.

———. "Sobre el estreno de Don Alvaro." In *Homenaje a Juan López Morillas,* 63–86. Madrid: Castalia, 1982.

Anonymous. *A Treatise Paraenetical, That Is to Say: An Exhortation.* In *The Black Legend: Anti-Spanish Attitudes in the Old World and the New,* ed. Charles Gibson, 48–53. New York: Knopf, 1971.

Appiah, Kwame Anthony. "Is the Post- in Postmodernism the Post- in Postcolonial?" In *Theory of the Novel: A Historical Approach,* ed. Michael McKeon, 882–99. Baltimore: Johns Hopkins University Press, 2000.

Aranguren, José Luis. *Moral y sociedad. La moral social española en el siglo XIX.* Madrid: Cuadernos Para el Diálogo, 1974.

Arce, Joaquín. *La poesía del siglo ilustrado.* Madrid: Alhambra, 1981.

Argullol, Rafael. "El Romanticismo como diagnóstico del hombre moderno." In *Romanticismo/Romanticismos,* ed. María Siguán, 205–13. Barcelona: Promociones y Publicaciones Universitarias, 1988.

Artola, Miguel. *Antiguo Régimen y revolución liberal.* Barcelona: Ariel, 1978.

———. *La burguesía revolucionaria (1808–1869).* Madrid: Alianza/Alfaguara, 1973.

Ayguals de Izco, Wenceslao. *La bruja de Madrid.* Barcelona: Taber, 1969.

Azorín (José Martínez Ruíz). *Clásicos y modernos. Obras completas.* Vol. 13. Madrid: Rafael Caro Ragio, 1919.

———. *Rivas y Larra.* Madrid: Espasa-Calpe, 1947.

Babitt, Irving. *Rousseau and Romanticism.* Boston: Houghton Mifflin, 1935.

Baker, Edward. "El Madrid de Larra: Del Jardín Público a la Necrópolis." *Sociocriticism* 4–5 (1986–1987): 185–206.

Balfour, Sebastian. *The End of the Spanish Empire: 1898–1923.* Oxford: Clarendon Press, 1997.

Barthes, Roland. *Mythologies.* New York: Hill and Wang, 1972.

Barnard, Frederick. *Herder's Social and Political Thought: From Enlightenment to Nationalism.* Oxford: Clarendon Press, 1965.

Basalisco, Lucio. "José Cadalso (1742–82): Scrittore esclusivamente *ilustrado* o anche araldo del romanticismo spagnolo?" *Quaderni del C.R.I.E.R.* 3 (1998): 5–19.

Bataillon, Marcel. *Erasmo y España.* Mexico City: Fondo de Cultura Económica, 1950.

Baucom, Ian. "Globalit Inc, or, The Cultural Logic of Global Literary Studies,"

PMLA 116, no. 1 (2001) (Special issue on "Globalizing Literary Studies"): 158–72.

Baudelaire, Charles. *Oeuvres completes.* Vol 2. Paris: Gallimard, 1976.

———. *Selected Writings on Art and Artists.* Middlesex: Penguin Books, 1972.

Benjamin, Walter. *Charles Baudelaire: A Lyric Poet in the Era of High Capitalism.* New York: Verso, 1997.

———. *Illuminations.* New York: Schoken Books, 1968.

Berlin, Isaiah. *The Roots of Romanticism.* Princeton: Princeton University Press, 1999.

———. *Three Critics of the Enlightenment: Vico, Hamann, Herder.* Princeton: Princeton University Press, 2000.

Berman, Marshall. *All That Is Solid Melts into Air: The Experience of Modernity.* New York: Penguin, 1982.

Bermúdez Cañete, Federico. "Cadalso en su contexto europeo." *Cuadernos Hispanoamericanos,* no. 389 (1982): 263–78.

Bernal, Antionio. *La lucha por la tierra en la crisis del antiguo régimen.* Madrid: Taurus, 1979.

Bhabha, Homi. "Afterword: A Personal Response." In *Rethinking Literary History: A Dialogue on Theory,* ed. Linda Hutcheon and Mario Valdés, 194–203. Oxford: Oxford University Press, 2002.

———. *The Location of Culture.* New York: Routledge, 1994.

Blanchot, Maurice. *Death Sentence.* Barrytown, NY: Barrytown Ltd., 1998.

Blanco, Alda. *Escritoras virtuosas: narradoras de la domesticidad en la España isabelina.* Granada: Universidad de Granada, 2001.

———. "El fin del imperio español y la generación del 98: nuevas aproximaciones." *Hispanic Research Journal* 4, no. 1 (2003): 3–18.

Blanco Aguinaga, Carlos. "On Modernism from the Periphery." In *Modernism and Its Margins: Reinscribing Cultural Modernity from Spain and Latin America,* ed. Anthony Geist and José Monleón, 3–16. New York: Garland Publishing, 1999.

Blaut, James. *The Colonizer's Model of the World: Geographical Diffusionism and Eurocentric History.* New York: Guilford Press, 1993.

———. *Eight Eurocentric Historians.* New York: Guilford Press, 2000.

Blecua, Alberto. "Introducción." In *Don Alvaro o la fuerza del sino,* by the Duke of Rivas [Angel Saavedra], 3–47. Barcelona: Planeta, 1988.

Bloom, Harold. "The Internalization of Quest Romance." In *Romanticism and Consciousness,* ed. Harold Bloom, 3–23. New York: Norton, 1970.

Blumenberg, Hans. *The Legitimacy of the Modern Age.* Cambridge, MA: MIT Press, 1983.

Botting, Fred. *Gothic.* London: Routledge, 1996.

Bourdieu, Pierre. *The Field of Cultural Production*. New York: Columbia University Press, 1993.

Bretón de los Herreros, Manuel. *Marcela, o ¿cual de los tres?* Ed. Francisco Serrano Puente. Logroño: Instituto de Estudios Riojanos. Sevicio de Cultura de la Excma Diputación Provincial, 1975.

Brown, Andrew. *Roland Barthes: The Figures of Writing*. Oxford: Clarendon Press, 1992.

Buckle, Henry Thomas. "Spanish Intellect from the Fifth to the Nineteenth Century." In *The Black Legend: Anti-Spanish Attitudes in the Old World and the New,* 129–38. New York: Knopf, 1971.

Burdiel, Isabel. "The Liberal Revolution, 1808–1843." In *Spanish History since 1808,* ed. Juan Alvarez Junco and Adrian Shubert. London: Oxford University Press, 2000.

Burgos, Carmen de. *"Figaro." (Revelaciones, "ella" descubierta, epistolario inédito).* Madrid: Imprenta "Alrededor del Mundo," 1919.

Bury, J. B. *The Idea of Progress: An Inquiry into Its Origin and Growth*. London: Macmillan, 1920.

Busquets, *Loreto. Rivas y Verdi: del "Don Alvaro" a "La forza del destino."* Quaderni della ricerca, 6. Rome: Bulzoni Editore, 1988.

Butler, Judith. *The Psychic Life of Power: Theories in Subjection*. Stanford: Stanford University Press, 1997.

Cadalso, José. *Cartas marruecas. Noches lúgubres*. Ed. Emilio Martínez Mata. Barcelona: Crítica, 2000.

———. *Cartas marruecas. Noches lúgubres*. Ed. Russell Sebold. Madrid: Cátedra, 2001.

———. *Escritos autobiográficos y epistolario*. Ed. Nigel Glendinning and N. Harrison. London: Tamesis, 1979.

Caldera, Ermanno. "Estudio Preliminar. La Revolución Romántica del *Don Alvaro.*" In *Don Alvaro o la fuerza del sino,* by the Duke of Rivas [Angel Saavedra], ed. Miguel Angel Lama, ix–xx. Barcelona: Crítica, 1994.

———. Introducción to *Don Alvaro o la fuerza del sino,* by the Duke of Rivas [Angel Saavedra], ed. Ermanno Caldera, 3–70. Madrid: Taurus, 1986.

Callahan, William. *Church, Politics, and Society in Spain, 1750–1874*. Cambridge: Harvard University Press, 1984.

Camarero, Manuel. "Didacticismo en las *Noches lúgubres*: el valor de la amistad." *Dieciocho* 9 (1986): 57–61.

———. "Las *Noches lúgubres*: historia de un éxito editorial." *Cuadernos Hispanoamericanos,* no. 389 (1982): 331–43.

Cano, José Luis. "Cienfuegos y la amistad." *Calavileño* 6, no. 34 (1955): 35–40.

Cardwell, Richard. "*Don Alvaro*, or the Force of Cosmic Injustice." *Studies in Romanticism* 13 (1973): 559–79.

Carnero, Guillermo. *La cara oscura del siglo de las luces*. Madrid: Cátedra, 1983.

———. *Los orígenes del romanticismo reaccionario español: el matrimonio Böhl de Faber*. Valencia: Universidad de Valencia, 1978.

Carr, Raymond, ed. *Spain: A History*. Oxford: Oxford University Press, 2000.

Casado, María Concepción. *Así nos vieron: la vida tradicional según los viajeros*. Salamanca: Diputación Provincial de Salamanca, 1996.

Casalduero, Joaquín. "Don Alvaro o el destino como fuerza." *La Torre* 7 (1959): 11–49.

Cascardi, Anthony. *Consequences of Enlightenment*. Cambridge: Cambridge University Press, 1999.

———. *Ideologies of History in the Spanish Golden Age*. University Park: Pennsylvania State University, 1997.

———. *The Subject of Modernity*. Cambridge: Cambridge University Press, 1992.

Caso González, José. *Los conceptos de rococo, neoclasicismo y prerromanticismo en la literatura española del siglo XVIII*. Oviedo: Facultad de Filosofía y Letras, Universidad de Oviedo, 1970.

Caso González, José Miguel, ed. *Ilustración y neoclasicismo*. Historia y crítica de la literatura española 4. Barcelona: Crítica, 1983.

Castro, Américo. *Les Grands Romantiques espagnols*. Paris: La Renaissance du Livre, 1922.

Cavell, Stanley. *In Quest of the Ordinary: Lines of Skepticism and Romanticism*. Chicago: University of Chicago Press, 1998.

Chakrabarty, Dipesh. *Provincializing Europe: Postcolonial Thought and Historical Difference*. Princeton: Princeton University Press, 2000.

Charnon-Deutch, Lou. *Gender and Representation: Women in Spanish Realist Fiction*. Amsterdam: John Benjamins Publishing, 1990.

Centeno, Augusto. "La Nochebuena de 1836 y su modelo horaciano." *Modern Language Notes* 41 (1935): 441–45.

Cirujano, Paloma. *Historiografía y nacionalismo español*. Madrid: CSIC, 1985.

Clark, Robert. *Herder: His Life and Thought*. Berkeley: University of California Press, 1969.

Clavero, Bartolomé. *Evolución histórica del constitucionalismo español*. Madrid: Tecnos, 1984.

Cortés, Cayetano. "Vida de don Mariano José de Larra conocido vulgarmente bajo el pseudónimo de Fígaro." *Biblioteca Virtual Miguel Cervantes*. www.cervantesvirtual.com (accessed December 2005).

Corwin, Arthur. *Spain and the Abolition of Slavery in Cuba.* Austin: University of Texas Press, 1967.

Cotarelo, Emilio. Prólogo to *Postfígaro. Artículos no coleccionados de D. Mariano José de Larra (Fígaro).* Vol. 1. Madrid: Tipografía Renovación, 1918.

Crick, Malcolm. "The Anthropologist as Tourist: An Identity in Question." In *International Tourism, Identity, and Change,* eds. Marie Francios Lanfant, John Allcock, and Edward Bruner, 205–23. London: Sage, 1995.

Cromwell, Oliver. "Speech at the Opening of Parliament, 1656." In *The Black Legend: Anti-Spanish Attitudes in the Old World and the New,* ed. Charles Gibson, 54–62. New York: Knopf, 1971.

Culler, Jonathan. "Semiotics of Tourism." *American Journal of Semiotics* 1, nos. 1–2 (1981): 127–40.

Del Vecchio, Eugene. "Larra and the Romantic Imagination." In *Resonancias románticas: evocaciones del romanticismo hispánico,* ed. John R. Rosenberg, 129–40. Madrid: José Porrua, 1988.

"Depression." In *National Institute of Mental Health Online.* www.nimh.nih.gov (accessed December 2005).

Derrida, Jacques. *Specters of Marx: The State of the Debt, the Work of Mourning, and the New International.* New York: Routledge, 1994.

Díaz, Nicomedes Pastor. *Obras políticas.* Ed. José Luis Prieto Benavent. Madrid: Fundación Caja de Madrid; Barcelona: Anthropos, 1996.

Diccionario de autoridades. Real Academia Española. Edición Facsímil. 3 vols. Madrid: Gredos, 1990.

Diccionario de la lengua castellana compuesto por la Real Academia Española. Madrid: Joaquín Ibarra, 1780.

Diccionario de la lengua castellana por la Real Academia Española. Madrid: Imprenta Nacional, 1822.

Diccionario de la lengua castellana por la Real Academia Española. Madrid: Imprenta de D. María Francisco Fernández, 1843.

Diez Taboada, María Paz. *La elegía romántica española: estudio y antología.* Madrid: Consejo Superior de Investigaciones Científicas, 1977.

Donovan, Richard. *The Liturgical Drama in Medieval Spain.* Toronto: Pontifical Institute of Medieval Studies, 1958.

Dowling, John. "Las *Noches lúgubres* de Cadalso y la juventud romántica del ochocientos." In *Coloquio Internacional sobre José Cadalso,* 105–24. Abano Terme: Piovan, 1985.

Durkheim, Emile. *Suicide: A Study in Sociology.* New York: Free Press, 1979.

Dussel, Ernique. "Beyond Eurocentrism: The World System and the Limits of Modernity." In *The Cultures of Globalization,* 3–31. Durham, NC: Duke University Press, 1998.

Eagleton, Terry. *Ideology: An Introduction.* London/New York: Verso, 1991.

——. *The Ideology of the Aesthetic.* Oxford: Blackwell, 1990.

——. *The Illusions of Postmodernism.* Oxford: Blackwell, 1996.

Edelstein, Ludwig. *The Idea of Progress in Classical Antiquity.* Baltimore: Johns Hopkins University Press, 1967.

Elias, Norbert. *The Civilizing Process.* 2 vols. Oxford: Blackwell, 1978 and 1982.

Ellingson, Ter. *The Myth of the Noble Savage.* Berkeley: University of California Press, 2001.

Engels, Friedrich. "Engels to Pyotr Lavrov in London." (1875). *Marx Engels Internet Archive,* 2000. www.marxists.org (accessed December 2005).

Escobar, José. "La canonización de Larra en el siglo XIX." *Biblioteca Virtual Miguel de Cervantes.* http://cervantesvirtual.com (accessed December 2005).

——. "Costumbrismo: Estado de la Cuestión," In *Romanticismo 6: Actos del VI Congreso del Centro Internacional de Estudios Hispánicos. El Costumbrismo Romántico,* 117–26. Rome, Bulzoni, 1996.

——. "Ilustración, romanticismo, modernidad." In *Entre Siglos,* ed. Ermanno Caldera et al., 123–33. Rome: Bulzoni, 1993.

——. "Larra: esperanza y melancolía." *Biblioteca Virtual Miguel Cervantes.* www.cervantesvirtual.com (accessed December 2005).

——. "Larra y la revolución burguesa." In *Resonancias románticas: evocaciones del romanticismo hispánico,* ed. John Rosenberg, 35–51. Madrid: José Porrua, 1988.

——. *Los orígenes de la obra de Larra.* Madrid: Prensa Española, 1973.

Farias García, Pedro. *Breve historia constitucional de España (1808–1978).* Madrid: Latina Universitaria, 1981.

Fayard, Janine. *Los miembros del Consejo de Castilla (1621–1746).* Madrid: Siglo XXI, 1982.

Fernández Almagro, Melchor. *La emancipación de América y su reflejo en la conciencia española.* Madrid: Instituto de Estudios Políticos, 1957.

Fernández Herr, Elena. *Les origines de l'Espagne romantique. Les récits de voyage 1755–1823.* Paris: Didier, 1973.

Flitter, Derek. *Spanish Romantic Literary Theory and Criticism.* Cambridge: Cambridge University Press, 1992.

Flórez Estrada, Alvaro. *Curso de economía política.* 2 vols. Madrid: Instituto de Estudios Fiscales, 1981.

Fontana, Josep. *La quiebra de la monarquía absoluta, 1814–1820. (La crisis del Antiguo Régimen en España).* Barcelona: Ariel, 1971.

Fontanella, Lee. "The Fashion and Styles of Spain's *Costumbrismo.*" *Revista Canadiense de Estudios Hispánicos* 6, no. 2 (1982): 175–89.

Ford, Richard. *A Handbook for Travellers in Spain and Readers at Home, Describing the Country and Cities, the Natives and Their Manners, the Antiquites, Religion, Legends, Fine Arts, Literature, Sports, and Gastronomy, with Notices on Spanish History.* Carbondale: Southern Illinois University Press, 1966.

Foucault, Michel. *The History of Sexuality: An Introduction.* Vol. 1. New York: Vintage, 1978.

———. *The Order of Things: An Archeology of the Human Sciences.* New York: Vintage, 1972.

Fox, Inman. *La invención de España: nacionalismo liberal e identidad nacional.* Madrid: Cátedra, 1997.

Frank, Waldo. *Virgin Spain.* New York: Boni and Liveright, 1926.

Freud, Sigmund. *The Freud Reader.* Ed. Peter Gay. New York: Norton, 1989.

———. *Three Essays on the Theory of Sexuality.* New York: Basic Books, 1961.

Froldi, Rinaldo. "Anticipaciones dieciochescas del costumbrismo romántico." In *Romanticismo 6: Actos del VI Congreso del Centro Internacional de Estudios Hispánicos. El Costumbrismo Romántico,* 163–70. Rome: Bulzoni, 1996.

———. "¿Literatura *prerromántica* o literatura *ilustrada?*" In *Simposio sobre el Padre Feijoo y su siglo,* 477–82. Oviedo: Cátedra Feijoo, 1983.

Fusi, Juan Pablo. *España: la evolución de la identidad nacional.* Madrid: Temas de Hoy, 2000.

Galdo, Juan Carlos. "Mestizaje, violencia y dialogismo en *Don Álvaro.*" *Romance Review* 11 (2001): 33-44.

García Fernández, Javier. *Esquemas del constitucionalismo español (1808–1976).* Madrid: Universidad Complutense (Facultad de Derecho), 1976.

García Mercadal, José. *España vista por los extranjeros.* Madrid: Biblioteca Nueva, 1918.

García Sanz, Angel, and Ramón Garrabou, eds. *Historia agraria de la España contemporánea.* Vol. 1. *Cambio social y nuevas formas de prosperidad (1800–1850).* Barcelona: Crítica, 1985.

Garcilaso de la Vega. *Obras completas.* Madrid: Castalia, 1981.

Geist, Anthony, and José Monleón, eds. *Modernism and Its Margins: Reinscribing Cultural Modernity from Spain and Latin America.* New York: Garland Publishing, 1999.

Geertz, Clifford. *The Interpretation of Cultures.* New York: Basic Books, 1973.

Gennette, Gerard. *Narrative Discourse: An Essay in Method.* Ithaca, NY: Cornell University Press, 1980.

———. *Narrative Discourse Revisited.* Ithaca, NY: Cornell University Press, 1988.

Gibson, Charles. Introduction. to *The Black Legend: Anti-Spanish Attitudes in the Old World and the New,* 3–27. New York: Knopf, 1971.

Gies, David. "*Ars amicitiae,* poesía y vida: el ejemplo de Cadalso." *Coloquio* (1985): 155–71.

―――. "Larra, la *Galería fúnebre*, y el gusto por lo gótico." *Atti del IV Congresso sul romanticismo spagnolo e ispanoamericano (Bordighera, 9–11 aprile 1987): La narrativa romántica.* Ed. Ermanno Caldera. Genoa: Biblioteca di Lett. *Romanticismo* 3–4 (1988): 60–68.

―――. "The Plurality of Spanish Romanticisms." *Hispanic Review* 49, no. 4 (1981): 427–42.

―――. *The Theater in Nineteenth-Century Spain.* Cambridge: Cambridge University Press, 1994.

Gillies, Alexander. *Herder.* Oxford: Blackwell, 1945.

Gilmore, Myron. *Humanists and Jurists: Six Studies in the Renaissance.* Cambridge: Harvard University Press, 1963.

Ginsberg, Morris. *The Idea of Progress: A Revaluation.* London: Methuen, 1953.

Glendinning, Nigel. Apéndices to *Noches lúgubres,* 99–109. Madrid: Espasa Calpe (Colección Austral), 1993.

―――. Introducción to *Noches lúgubres,* 9–52. Madrid: Espasa Calpe (Colección Austral), 1993.

―――. Prólogo to *Noches lúgubres,* vii–lxvi. Madrid: Espasa Calpe (Clásicos Castellanos), 1961.

Godin, David. "Cadalso's *Noches lúgubres*: Autobiography and Fiction." *Hispanic Journal* 5, no. 2 (1984): 127–36.

Gollich, Graeme. *Myth and Metropolis: Walter Benjamin and the City.* Cambridge: Polity, 1996.

Gómez de la Serna, Ramón. "El primer romántico de España, Cadalso el desenterrador." In *Mi Tía Carolina Coronado,* 33–41. Buenos Aires: Emecé, 1942.

Graf, E. C. "Necrophilia and Materialist Thoughts in José Cadalso's *Noches lúgubres*: Romanticism's Anxious Adornment of Political Economy." *Journal of Spanish Cultural Studies* 2, no. 2 (2001): 211–30.

Granjel, Luis. *La medicina española del siglo XVIII.* Salamanca: Universidad de Salamanca, 1979.

Gray, E. "Satanism in Don Alvaro." *Roanische Forschunge* 80 (1968): 292–302.

Green, Otis. *Spain and the Western Tradition: The Castilian Mind in Literature from El Cid to Calderón.* Vol. 1. Madison: University of Wisconsin Press, 1968.

Greenblatt, Stephen. "Racial Memory and Literary History." *PMLA* 116, no. 1 (2001): 48–63.

Gunn, Giles, coordinator. *Globalizing Literary Studies. PMLA* 116 (2001): 1–272.

Habermas, Jürgen. *The Philosophical Discourse of Modernity: Twelve Lectures.* Cambridge, MA: MIT Press, 1987.

————. *The Structural Transformation of the Public Sphere.* Cambridge, MA: MIT Press, 1989.

Hafter, Monroe. *Pen and Peruke: Spanish Literature of the Eighteenth Century.* Ann Arbor: Department of Romance Languages, University of Michigan, 1992.

Haidt, Rebecca. *Embodying Enlightenment: Knowing the Body in Eighteenth-Century Spanish Literature and Culture.* New York: St. Martin's Press, 1998.

————. "Gothic Larra." *Decimonónica* 1, no. 1 (2004): 52–66. www.decimononica.org (accessed December 2005).

Halecki, Oscar. *The Limits and Divisions of European History.* Notre Dame, IN: University of Notre Dame Press, 1962.

Hardison, O. B. *Christian Rite and Christian Drama in the Middle Ages.* Baltimore: Johns Hopkins University Press, 1965.

Harris, John. *Medieval Theater in Context: An Introduction.* London: Routledge, 1992.

Harris, Marvin. *Cultural Materialism: The Struggle for a Science of Culture.* Lanham, MD: Rowman and Littlefield, 2001.

Hart, Michael, and Antonio Negri. *Empire.* Cambridge: Harvard University Press, 2000.

Harvey, David. *Paris, Capital of Modernity.* New York: Routledge, 2003.

Hegel, Georg. *Phenomenology of the Spirit.* Oxford: Clarendon Press, 1977.

Helman, Edith. "Caprichos and Monstruos of Cadalso and Goya." *Hispanic Review* 26 (1958): 200–22.

————. Introducción to *Noches lúgubres,* by José Cadalso, 9–65. Madrid: Taurus, 1968.

Herr, Richard. *The Eighteenth-Century Revolution in Spain.* Princeton: Princeton University Press, 1958.

————. *An Historical Essay on Modern Spain.* Berkeley: University of California Press, 1974.

Herrero, Javier. Review of *Colonel don José Cadalso,* by Russell Sebold. *Modern Language Notes* 93 (1978): 356–59.

Herzberger, David. *Narrating the Past: Fiction and Historiography in Post-War Spain.* Durham, NC: Duke University Press, 1995.

Hibbert, Christopher. *The Grand Tour.* London: Weidenfeld and Nicolson, 1969.

Hillgarth, J. N. *The Mirror of Spain 1500–1700: The Formation of a Myth.* Ann Arbor: University of Michigan Press, 2000.

Hobbes, Thomas. *Leviathan.* New York: Norton, 1997.

Hobsbawm, Eric. *The Age of Extremes: A History of the World, 1914–1991.* New York: Vintage, 1998.

Holt, Edgar. *The Carlist Wars in Spain.* Cheter Springs, PA: Dufour Editions, 1967.

Hoffman, Leon-Francois. *Romantique Espagne: l'image d'Espagne en France entre 1800 et 1850.* Princeton: Department of Romance Languages, Princeton University, 1961.

Horkheimer, Max, and Theodor Adorno. *Dialectic of Enlightenment.* New York: Continuum, 1997.

Hugo, Victor. *Le Préface de Cromwell.* Ed. Maurice Souriau. Paris: Boivin, 1897.

Hume, David. *An Enquiry Concerning the Principles of Morals.* Oxford: Clarendon Press, 1998.

Hutcheon, Linda. "Rethinking the National Model." In *Rethinking Literary History: A Dialogue on Theory,* ed. Linda Hutcheon and Mario Valdés, 3–49. Oxford: Oxford University Press, 2002.

Iarocci, Michael. "Between the Liturgy and the Market: Bourgeois Subjectivity and Romanticism in 'La Nochebuena de 1836.' " *Revista de Estudios Hispánicos* 33 (1999): 41–63.

Iglesias, María Carmen. "Montesquieu and Spain: Iberian Identity as Seen through the Eyes of a Non-Spaniard of the Eighteenth Century." In *Iberian Identity: Essays on the Nature of Identity in Portugal and Spain,* ed. Richard Herr and John Polt, 143-55. Berkeley: Institute of International Studies (University of California), 1989.

Ilie, Paul. *The Age of Minerva: Counter-rational Reason in the Eighteenth Century. Goya and the Paradigm of Unreason in Western Europe.* Philadelphia: University of Pennsylvania Press, 1995.

———. "Larra's Nightmare." *Revista Hispánica Moderna* 38, no. 4 (1974/75): 153–66.

Jagoe, Catherine. *Ambiguous Angels: Gender in the Novels of Galdós.* Berkeley: University of California Press, 1994.

Jameson, Fredric. *The Political Unconscious: Narrative as Socially Symbolic Act.* Ithaca, NY: Cornell University Press, 1981.

———. *A Singular Modernity: Essay on the Ontology of the Present.* London: Verso, 2002.

Jarvis, Simon. *Adorno: A Critical Introduction.* New York: Routledge, 1998.

Jenks, Chris. "Watching your Step: The History and Practice of the Flaneur." In *Visual Culture,* ed. Chris Jenks. New York: Routledge, 1995.

Juderías, Julián. *La leyenda negra.* Barcelona: Araluce, 1917.

Juretschke, Hans. *La época del romanticismo.* Madrid: Espasa Calpe, 1996.

———. *Origen doctrinal y génesis del romanticismo español.* Madrid: Ateneo, 1954.

————. "La presencia del ideario romántico alemán en la estructura y evolución teórica del romanticismo español." In *El romanticismo,* ed. David Gies, 215–41. Madrid: Taurus, 1989.

Kamen, Henry. *The Spanish Inquisition: An Historical Revision.* London: Westfield and Nicolson, 1997.

Kant, Immanuel. *Critique of Pure Reason.* New York: St. Martin's Press, 1965.

Kagan, Richard. *Students and Society in Early Modern Spain.* Baltimore: Johns Hopkins University Press, 1974.

————, ed. *Spain in America: The Origins of Hispanism in the United States.* Urbana: University of Illinois Press, 2002.

Kerrigan, William, and Gorden Braden. *The Idea of the Renaissance.* Baltimore: Johns Hopkins University Press, 1989.

Kierkegaard, Soren. *A Sickness unto Death: A Christian Psychological Exposition for Upbuilding and Awakening.* Princeton: Princeton University Press, 1980.

Kincaid, James. "Resist Me, You Sweet Resistable You." *PMLA* 118, no. 5 (2003): 1325–33.

Kinsbruner, Jay. *Independence in Spanish America: Civil Wars, Revolutions, and Underdevelopment.* Albuquerque: University of New Mexico Press, 1994.

Kirkpatrick, Susan. "Constituting the Subject: Race, Gender and Nation in the Early Nineteenth Century." In *Culture and the State in Spain (1550–1850),* 225–51. New York: Garland Publishing, 1999.

————. "The Ideology of Costumbrismo" *Ideologies and Literature* 2, no. 7 (1978): 28–44.

————. *Larra: el laberinto inextricable de un romántico liberal.* Madrid: Gredos, 1977.

————. *Las Románticas: Women Writers and Subjectivity in Spain 1835–1850.* Berkeley: University of California Press, 1989.

————. "Spanish Romanticism and the Liberal Project: The Crisis of Mariano José de Larra." *Studies in Romanticism* 16, no. 4 (1977): 451–72.

Kittay, Jeffery, and Wlad Godzich. *The Emergence of Prose: An Essay in Prosaics.* Minneapolis: University of Minnesota Press, 1987.

Klibansky, Raymond, Erwin Panofsky, and Fritz Saxl. *Saturn and Melancholy: Studies in the History of Natural Philosophy and Art.* London: Thomas Nelson and Sons, 1964.

Kristeva, Julia. *Black Sun: Depression and Melancholia.* New York: Columbia University Press, 1989.

Labanyi, Jo. *Gender and Modernization in the Spanish Realist Novel.* Oxford: Oxford University Press, 2000.

————, ed. *Constructing Identity in Contemporary Spain: Theoretical Debates and Cultural Practice.* Oxford: Oxford University Press, 2002.

Lama, Miguel Angel. "Escribir un cuadro y pintar un poema: del arte de Rivas en Don Alvaro o la fuerza del sino." *Glosa* 3 (1992): 199–219.

———. "Las *Noches lúgubres* de Cadalso o el teatro a oscuras." *Hispanic Review* 51 (1993): 1–13.

———. Prólogo to *Don Alvaro o la fuerza del sino*, by the Duke of Rivas [Angel Saavedra], ed. Miguel Angel Lama, 1–76. Barcelona: Critica, 1994.

Lancha, Charles. *Alvaro Florez Estrada, 1766–1853, ou Le liberalisme espagnol.* Grenoble: Université de Langues et Lettres de Grenoble, 1984.

Lanfant, Marie Franciose. Introduction to *International Tourism, Identity and Change,* ed. Marie Francios Lanfant, John Allcock, and Edward Bruner. London: Sage, 1995.

Larra, Mariano José. *Figaro. Colección de artículos dramáticos, literarios, políticos y de costumbres.* Ed. Alejandro Pérez Vidal. Barcelona: Critica, 1997.

LaRubia-Prado, Francisco. "Historia desde la cripta: terror y fascinación del cadaver en *Noches lúgubres* de José de Cadalso." *Dieciocho* 25, no. 1 (2002): 65–74.

Latour, Brouno. *We Have Never Been Modern.* Cambridge: Harvard University Press, 1993.

Levinas, Emmanuel. "Reality and Its Shadow." In *The Continental Aesthetics Reader,* ed. Clive Cazeaux, 117–28. New York: Routledge, 2000.

Lewis, Martin, and Kären Wigen. *The Myth of Continents: A Critique of Metageography.* Berkeley: University of California Press, 1997.

Llobera, Josep. *The God of Modernity: The Development of Nationalism in Western Europe.* Oxford: Berg, 1994.

Llorens, Vicente. *El romanticismo español.* Madrid: Fundación Juan March/Castalia, 1979.

López, Francois. *Juan Pablo Forner et la crise de la conscience espagnole au XVIIIe Siècle.* Bordeaux: Université de Bordeaux, 1976.

López Cepero, José. *España vista por los extranjeros. Antología.* Madrid: Doncel, 1918.

Loureiro, Angel. "Spanish Nationalism and the Ghost of Empire." *Journal of Spanish Cultural Studies* 4, no. 1 (2003): 65–76.

Lowenthal, David. *The Past Is a Foreign Country.* Cambridge: Cambridge University Press, 1985.

Löwith, Karl. *Meaning in History.* Chicago: University of Chicago Press, 1970.

Löwy, Michael, and Robert Sayre. *Romanticism against the Tide of Modernity.* Durham, NC: Duke University Press, 2001.

Lunardi, Ernesto. *La crisi del Settecento. José Cadalso.* Genova: Romano Editrice Moderna, 1948.

Lukàcs, Georg. *The Historical Novel.* Lincoln: University of Nebraska Press, 1983.

———. *History and Class Consciousness: Studies in Marxist Dialectics.* Cambridge, MA: MIT Press, 1971.

Luzán, Ignacio. *Poética.* Ed. Russell Sebold. Barcelona: Labor, 1977.

MacCannell, Dean. *The Tourist: A New Theory of the Leisure Class.* New York: Schocken, 1976.

MacCurdy, G. Grant. "Romantic Expressionism and the Last Days of Larra." In *Resonancias románticas: evocaciones del romanticismo hispánico,* ed. John R. Rosenberg, 141–52. Madrid: José Porrua, 1988.

Maltby, William. *The Black Legend in England: The Development of Anti-Spanish Sentiment, 1558–1660.* Durham, NC: Duke University Press, 1971.

Mansour, George. "Concerning Rivas' Unexplained Localization of Don Alvaro in the Eighteenth Century." *Romance Notes* 18 (1978): 349.

Marcuse, Herbert. *The Aesthetic Dimension: Toward a Critique of Marxist Aesthetics.* Boston: Beacon Press, 1978.

Maravall, José Antonio. *Antiguos y modernos: la idea del progresso en el desarrollo inicial de una sociedad.* Madrid: Sociedad de Estudios y Publicaciones, 1966.

———. "La estimación de la sensibilidad en la cultura de la Ilustración." In *Estudios de la historia del pensamiento español (siglo XVIII),* ed. M. C. Iglesias, 269–90. Biblioteca Mondadori 19. Madrid: Mondadori, 1991.

Maravall, José María. *Mentalidad burguesa e idea de la historia en el siglo XVIII. Revista de Occidente.* Vol. 107. Madrid: Galo Sáez, 1972.

Martínez Cachero, Luis. *Alvaro Florez Estrada: su vida, su obra política y sus ideas económicas.* Oviedo: Universidad de Oviedo, 1961

Martínez Mata, Emilio. Footnotes to *Cartas marruecas. Noches lúgubres,* by José Cadalso. Barcelona: Crítica, 2000.

———. Notas Complementarias. to *Cartas marruecas. Noches lúgubres,* by José Cadalso, 301–86. Barcelona: Crítica, 2000.

———. Prólogo to *Cartas marruecas. Noches lúgubres,* by José Cadalso, xxxi–lxxxix. Barcelona: Crítica, 2000.

Martínez Torrón, Diego. *El alba del romanticismo español.* Seville: Alfar, 1993.

Marun, Gioconda. *Orígenes del costumbrismo ético-social. Addison y Steele, antecedentes del costumbrismo español y argentino.* Miami: Ediciones Universal, 1983.

Marx, Karl. *Economic and Philosophical Manuscripts of 1844.* New York: Prometheus Books, 1988.

———. *The Eighteenth Brumaire of Louis Bonaparte.* New York: International Publishers, 1963.

————. *The German Ideology.* New York: Prometheus Books, 1998.

————. *Das Kapital: A Critique of Political Economy.* Washington, DC: Regenery Publishing, 1996.

Masters, Roger. "Rousseau and the Rediscovery of Human Nature." In *The Legacy of Rousseau,* ed. Clifford Orwin and Nathan Tarcov. Chicago: University of Chicago Press, 1997.

McCarthy, Thomas. Introduction to *The Philosophical Discourse of Modernity: Twelve Lectures,* by Jürgen Habermas, vii–xvii. Cambridge, MA: MIT Press, 1987.

McFarland, Thomas. *Romanticism and the Heritage of Rousseau.* Oxford: Clarendon Press, 1995.

Mead, William. *The Grand Tour in the Eighteenth Century.* New York: Houghton Mifflin, 1914.

Menéndez Pelayo, Marcelino. *Historia de las ideas estéticas en España.* Vol. 3. Madrid: Centro de Investigaciones Científicas, 1940.

Mesa, Roberto. *La idea colonial en España.* Valencia: Fernando Torres, 1976.

Mesonero Romanos, Ramón. *Escenas y tipos matritenses.* Ed. Enrique Rubio Cremades. Madrid: Cátedra, 1993.

Mignolo, Walter. "Globalization, Civilization Processes, and the Relocation of Languages and Cultures." In *Cultures of Globalization,* ed. Fredric Jameson and Masao Miyoshi. Durham, NC: Duke University Press, 1998.

————. *Local Histories/Global Designs: Coloniality, Subaltern Knowledges, and Border Thinking.* Princeton: Princeton University Press, 2000.

————. "Rethinking the Colonial Model." In *Rethinking Literary History: A Dialogue on Theory,* ed. Linda Hutcheon and Mario Valdés, 155–93. Oxford: Oxford University Press, 2002.

Monleón, José. "Estrategias Para Entrar y Salir del Romanticismo." *Revista Hispánica Moderna* 53 (2000): 5–21.

Montesinos, José. *Costumbrismo y novela: ensayo sobre el redescubrimiento de la realidad española.* Madrid: Castalia, 1980.

Montesquieu, Charles de Secondat, baron de. *The Spirit of the Laws.* Cambridge: Cambridge University Press, 1989.

Moratín, Leandro Fernández. *Viaje a Italia.* Madrid: Espasa Calpe, 1991.

Moreno Alonso, Manuel. *Historiografía romántica española.* Seville: Universidad de Sevilla, 1979.

Moretti, Franco. "Conjectures on World Literature." *New Left Review* ns 1 (2000): 54–68.

Mulhern, Francis, ed. *Contemporary Marxist Literary Criticism.* London: Longman, 1992.

Nancy, Jean-Luc, and Phillipe Lacoue-Labarth. *L'absolu littéraire: Théorie de la littérature du romantisme allemand.* Paris: Seuil, 1978.

Navarro Azcue, Concepción. *La abolición de la esclavitud negra en la legislación española, 1870–1886.* Madrid: Instituto de Cooperación Iberoamericana/ Ediciones Cultura Hispánica, 1987.

Navas Ruiz, Ricardo. *El romanticismo español.* Madrid: Cátedra, 1982.

———, ed. *Don Alvaro o la fuerza del sino. Lanuza.* By the Duke of Rivas [Angel Saavedra]. Madrid: Anaya, 1986.

Nesbit, Robert. *History of the Idea of Progress.* New York: Basic Books, 1980.

Nietzsche, Friedrich. *The Complete Works of Friedrich Nietzsche.* Vol 2. Part 2. *Thoughts Out of Season.* London: T. N. Foulis, 1910.

Núñez Florencio, Rafael. *Sol y sangre. La imagen de España en el mundo.* Madrid: Espasa Calpe, 2001.

Onainda, Mario. *La construcción de la nación española: republicanismo y nacionalismo en la Ilustración.* Barcelona: Ediciones B, Grupo Zeta, 2002.

Orange, William of. [William the Silent (1533–1584)]. "Apologia." In *The Black Legend: Anti-Spanish Attitudes in the Old World and the New,* ed. Charles Gibson, 41–47. New York: Knopf, 1971.

Oyarzun, Román. *La historia del carlismo.* Madrid: Pueyo, 1965.

Parker, Alexander. "The Spanish Drama of the Golden Age: A Method of Analysis and Interpretation." In *The Great Playwrights.* Vol. 1. *Twenty-five Plays with Commentaries by Critics and Scholars Chosen and Introduced by Eric Bently,* 679–707. New York: Doubleday, 1970.

Passerin d'Entrèves, Maurizio, and Seyla Benhabib, eds. *Habermas and the Unfinished Project of Modernity: Critical Essays on* The Philosophical Discourse of Modernity. Cambridge, MA: MIT Press, 1997.

Pattison, Walter. "The Secret of Don Alvaro." *Symposium* 21 (1967): 67–81.

Payne, Stanley. *Spanish Catholicism. An Historical Overview.* Madison: University of Wisconsin Press, 1984.

Paz, Octavio. "La búsqueda del presente" Nobel Conference, 1990. In *Convergencias,* 7–22. Barcelona: Seix Barral, 1991.

Peers, Edgar Allison. "Angel de Saavedra, Duque de Rivas: A Critical Study." *Revue Hispanique* 57 (1923): 417–42.

———. *A History of the Romantic Movement in Spain.* Vol. 1. Cambridge: Cambridge University Press, 1935.

Pérez Magallón, Jesús. *Construyendo la modernidad: la cultura española en el tiempo de los novatores (1675–1725).* Madrid: Consejo Superior de Investigaciones Científicas, 2002.

Pérez Vidal, Alejandro. Footnotes to *Fígaro. Colección de artículos dramáticos, liter-*

arios, políticos, y de costumbres, by Mariano José de Larra. Barcelona: Crítica, 1997.

Perry, Leonard. "Larra's View of the Middle Classes as Perceived through His *Artículos costumbristas*." *Revista de Cultura* 11 (1982): 93–98.

Peters, Edward. *Inquisition.* New York: Free Press, 1998.

Piave, Francesco Maria. *The Force of Destiny (La Forza del Destino).* New York: Riverrun Press, 1983.

Picoche, Jean-Louis. "Existe-t-il une drame romantique espagnol?" In *Romantisme, realisme, naturalisme en Espagne et en Amérique Latine (Actes du II Colloque de Centre d'Etudes Ibériques et Ibéro-Américaines du XIXéme siècle, Lille, 1975).* Vol. 3, 47–55. Villeneuve d'Ascq: Université de Lille, 1978.

Pitollet, Camille. *La Querelle caldéronienne de Johan Nikolas Böhl von Faber et José Joaquín de Mora, reconstituée d'après les documents originaux.* Paris: Félix Alcan, 1909.

Poggioli, Renato. *The Theory of the Avant Garde.* Trans. Gerald Fitzgerald. Cambridge: Harvard University Press, 1968.

Polt, John. *Batilo: estudios sobre la evolución estilística de Meléndez Valdés.* Berkeley: University of California Press; Oviedo: Centro de Estudios del Siglo XVIII, 1987.

Pope, Randolph. "Intrusos en el templo: profanando tumbas en las *Noches lúgubres*." *Dieciocho* 21 (1998): 21–34.

Pratt, Mary Louise. *Imperial Eyes: Travel Writing and Transculturation.* London: Routledge, 1992.

Penas Varela, Ermitas. "Las firmas de Larra." *Cuadernos Hispanoamericanos* 361–362 (1980): 227–51.

Preston, Joseph. "Was There an Historical Revolution?" *Journal of the History of Ideas* 38 (1977): 253–364.

Punter, David, and Glennis Byron. *The Gothic.* Oxford: Blackwell, 2004.

Quevedo, Francisco de. *Poesía original completa.* Barcelona: Planeta, 1981.

Quijano, Anibal. "Colonialidad y modernidad-racionalidad." In *Los conquistadores,* ed. H. Bonilla, 437–47. Bogota: Tercer Mundo, 1992.

Quinn, David. "Rivas' Unexplained Localization of *Don Alvaro* in the Eighteenth Century." *Romance Notes* 16 (1975): 483–85.

Quinziano, Franco. "Le *Noches lúgubres* e il modello cadalsiano della sensibilità ilustrata: Tediato, *espíritu fuerte e corazón sensible*." In *Scrittori "contro": modelli in discussione nelle letterature iberiche,* 95–109. Rome: Bulzoni, 1996.

Radden, Jennifer. *The Nature of Melancholy: From Aristotle to Kristeva.* Oxford: Oxford University Press, 2000.

Raimondi Capasso, Maddalena. "Cadalso e Rousseau." *Annali della Facoltà di Filosofia e Lettere de Milano* 20, no. 1 (1967): 97–115.

Ramírez, Angel. *José Zorrilla: Biografía anecdótica*. Madrid: Mundo Latino, n.d.

Real de la Riva, César. "La escuela poética salmantina del siglo XVIII." *Boletín de la Biblioteca Menéndez y Pelayo* 24 (1948): 321–64.

Rey Hazas, Antonio. "La insólita estructura de Don Alvaro o la fuerza del sino." *Anuario de Estudios Filológicos* 9 (1986): 249–62.

Richards, Michael. *A Time of Silence: Civil War and the Culture of Repression in Franco's Spain, 1936–1945*. Cambridge: Cambridge University Press, 1998.

Ricoeur, Paul. *Time and Narrative*. Vol. 1. Chicago: University of Chicago Press, 1984.

Ringrose, David. *Spain, Europe and the "Spanish Miracle."* Cambridge: Cambridge University Press, 1996.

Río, Angel del. "Present Trends in the Conception and Criticism of Spanish Romanticism." *Romanic Review* 39, no. 2 (1948): 229–48.

Ríos-Font, Wadda. *The Canon and the Archive: Cofiguring Literature in Modern Spain*. Lewisburg, PA: Bucknell University Press, 2004.

Ripodas Ardanaz, Daysi. *El indiano en el teatro español del setecientos*. Madrid: Atlas, 1986.

Rodríguez, Juan. "Una lectura romántica de las *Noches lúgubres* de Cadalso." In *El mundo hispánico en el siglo de las luces*. Vol. 2, 1111–25. Madrid: Editorial Complutense, 1996.

Romero Tobar, Leonardo. "Estudio Preliminar." In *Fígaro. Colección de artículos dramáticos, literarios, políticos y de costumbres*, by Mariano José Larra, ed. Alejandro Pérez Vidal, ix–xxv. Barcelona: Critica, 1997.

———. "Larra y los Seudónimos Transmigratorios." In *Estudios de la literatura española de los siglos XIX y XX: Homenaje a Juan María Díez Taboada*, 359–65. Madrid: Consejo Superior de Investigaciones Científicas, 1998.

Rorty, Richard. *Contingency, Irony, and Solidarity*. Cambridge: Cambridge University Press, 1989.

Rosenberg, John. "Between Delirium and Lumninosity: Larra's Ethical Nightmare." *Hispanic Review* 61 (1993): 379–89.

Rosenblum, Nancy. *Another Liberalism: Romanticism and the Reconstruction of Liberal Thought*. Cambridge: Harvard University Press, 1987.

Rousseau, Jean-Jacques. *Rousseau's Political Writings*. Ed. Alan Ritter and Julia Conaway. New York: Norton, 1988.

Rudat, Eva. "Artificio, afecto y equilibrio clásico: ubicación estética en la obra de Cadalso." In *Coloquio Internacional sobre José Cadalso*, 193–210. Abano Terme: Piovan, 1985.

———. "Lo *prerromántico*. Una variante neoclásica en la estética y literaturas españolas." *Iberoromania* 15 (1982): 47–69.

Rueda Hernanz, Germán. *La desamortización de Mendizábal y Espartero en España*. Madrid: Cátedra, 1986.

Ruiz, Juan [Archipreste de Hita]. *Libro de buen amor*. Barcelona: Planeta, 1983.

Saavedra, Angel [Duke of Rivas]. *Don Alvaro o la fuerza del sino*. Barcelona: Crítica, 1994.

———. *El moro expósito, o Córdoba y Burgos en el siglo décimo*. Madrid: Espasa Calpe, 1982.

Saco, José Antonio. *Historia de la esclavitud de la raza africana en el nuevo mundo*. 4 vols. Havana: Cultural S.A., 1938.

Saglia, Diego. *Poetic Castles in Spain: British Romanticism and Figurations of Iberia*. Amsterdam: Rodopi, 1999.

———. "'The True Essence of Spanish Romanticism': Romantic Theories of Spain and the Question of Spanish Romanticism." *Journal of Iberian and Latin American Studies* 3, no. 2 (1997): 127–45.

Said, Edward. *Culture and Imperialism*. New York: Knopf, 1993.

———. *Orientalism*. New York: Pantheon, 1978.

Sánchez, Joseph. *The Spanish Black Legend: Origins of Anti-Hispanic Stereotypes*. Albuquerque: National Park Service Spanish Colonial Research Center, 1990.

Sánchez Marcos, Fernando. "La historiografía sobre la Edad Moderna." In *Historia de la historiografía española*, coord. José Andrés-Gallego. Madrid: Ediciones Encuentro, 1999.

Sánchez-Blanco Parody, Francisco. "Una ética secular; la amistad entre los ilustrados." *Cuadernos de Estudios del Siglo XVIII* 2 (1992): 97–116.

Santiáñez, Nil. *Investigaciones literarias: modernidad, historia de la literatura, y modernismos*. Barcelona: Crítica, 2002.

Sarrailh, Jean. *La España ilustrada de la segunda mitad del siglo XVIII*. México: Fondo de Cultura Económica, 1957.

Schiller, Friedrich. *On the Aesthetic Education of Man: In a Series of Letters*. Oxford: Clarendon Press, 1982.

Schlegel, August Wilhelm. *A Course of Lectures on Dramatic Art and Literature*. 2 vols. London: Baldwin, Craddock and Joy, 1815.

Schulze, Hagen. *States, Nations, and Nationalism: From the Middle Ages to the Present*. Oxford: Blackwell, 1996.

Schurlknight, Donald. "Another Document in Support of Cadalso's Romanticism." *Romance Notes* 27, no. 2 (1986): 163–66.

———. "Larra and the Mixing of the Classes." In *Resonancias románticas: evocaciones del romanticismo hispánico*, ed. John R. Rosenberg, 77–91. Madrid: José Porrua, 1988.

Sebold, Russell. *Cadalso: el primer romántico "europeo" de España*. Madrid: Gredos, 1974.

———. "Cadalso y Larra: una inseguridad romántica en dos tiempos." *Biblioteca Virtual Cervantes*. www.cervantesvirtual.com (accessed December 2005).

———. *Colonel don José Cadalso*. New York: Twayne, 1971.

———. *De ilustrados y románticos*. Madrid: El Museo Universal, 1992.

———. *Descubrimiento y fronteras del neoclasicismo español*. Madrid: Fundación Juan March-Cátedra, 1985.

———. "Jovellanos, dramaturgo romántico." *Anales de Literatura Española* 4 (1985): 415–37.

———. "Larra y la Misión de Zorrilla." *American Hispanist* 3, no. 26 (1978): 7–12.

———. "Nuevos Cristos en el drama romántico español." *Cuadernos Hispanoamericanos* 431 (1986): 126–32.

———. Prólogo to *Poética*, by Ignacio Luzán. Barcelona: Labor, 1977.

———. *El rapto de la mente. Poética y poesía dieciochescas*. Barcelona: Anthropos, 1989.

———. *Trayectoria del romanticismo español. Desde la Ilustración hasta Bécquer*. Barcelona: Crítica, 1983.

———, ed. *Noches lúgubres,* by José Cadalso. Madrid: Taurus, 1993.

Sedwick, Brian. "Rivas's Don Alvaro and Verdi's La forza del destino." *Modern Language Quarterly* 16 (1955): 124–29.

Shade, Patrick. *Habits of Hope: A Pragmatic Theory*. Nashville: Vanderbilt University Press, 2001.

Shaw, Donald. "Acerca de la estructura de Don Alvaro." In *Romanticismo I. Atti del II Congreso sul Romanticismo Spagnolo e Ispanoamericano. Spetti e problemei del teatro romantico,* 61–69. Genova: Biblioteca di letterature, 1982.

———. "The Anti-Romantic Reaction in Spain." *Modern Language Review* 63 (1968): 606–11.

———. *The Generation of 1898 in Spain*. London: E. Benn; New York: Barnes and Nobel, 1975.

———. *The Nineteenth Century*. London: Benn, 1972.

———. "Towards an Understanding of Spanish Romanticism." *Modern Language Review* 58 (1963): 190–95.

Shih, Shu-mei. "Global Literature and the Technologies of Recognition." Literatures at Large. *PMLA* 119 (2004): 16–30.

Shubert, Adrian. *A Social History of Modern Spain*. London: Unwin Hyman, 1990.

———. "Spanish Historians and English-Speaking Scholarship." *Social History* 29, no. 3 (2004): 358–63.

Silver, Philip. *Ruin and Restitution: Reinterpreting Romanticism in Spain.* Nashville: Vanderbilt Univeristy Press, 1997.

———. "Towards a Revisionary Theory of Spanish Romanticism." *Revista de Estudios Hispánicos* 28 (1994): 293–302.

Simmel, Georg. *The Philosophy of Money.* New York: Routledge, 1990.

Simon Segura, Francisco. *La desamortización española del siglo XIX.* Madrid: Instituto de Estudios Fiscales, 1973.

Smith, Adam. *An Inquiry into the Nature and Causes of the Wealth of Nations.* Oxford: Clarendon Press, 1976.

———. *The Theory of Moral Sentiments.* Cambridge: Cambridge University Press, 2002.

Sohn-Rether, Alfred. *Intellectual and Manual Labor: A Critique of Epistemology.* Atlantic Highlands, NJ: Humanities Press, 1977.

Southworth, Herbert. *Conspiracy and the Spanish Civil War: The Brainwashing of Francisco Franco.* London: Routledge, 2002.

Spell, J. R. *Rousseau in the Spanish World before 1833: A Study on Franco-Spanish Literary Relations.* Austin: University of Texas Press,1938.

Subirats, Joan. *Después de la lluvia: sobre la ambigua modernidad española.* Madrid: Temas de Hoy, 1993.

———. *La ilustración insuficiente.* Madrid: Taurus, 1981.

Talens, Jenaro. *Romanticism and the Writing of Modernity: Espronceda and the Collapse of Literature as Institutionalized Discourse.* Austin: Studia Hispanica, 1989.

Tarr, Courtney. *Romanticism in Spain and Spanish Romanticism.* Liverpool: Institute of Hispanic Studies, 1939.

Taylor, Peter. *Modernities: A Geohistorical Interpretation.* Minnneapolis: University of Minnesota, 1999.

Teichmann, Reinhard. *Larra: sátira y ritual mágico.* Madrid: Playor, 1986.

Ter Ellingson, Terry. *The Myth of the Noble Savage.* Berkeley: University of California Press, 2001.

Tomás y Valiente, Francisco. *El marco político de la desamortización en España.* Barcelona: Ariel, 1973.

Tortella, Gabriel. *The Development of Modern Spain: An Economic History of the Nineteenth and Twentieth Centuries.* Cambridge: Harvard University Press, 2000.

———. Los orígenes del capitalismo en España. Banca, industria y ferrocarriles en el siglo XIX. Madrid: Tecnos, 1973.

Torrecilla, Jesús. *España exotica: La formación de la identidad española moderna.* Boulder: University of Colorado, 2004.

————. *La imitación colectiva: modernidad vs. autenticidad en la literatura española*. Madrid: Gredos, 1996.

————. *El tiempo y los márgenes*. Chapel Hill: University of North Carolina Press, 1996.

Ullman, Pierre. *Mariano de Larra and Spanish Political Rhetoric*. Madison: University of Wisconsin Press, 1971.

Urrutia, Jorge, ed. *Poesía española del siglo XIX*. Madrid: Cátedra, 1995.

Urry, John. *The Tourist Gaze: Leisure and Travel in Contemporary Societies*. London: Sage, 1990.

Valis, Noël. *The Culture of Cursilería: Bad Taste, Kitsch, and Class in Modern Spain*. Durham, NC: Duke University Press, 2002.

————. "Romanticism, Realism, and the Presence of the Word." *Letras peninsulares* 3, nos. 2–3 (1990): 321–39.

Van Aken, Mark. *Pan-Hispanism: Its Origin and Development to 1866*. Berkeley and Los Angeles: University of California Press, 1959.

Van Doren, Charles. *The Idea of Progress*. New York: F. A. Praeger, 1967.

Varela, Javier. *La novela de España: los intelectuales y el problema español*. Madrid: Taurus, 1999.

Vázquez de Castro, Isabel. "Hacia un nuevo sentido de lo sublime: un aspecto del léxico de Cadalso." In *Coloquio Internacional sobre José Cadalso. Bolonia, 26–29 de octubre de 1982)*, 317–45. Bologna: Abano Terme, 1985.

Voloshinov, V. N. *Marxism and the Philosophy of Language*. Cambridge: Harvard University Press, 1986.

Weber, Max. *The Protestant Ethic and the "Spirit of Capitalism."* London: Fitzroy Dearborn, 2001.

————. "Science as Vocation." In *Max Weber's "Science as Vocation,"* ed. Peter Lassman and Irving Velody. London: Unwin Hyman, 1989.

Wagar, Warren, ed. *The Idea of Progress since the Renaissance*. New York: Wiley, 1969.

Waltz, Otto. *Eine historische skizze*. Bonn: M. Hager, 1905.

Wallerstein, Immanuel. *The Modern World System: Capitalist Agriculture and the Origins of the European World Economy in the Sixteenth Century*. New York: Academic Press, 1974.

Wellek, René. "The Concept of Romanticism in Literary History." In *Concepts of Criticism*, 128–98. New Haven: Yale University Press, 1963.

Williams, Raymond. *Marxism and Literature*. Oxford University Press, 1977.

————. *Problems in Materialism and Culture*. London: Verso, 1980.

Wilson, Bryan. "Secularization: The Inherited Model." in *The Sacred in a Secular Age : Toward Revision in the Scientific Study of Religion*, ed. Phillip E. Hammond, 9–20. Berkeley: University of California Press, 1985.

Wolf, Eric. *Europe and the People without History*. Berkeley: University of California Press, 1982.

Young, Karl. *The Drama of the Medieval Church*. Oxford: Clarendon Press, 1933.

Zavala, Iris. "La literatura: romanticismo y costumbrismo." In *Ramon Menéndez Pidal Historia de España. XXXV: La época del romanticismo (1808–1874)*. Vol. 2. *Las letras, las artes, la vida cotidiana*. Madrid: Espasa Calpe, 1996.

Zea, Leopoldo. *The Role of the Americas in History*. Savage, MD: Roman and Littlefield, 1992.

Zizek, Slavoj. *The Sublime Object of Ideology*. New York: Verso, 1989.

Index